To Lorri —
Great meeting you!

My Oregon III

Final collection of RG columns, 2009-2015

BOB WELCH

The Register-Guard

 AO FILMS

Eugene, Oregon

 **AO FILMS**

Published by AO Films
2350 Oakmont Way
Suite 110
Eugene, OR 97401

www.aofilms.com

Front cover: Five-year-old Keaton Welch, one of the author's five
grandchildren, jumps a Fourth of July sunset in Yachats. (Photo by
Bob Welch.)

ISBN: 978-1512131703

Author information:

web: www.bobwelch.net
email: info@bobwelch.net
twitter: @bob_welch

Table of Contents

Also by Bob Welch

Lessons on the Way to Heaven
  (with Michael Fechner Jr.)
52 Little Lessons from a Christmas Carol
The Keyboard Kitten Gets Oregonized
52 Little Lessons from Les Misérables
The Keyboard Kitten
Cascade Summer
52 Little Lessons from It's a Wonderful Life
Resolve
My Oregon II
Easy Company Soldier (with Don Malarkey)
My Oregon
Pebble in the Water
American Nightingale
The Things That Matter Most
My Seasons
Stories from the Game of Life
Where Roots Grow Deep
A Father for All Seasons
More to Life Than Having It All
Bellevue and the New East Side

To Jim Godbold, who believed in me.

To look at the paper is to raise a seashell to one's ear and to be overwhelmed by the roar of humanity.

— Alain de Botton,
The Pleasures and Sorrows of Work

Author's note

In 1974, as a University of Oregon sophomore, I had just finished a sports shift at *The Register-Guard* in Eugene. I took the elevator down to the pint-sized cafeteria, bought a hot dog and stuck it in one of those new-fangled gizmos called a microwave oven.

It was a miracle.

Not just that my hot dog would be fully cooked in 90 seconds but that I was working part-time at one of the finest mid-sized daily newspapers in the United States.

Someday, I told myself, I want to work here full-time.

I thought "someday" would come in a couple of three years. Instead, it took me 13 — stints in Bend, Ore., and Bellevue, Wash. — before I landed a job at the paper I'd revered since I was in high school. But when then-features editor Jim Godbold called me in July 1989 to offer me a job, it was a landmark moment in my life.

Twenty-four years of landmark moments followed. As a features writer, features editor and columnist, I experienced new adventures every day.

That's what I loved about the newspaper business — that it allowed you to meet, and learn about, people who you'd never get to meet in most other jobs. That many of those people allowed me to plumb the depths of their lives. That you could be hanging out with a homeless guy in the morning, standing in a millionaire's lakeside mansion in the afternoon and doing a phone interview in between with a guy who was sure he'd been abducted by a UFO.

To have the chance to write columns amid such diversity is to understand the word "privilege." For 14 years, *The Register-Guard* basically let me decide what I wanted to write three times a week.

What follows on these pages is the third, and final, collection of columns that, I hope, reflects not so much who I am, but who *we* are. As Oregonians. As a community. As a group of people unlike any group of people anywhere, defined by everything from winter rain to Bill Bowerman to Saturday Market to the wonder of being able to start a day at sea level and end it atop a 10,000-foot mountain — all while staying in Lane County.

Since leaving *The Register-Guard* in December 2013, I've written books, given speeches, taught Beachside Writers Workshops and launched the "Bob Welch & Friends" live performances at Eugene's Hult Center and the Florence Events Center.

But none of that has been as satisfying as my years of simply telling stories of the people, places and passion of this place we call home.

Bob Welch
Eugene, Oregon
September 2015

1.

Eugene

Childlike faith

Aug. 1, 2010

It was in the last 60-meter-dash of Wednesday's Oregon Track Club All-Comers meet at Hayward Field that Karaline Glenn went astray.

The 2-year-old Creswell girl was barreling down the east straightaway with a smile on her face roughly the size of the Nike swoosh on the nearby video display.

Suddenly, she veered right, going from Lane 5 to Lane 4 to Lane 3. It was like watching a drink slide sideways on the galley shelf of a heeling sailboat.

About 10 yards from the finish line — her stride, smile and course unwavering — Karaline crossed from Lane 2 to Lane 1.

Then, with true childlike faith, she leapt into the air, into the waiting arms of her father, Tim, who celebrated her passionate, if not quite complete, race with a hug.

Watching one of OTC's Ages 1-though-12 All-Comers Meets is like eating a fresh fruit salad on your back deck: bursts of alluring flavors that, thrown together in a single place, say "summer in Eugene."

When Bill Bowerman started such meets for grade-school kids at Hayward Field in 1949, 15 people showed up. Wednesday night, there were some sprint heats with that many entrants, though, in one case, a kid literally got lost en route to the finish line, later being tear-fully reunited with his parents.

(With athletic trauma like this, who needs the agony of defeat?)

"In the 'diaper dashes,' as we call them, kids make up their own races as they go," says Liz James, a former University of Oregon runner who coordinates the 50 volunteers. "It's kind of up in the air whether they're going to make it to the finish line or not."

The meet is the taste of comedy, community and competition, all of it playing out in a venue where track and field history is imbedded as indelibly as the spike marks in the steps of the 91-year-old East Grandstand.

It is the sound of "runners to your mark, set, go." Of Danette Bloomer, a volunteer official in the Age 1-3 softball throw, announc-ing a competitor's distance thusly: "About 14 feet!" Of kids, between events, showing off with cartwheels on the well-trimmed grass of the infield.

It is the sight of 3-year-olds proudly waving orange "Participant" ribbons, not knowing exactly what they mean but based on gone-wild parents, figuring it's something pretty darn good.

Oh, the meet isn't perfect. Here and there, you see a spark of par-ent-child tension. And you see the little boy who, braced to throw the softball, freezes like a statue, no amount of parental coaxing getting him to release that ball.

But what makes it special is as much about what you don't see as what you do. Unlike at too many Kidsports baseball games I've seen, there are no parents screaming at officials over what they think is a bad call.

No exclusivity among the 500 kids who have shown up on this near-perfect summer evening, all skill levels treated equally.

No win-or-else coaches forgetting that it should be about learning, improving and having fun.

Indeed, the story is told of a 7-year-old boy who, years ago in this meet, finished fourth in the then-220-yard dash.

"How fast did you run?" an adult asked.

Eyes wide, he replied: "As fast as I could!"

If the meet is well-organized, the feel is still laid back, from the barefoot long jump official to a family settling down for a quick din-ner of rice cakes on the infield. (A menu reminding you that, no, this isn't baseball.)

"With all the volunteers, you can see that 'takes-a-village' theme to run the meet," says James.

One of the long-jump officials is former UO women's track and field coach Tom Heinonen, who's been around long enough that he's marking the sand splashes of children whose parents he once did the same for.

The kids' all-comers meet is part picnic, part 17-ring circus, part Olympics.

For the older kids who know the stories of Steve Prefontaine, Annette Peters and other Olympic athletes who've left their marks here, competing at Hayward Field is pure magic.

For the younger kids, the meet would be no less fun were it held in a Harrisburg grass seed field.

I see Miguel Huhndorf-Lima throw the softball — while wearing baby-blue rain galoshes, known as his "super boots." "I wanna throw it again!" he immediately says.

I see 9-year-old Madelyn Hubbs of Eugene tumble to the track after hitting her final hurdle, then get up and still win. Inspiring stuff, that.

I see grandparents cheering from infield lawn chairs and Gen-X and New Millennial parents following their toddlers down the track with cameras and encouragement, some fathers later showing iPhonian instant replays.

But mainly what I see is a delicious slice of summer, served up in a way only Eugene can.

The airport angel

June 13, 2010

If places mark time in relation to their iconic features, then consider this a coming-of-age moment for the Eugene Airport, if not Eugene itself.

It's that little 10-month-old "angel," probably the youngest of the 130 people photographed for the airport's beloved "Flying People" mural.

She graduates from the University of Oregon on Monday.

"When we photographed people, we were very concerned about

costuming and hairstyles so there wouldn't be anything out of date," says Kacey Joyce, wife of the late David Joyce, the artist who did the mural. "We weren't thinking of the people aging. Suddenly, you realize: The kids have all grown up!"

Even if she wasn't yet a year old, Dayna Klute, now 22, managed to play a role in her being among the fortunate few to grace the wall on the second-level corridor leading to the "A" gates. However, her father, Daniel, wasn't as fortunate.

It was November 1988. Daniel and wife Sandy Alperin were enjoying watching Dayna, born the previous January, learn to crawl.

"I bumped something and managed to break a lamp," Dayna recalled last week.

Thus Daniel, at the time a 38-year-old intern in an architectural firm, found himself downtown with his daughter in search of a new lamp when he saw it: a sort of "fly-in studio" on Olive Street where David Joyce, then 42, was photographing people.

A woman, perhaps Kacey, invited them to be photographed for the mural.

David Joyce stood on a ladder, shooting down.

"I laid Dayna down on this mat and I laid down next to her, pretending to fly, and he took a couple of shots of us together, then we left," says Daniel Klute. "I never heard another thing about it."

Until a year or so later when he was in the Eugene Airport. Behold, there was his wonderful daughter, Dayna, among the wall's whimsical fliers. West end, nearest the gates, powered by angel wings.

Alas, Daniel's image was nowhere to be seen. Photoshop 1.0 wouldn't be released until a few months later. "But it's clear that I had been X-Acto-knifed out of the picture," he says, laughing.

The fanciful mural was commissioned — for $15,000 — as part of the remodeling of the airport. Joyce had worked with large photo cutouts for years and, while sitting at the Fifth Street Public Market one day, got an idea.

"Photo cutouts of all man's early attempts at flight," he told *The Register-Guard*'s Bob Keefer in 1999, the 10-year anniversary of the piece of art that's officially called "Flight Patterns." "I was going to make a hanging mobile. Then I thought, 'Wow, what if you could just hold out your arms and fly yourself? Superman! Mighty Mouse!'"

Naw, he countered, too wacky. Then he remembered where he lived. Eugene. A place where "Why be normal?" bumper stickers are normal. Where *Animal House* was filmed.

He decided to go with flying people.

Daniel Klute wasn't the only one to not make the cut; 70 of the 200 people photographed were not chosen. Among those who were: cartoonist Jan Eliot before she was famous; former *Register-Guard* columnist Don Bishoff, with a laptop computer so dated it looks as if Horace Greeley might have used it; and author/humorist Garrison Keillor, the only non-local used. (He happened to be in town doing a show.)

Once put in place in August 1989, the mural quickly became a favorite. Never mind that a few people have been removed. A child molester. And a former student of David Joyce's at Lane Community College who'd borrowed some equipment that hadn't been returned. Some minorities were added. A cop was stolen and never recovered.

Sadly, Joyce died in 2003 at age 57 of non-Hodgkin's lymphoma. But the flying people mural lives on as a legacy of a man who captured the essence of Eugene perfectly.

"It's a nice mix," says Phil Groshong, the airport's general aviation and tenant manager. "You have an airport with a state-of-the-art instrument landing system and nostalgia."

"Seeing the mural is a 'Eugene moment,'" says Dayna Klute.

And she's proud to be part of it.

She is a Eugene native, has volunteered at Birth to Three and Womenspace, and has a 3.57 GPA.

"I love everything Eugene," says Klute, a South Eugene High graduate. "I'm a big Country Fair fan. I go to Saturday Market. I'm a huge Duck fan."

Never mind that the day after she graduates from UO with a Family & Human Services degree, she's flying off to enter the University of Southern California's School of Social Work graduate program.

Like the others, she's there to remind us that, in a sense, we're forever young.

Goodbye, Civic

Aug. 23, 2009

I said my goodbyes to 71-year-old Civic Stadium Tuesday night. It was, I suppose, a little like your last visit with a dying relative and yet I didn't walk away all weepy. That moisture on my cheeks was sweat; the right-field digital thermometer read 96 degrees at game's start. And that pit in my stomach had nothing to do with loss; instead, I was having sympathy pains for my 4-year-old grandson who downed a Pepsi, batting helmet of Oreo ice cream and a bubble gum snow cone — all in the span of two-plus innings.

He didn't quite last three, though by then we'd gotten our money's worth: 13 runs, two homers and seeing a foul ball land near us in the snow-cone line, though we couldn't nab it.

"Let's see if we can find one of those balls that was hit over the fence," said Cade in one of his rare moments between gulps, sips and licks.

"That'll be hard to do," I said. "Some other kids probably got them. Or they're lost in the tall grass."

Back in our first-baseline seats, I was reminded of how perfect it always seems at Civic: the orange-tinged sun bathing the Douglas firs of Hendricks Hill, the American flag waving lazily in the outfield and the guy placing wooden numbers on the scoreboard.

The scene always captures that wonderful "I-don't-care-if-I-ev-er-get-back" escapism of which "Take Me Out to the Ball Game" speaks.

So why wasn't I getting all sentimental? This, after all, would probably be the last game I'd see at the stadium. The Eugene Em-eralds, by all indications, are headed for PK Park in the shadows of Autzen Stadium next summer. And my schedule isn't lining up for any of the other six home games left this season.

For starters, my guest wasn't into memories; he was into food and getting a home-run ball and having the balloon man tie him a yellow "bug hat" with two green antennae.

I could have said: "Cade, in the old days the vendors would throw back your change in a tennis ball with a slit in it." And he would have said something like, "Can I get a hot dog?" Or: "Can we go look for those baseballs over the fence now?"

What's more, I'm not a Civic Stadium regular like some Ems die-hards. My summer pies get sliced into so many pieces that I might only get to a game or three each year.

But in two decades, I've come to believe that a summer without watching baseball at Civic Stadium is not a summer.

Still, you can't program sentimentality; it's like trying to cry when you're happy, which I was Tuesday night, eating concession-stand food with my grandson while occasionally watching a pitch or two of baseball.

Finally, the death of a ball park is not the death of watching minor league baseball in Eugene on warm summer nights.

Will PK Park have Civic's ambiance, soul or venerability? Nope. Only time, memories and stadium decay can create as much. But anyone who believes you can't find that "don't-care-if-I-ever-get-back" feeling in newer stadiums has never been to, say, Seattle's Safeco Field or Denver's Coors Field.

Such stadiums remind us that it's not just the age of the stadium that matters, it's how fan-friendly it is. How it looks. Feels. Whether it respects the traditions of the game.

And PK, despite its untraditional artificial turf, has the potential to be a beautiful ball park on a summer's eve. The permanent stands will give it the coziness it lacked last spring. And the view beyond the outfield fences, like at Civic, is of green Oregon trees. Yes, it'll need some aging to round off the edges; relationships take time to develop as, I imagine, was the case with a spanking-new Civic Stadium.

Even then, it's important to remember that baseball is more than a venue. It's the game on the field. The fans. The magic of sport, period, which you can find in a multimillion-dollar stadium or on a Haitian soccer field that uses rocks for goals.

Save Civic? Sure, if a practical way to do so can be found. But let's not forget that baseball is bigger than the place where it's played. And not forget that a new venue needn't invalidate our great memories of the old one.

Like the final memory I'll take away from Civic. As Cade and I headed for home, near the Amazon Parkway footbridge, we saw a 40-something guy with a backpack poking around the tall grass beyond the left-field fence.

He dipped down and found a ball. Then — hot dog! — another. He walked toward us, eyed Cade and graciously handed him one.

A final gift from a ball park that gave so much.

Editor's note: After a citizens group bought the property with plans to turn it into a youth sports complex, an arson-set fire burned Civic Stadium to the ground on June 29, 2015.

Behind Silva's ceiling

Jan. 13, 2011

It's time. In an industrial district off Springfield's Laura Street, the tools and other equipment of Benny Bartel Co. are being organized for a liquidation sale.

In the next few months, the 63-year-old plastering and drywall company — among Lane County's oldest construction-related businesses — will shut its doors for good.

But among its many legacies will be a Eugene architectural icon: the basket weave ceiling and the curving balcony fascias of the Silva Concert Hall.

"It's one-of-a-kind anywhere," says Jerry McDonnell of Eugene, the on-site architect for the Hult Center for Performing Arts Center that opened in 1982.

Plenty about the Hult project was eye-opening, not the least of which was Eugene voters, in iffy economic times, passing an $18.5 million bond measure to help fund it. But the *coup de grace* of creativity was the ceiling of the main concert hall. It would defy the traditional straight-wall, flat-ceiling look and, instead, give people a sense that they were sitting in, well, a giant, upside-down woven basket.

"Everything that is important in this remarkable hall is the first of its kind — including, most spectacularly, the ceiling," wrote *Architectural Record* magazine in 1983. "The present shape was first thought of (so it has been said) when one of its architects held an inverted peach basket up to the sky..."

When Benny Bartel heard what was being planned, he couldn't wait to bid on the job. In business since 1948, he was a diehard, old-school plaster man. "To me, sheetrock is a nasty word," says Bartel, now 91, silver-haired and rosy-cheeked.

Bartel did the original Lane County Courthouse in the mid-1950s, the Ya-Po-Ah Terrace, Patterson Towers and numerous dormitories at the University of Oregon and Oregon State University. But the Hult project, well, that was the major leagues.

"I wanted it bad," says Bartel, "because it was a monument to Eugene, and I had a lot of pride in Eugene. I was born here (1919) and grew up with the place."

Lots of other companies wanted the project, too, but because of its complexities — beyond aesthetics, the panels would offer acoustical value — all but Bartel and one other bowed out before the bid deadline.

Bartel landed the job with his $1.5 million offer.

At first, however, the New York-based architecture firm, Hardy Holzman Pfeiffer Associates, wondered if Bartel could handle it. "Then I told them I was a plaster man," Bartel says. "They said, 'That does it. You've got the job.'"

It would be the largest project he would ever do. Would take 18 months to complete. And would require, a times, 90 workers.

A total of 138, one-ton convex arcs were designed and fabricated, each in the 18-foot-by-21-foot range but no two alike.

It took about a week to 10 days to make each one, the plaster smoothed onto a wire mesh atop 3/4-inch iron.

"Benny looked at it as a challenge," McDonnell says. "How is one to build that?"

The Hult is, at first, a giant box. But in the Silva there's a dome-like "trapeze ceiling" beneath its lid to which the panels needed to be affixed.

"It's like you have this upside-down bowl upon which you're attaching panels that have the opposite curve," says son Gary Bartel, who became company president two years after the Hult opened.

"What Benny did was very clever," says McDonnell, who came to Eugene from Colorado to do the project and never left. "Because there was scaffolding everywhere, he built the panels off-site, then brought them in and put them up one at a time."

Each panel overlapped the other by about a foot. Gradually, the ceiling began taking shape, a paint contractor adding the sage-and-tan final touches.

"One really didn't have a sense of what was happening until the scaffolding was all taken away," McDonnell says. "Then, you realized it was rather extraordinary."

Benny Bartel Co. not only did the ceiling, but the artsy, curved balcony fascias — all by hand.

Twenty-nine years later, Gary, now 68, wants to retire, and this isn't the economic climate to be selling a business; thus, the decision to call it quits.

Though the business did scores of other jobs — many with Benny's much-loathed sheetrock — none was remotely like the Hult.

The project won the company the Northwest Lath and Plaster Bureau's Project of the Year award for 1982-83.

"Sure, I look up when I'm there," says Benny. "You do something like that, and you feel proud of it."

And rightly so.

It's a one-of-a-kind ceiling for a one-of-a-kind place.

Woo-woo way back

July 8, 2010

According to the Eugene lunar calendar, this weekend's Oregon Country Fair is when the stars line up for ultimate weirdness. But given Eugene's general weirdness, is the fair really all that bizarre?

Consider these nonfair occurrences over the years:

In 2001, on the Victor Boc radio show, a Eugene caller blames the Seattle Earthquake on the overcutting of old growth forests.

In the '90s, conservative talk show host Michael Medved reports that a Eugene woman is blaming George Bush Sr. for the murder of President John F. Kennedy.

In a back-to-school riot in 2002, drunken University of Oregon students burn mattresses, furniture and street signs while chanting "USA, USA, USA." (No, the riot had nothing to do with the Olympics or World Cup.)

A Eugene woman blames the aforementioned riot on "karmic debt" owed to the Eugene Police Department for its alleged overzealous reaction to more civilized protests.

Eugene's 2008 State of the City event includes an angry rap in which listeners are encouraged to stop driving cars and shopping at Wal-Mart.

In 2000, from her Lane County Jail holding cell, an anarchist who says "it might take a little window breaking and sabotage to wake people out of their trances" complains about having to endure peanut butter sandwiches and Muzak.

In 2007, an Oregon couple appearing on the TV show "Wife Swap" tell of eschewing toilet paper (wasteful) and using their own urine to moisten their compost piles.

In December 2000, Eugene's city manager joins the holiday spirit by banning Christmas trees from public places.

In July 1998, Saturday Market plays host to a wedding featuring a couple wearing all-hemp clothing.

In 2002, a Eugene artist chagrined at never having had his more conventional artwork chosen to be part of the Mayor's Art Show enters a paint-splotched section of a wall — and it's accepted.

Protesters at a human rights celebration in 1998, unhappy about Mayor Jim Torrey's views on a tree protest, graze him with one pie and smash another on his head.

Not long before building a 2010 state-of-the-art academics center for student athletes, the UO hires a college dropout to be its athletic director.

In the '90s, when a reggae concert gets unruly and Eugene police intervene, a Eugene woman credits her "sun dance" with restoring peace, saying her "healing white light" quelled the uprising.

In May 2005, *Eugene Weekly* — in commemoration of Mother's Day — runs a column decrying the exploitation of female pigs, cows and chickens for only their reproductive qualities, calling it a "slap in the face to motherhood."

In 2000, a 20-year-old man is slapped with a 20-day contempt of court sentence for yawning three times and making "vocal interruptions" during an arraignment, though his attorney later argues he yawned only once.

In 1998, a self-professed "animal communicator" from Eugene channels a one-page, single-spaced letter from Keiko after the whale has been transported from Newport to Iceland. Among Keiko's alleged thoughts: "I am quite content for the moment."

On Jan. 20, 2005, when McArthur Court announcer Don Essig introduces the national anthem on the inauguration day of George W. Bush, a smattering of fans begin chanting "Four More Wars, Four More Wars."

In February 2008, after author and Olympian Kenny Moore has written about how athletics can bridge human divides, a letter writer denounces competition, lamenting, "Why, exactly, is it important to run faster than someone else?"

Among the winning parade entries in the 2000 Eugene Celebration is Planned Parenthood for a theme featuring a sunglass-wearing character named "Joe Sperm."

In 2000, two Eugene men file an initiative proposal restricting the repetitive music that ice cream trucks play as they cruise neighborhoods.

In 2000, after speaking at the UO, the top environmental adviser to then-Vice President Al Gore has a 20-pound Chinook salmon thrust in her face.

During a 2000 speech at the UO, tree-sitter Julia "Butterfly" Hill is heckled to tears by a masked trio who claimed that after a two-year protest perched in a California redwood, she "sold out" to a logging company.

In 2008, nude protesters ride bicycles around town to denounce the country's dependence on oil and other nonrenewable energy.

A lining up of weirdness stars? Perhaps not. Then again, it's not easy dismissing dozens of full moons.

Mac's final night

Jan. 2, 2011

It was fitting that my walk to attend the final men's basketball game at the University of Oregon's McArthur Court was through the Pioneer Cemetery.

The experience evoked at least a touch of death.

Many of the game's 7,165 fans, after all, were saying goodbye to a place that's provided us decades of fond memories. Now, after nearly 84 years, it's giving way to the new Matthew Knight Arena.

The UO's women's team has the honor of playing the final Mac Court game this Saturday, but last night was my farewell. And the farewell for men's basketball, which played the first game in the building on Jan. 14, 1927.

UO won that opener, over Willamette, but couldn't close with a victory, falling 60-55 to Arizona State.

Fans seemed to be in a fairly forgiving mood; after all, this night was as much about the past as the present.

Everywhere you looked, people were snapping photos. The trivia questions during timeouts focused on Mac Court memories. And among the loudest ovations of the evening were for ex-Ducks Aaron Brooks, now with the Houston Rockets, and Rear Adm. John Dick, one of the "Tall Firs" who won UO's lone NCAA championship, in 1939.

If you can stroll down memory lane at Mac Court — not easy given the crowds in the narrow concourse — I did just that, arriving first at a Neil Young concert Jan. 10, 1971, as a high school junior. Though captivated by Young's all-acoustic show, I was also enamored by a sold-out McArthur Court, though it wasn't love at first sight.

Only time and experiences can forge such a bond between person and place.

Twenty months later, I registered for my first semester of UO classes on Mac Court's wooden floor, knowing nothing of the history already sealed into a building that opened in 1927: Jack Dempsey's powerful punches, Bob Hope's eye-rolling jokes, Robert F. Kennedy's hopeful words.

That fall, I interviewed, in the stands, an unknown-at-the-time freshman basketball player, Ronnie Lee, for the *Oregon Daily Emerald*. And, in the next few years, watched the Lee-led "Kamikaze Kids" turn Mac Court into "The Pit," an amped-up venue that became an intoxicating blend of basketball, prizefighting and Woodstock.

Before games and during timeouts, a student "Lone Ranger" rode a stick pony around the floor to rev up the crowd as the UO band blared "The William Tell Overture."

Students camped out after Friday night games so they'd get prime seats for Saturday's.

The Ducks played, in the words of Wichita State coach Harry Miller, like "kamikaze pilots." They pounced on loose balls. Dived into the stands to make saves. And basically antagonized the life out of their often more-talented opponents.

Coach Dick Harter, often in plaid pants, fueled a fanaticism that sometimes spun out of control. After a 1974 win over No. 1 UCLA, announcer Don Essig interrupted the postgame celebration thusly: "Will the students please get off the backboards?"

In 1975, a fan took a swing at a referee, UCLA's Dave Meyers took a Frisbee in the leg and, of course, who can forget the streaker?

But among my favorite Mac Court memories was when, in 1976, a handful of University of Washington players donned Groucho Marx glasses to counter Oregon's pregame tradition of staring down their opponents at mid-court — noses to really-big noses — then won the game. *Touché!*

Over the years, I've sat in probably two dozen locales at Mac Court, from press row to where my season tickets were for the last decade: second-row-from-the-top in Section 316. Weirdly, my favorite location.

Plywood seats that looked as if made in a high school shop class. Parents who'd punch out the bottoms of popcorn boxes and duct-tape the containers to the wall so their kids could play halftime hoops. A visual jungle: two-by-fours, catwalks, pipes and thick, wooden beams. Given the horizontal strands of wire we had to look through, we joked that our seats came with cable vision.

Indeed, there was no pretense about the upper deck. A friend of mine, Sandy Silverthorne, likened it to bunking in steerage on the *Titanic*. "Every time I open the door, I expect to see Leonardo DiCaprio leading the other passengers in an Irish folk dance."

I won't miss certain things about Mac Court, say, the tiny men's bathrooms, which were like mosh pits with urinals. But as the final minutes of Oregon's loss to Arizona State ticked down Saturday night, I wanted to call a permanent timeout so the ambiance wouldn't have to end — nor would the memories.

Because Mac Court has been more than a basketball arena. It's been like a microcosm of Eugene itself: unique, quirky, full of the flavor that Civic Stadium had and Hayward Field still has. The stuff money can't buy — not that the new arena won't create an identity all its own and memories for, say, some 16-year-old kid who'll attend a concert or game there the first time this season.

But also stuff that can never be replicated, the moments we Mac lovers will take with us:

Like two heavyweight fighters, UCLA outlasting Oregon 107-103 in a 1975 game in which the two teams scored more points than in any other game, my voice so hoarse afterward I could hardly order a pizza ... Luke Jackson's 29 straight against Colorado in 2004 ... Luke Ridenour's three-point bombs ... Arizona Coach Lute Olson, after a tirade-triggered technical foul, turning boos to cheers when he bowed to the crowd in all four directions ... Bev Smith's first team rising from the dead to win the 2002 Women's National Invitation Tournament ... the smell of popcorn greeting you as soon as you got through the front doors ... "Bingo cards, get your halftime bingo cards!" ... and, finally, after some spectacular shot, the foot-stomping, hand-clapping, basket-shaking joy that seemed to meld 9,000-plus people in a rare sense of sweat-tinged oneness.

Change is inevitable; as a Neil Young song says: "Comes a time."

On Saturday, that time came at 8:57 p.m. when the last men's game officially ended.

"Thanks a lot, Mac Court," Essig said. "We'll never forget."

John Dick, 91, with the help of a cane and a friend, slowly left the court he'd played on 71 years ago. And I headed back to my car through the cemetery, looking back one final time.

2.

Seasons

Forgetting our soggy roots

Dec. 20, 2011

I walked out to get the paper the other morning — one of life's small pleasures — when I realized something was wrong.

Once again, it was not raining.

As if I were in the way of an errant emotional javelin, I was stabbed instantly with guilt. It hadn't been raining for weeks, and yet I had noticed only now.

Do you see what's happening? Maybe it's happening to you.

We're not missing the very thing that defines us as Oregonians. Rain.

We're thinking this cold, clear, Christmasy weather is kind of nice.

We're starting to think we're just like every other dry-and-mighty place.

And that's dangerous. Because we're not.

"I don't mind the rain, but I don't miss it," a friend says flippantly.

Dangerous thinking, that.

Here are the hard, cold facts — as opposed to the usual soggy, mild facts:

In the historically wettest month of the year, December, we haven't had a single day with measurable precipitation.

We've had precipitation on only four of the past 19 days.

We've had only 0.66 inches of precipitation since Thanksgiving, and nearly three-fourths of that trifling amount came in a single day: Nov. 27.

Do you remember that afternoon and evening? It was a Sunday. I was halfway through putting up our outdoor Christmas lights when the rain came, inspiring me to tackle the uninspiring job of cleaning my gutters while on the ladder.

It hasn't rained since.

So pour that into my guilt bucket, too: the fact that cleaning my gutters for the first time since roughly 1991 triggered our current mini-drought.

The weather gods, to spite me for my laziness, fiendishly have placed a moratorium on those nimbostratus clouds that drip rain like saturated, coal-dark towels. And I was so looking forward to seeing if my poor man's Roto-Rooter job worked on the downspouts.

But now I must wait. And how long?

The five-day forecast suggests only chances of rain here and there — Wednesday afternoon at the soonest. At the current rate, we might be headed for the driest December — 7.83 inches is average — on record: 1976, when only 1.24 inches of precipitation fell amid a true drought winter.

That was a fun year for me. I lived in Bend, and with no snow, I played hockey on ice-covered Devils Lake at the foot of South Sister, using tuna fish cans for goals.

That said, droughts aren't good, which is where more guilt comes into play for those of us who wake up and realize we're not missing the rain as much as we should be.

What about the skiers, snowboarders and lift operators?

What about the Eugene Water & Electric Board and the Springfield Utility Board, which buy all that dam-produced energy and bill us accordingly — more, generally, in low-snowpack years, which this is shaping up to be?

What about the farmers who need storage in the reservoirs this winter for irrigation come spring?

What about sailors who need keel clearance at shallow Fern Ridge Lake come summer?

Wait a minute. That's me!

Alas, I've blithely blundered into the mass of ignorance-is-bliss folks, the immediate-gratification types who welcome each rainless day as if there were no rainy tomorrow.

At last Saturday's Holiday Market, browsers brazenly walked by without umbrellas in their hands.

On Sunday, at the Off the Waffle restaurant on Willamette Street, people wolfed down breakfasts without even glancing pensively to see if it was raining outside.

Later, as fans filed in for a Kidsports basketball game at Monroe Middle School, nobody's shoes squeaked from having sloshed through puddles to get there.

And here's the thing: We all acted as if this were normal.

As if this were an-every-December occurrence.

As if we were non-cinematic Ariels, *The Little Mermaid* who dared to boldly live beyond the water.

Ah, but she's chastised by her father, Triton, after she admits she liked it.

"Not another word," he booms. "I am never, never to hear of you going to the surface again. Is that clear?"

Kathie Dello, deputy director of Oregon Climate Service in Corvallis, brings no such warning.

"Winter's just beginning and it's not time to panic," she says, "but this is unusual."

"Things can change really fast," says George Taylor, president of Applied Climate Services in Corvallis.

We can only hope so, lest we forget our soggy roots as Oregonians. And are parched by our guilt in doing so.

The snow flake

March 22, 2012

When spring unlocks the flowers to paint the laughing soil ..."
The English poet Reginald Heber penned those words two centuries ago. And Tuesday night, as I drove through our daffodil-sprinkled neighborhood, I was ready for the manifestation of such here in the Valley of Perpetual Drizzle.

I was ready for painting flowers and laughing soil.

But spring has not thusly sprung. It has, instead, crashed down on us with all the subtlety of a snow-laden oak branch shattering a backyard arbor.

It has seeped into our shoes in the form of icy water from parking lots that look and feel like a really large but shallow Slurpee.

It has snarled our commutes and closed our schools and stopped our EmX buses literally in their tracks, like frozen slugs.

The Willamette Valley soil is not laughing. Instead, it is considering a breach-of-contract lawsuit against the weather gods, whose March 20 promise of spring was shattered by a 7-inch-plus snowstorm that arrived early Wednesday morning.

Like Muhammad Ali, it floated like a butterfly, then stung like a bee, the beauty of snow at dawn giving way to falling trees. Power outages. Limb-sanity.

The result? The true allegiance of self-proclaimed snow lovers is at stake.

It is one thing to love snow when it whitens the backdrop of Christmas lights; another to love it when it crumples your rhodies only 10 days short of April.

One thing to love it when it melts by 9 a.m.; another to love it, like Wednesday, when it hangs around like *Christmas Vacation's* Cousin Eddie. "Don't you go falling in love with (my RV) now, because we're taking it with us when we leave here next month."

One thing to love it when it's soft and feathery; another to love it when it's wet and heavy and seeping through your garage roof, courtesy of the hole it helped inflict with that snapped fir branch.

Earlier in the week, Sheldon High baseball Coach Stan Manley mumbled something to me in a downpour about putting in a plea to the weather gods to end the incessant rain; two of his team's three games had been scrubbed.

"I should have been more specific in my request," he told me Wednesday while talking by cell phone at the school's white-glazed ballpark. "Two geese just landed in right field. We open spring break in Arizona against New Mexico's defending state champs — and we haven't even been outside in two weeks."

So, where do I stand on snow?

Lately, everywhere, though I sink quickly because the stuff has the density of mixed concrete.

But, no, I still pledge my allegiance to the united skates of a miracle — our collective boot-wrapped feet slip-sliding in oneness to celebrate this rare phenomenon of frozen ice crystals.

Yup, even if it's spring, even if it was 85 in Chicago on Wednesday, even if I might yet wind up power-less, I am still a snow flake.

Snow makes you a kid again. OK, so maybe you're not making snow angels in the front yard or hammering your neighbor with a fat one in the ear, but you're remembering such days. You're 10 again and school's canceled and you're sledding in Corvallis' Corl's Field.

Snow brings the present-day kids out of the video game woodwork. Around the neighborhood, kids are laughing and rolling snowballs and trying to snowboard down nearly flat driveways — kids whom you might not see the rest of the year. A snowman welcomes you at the Starbucks on Seventh and Washington. People's moods are lighter than usual.

Snow brings us together and, in some cases, bonds us. While getting the morning paper, a neighbor is using a broom to lighten the snowy load on our Japanese maple. Elsewhere, folks give power-out neighbors juice via extension cords. Others pitch in to help cut up a road-blocking tree.

On Facebook, photos feature parents and kids building snow people, baking cookies, playing Monopoly. (Instead of war, why don't world leaders just play a spirited game of Monopoly during a snowstorm and call it good?)

Snow throws off routines. We live much of our lives as if straight from the movie *Groundhog Day.* But snow snarls everything. It humbles us. Reminds us that though we can plan and plan and plan, nature bats last. Reminds us that everything we thought was so critically important might not be as important as watching the beauty of falling snow.

In defending my allegiance to snow, I realize that such weather causes some people serious problems. It can do more than inconvenience us. It can be dangerous. It can cut people off from services they need. I'm not championing that.

I also realize some may chide my childish take on this. But what worries me isn't being an adult and letting snow bring out the kid in me. What worries me is that someday I might not.

Summer dreams

Feb. 7, 2012

In the past few days, I've lunched at a cafe on the Place du Tertre in Paris; watched the northern lights while on a boat off Seward, Alaska; feasted on fresh Willamette Valley corn; and listened to ballgame cheers at old Civic Stadium.

All without leaving Eugene. Or winter.

Thanks to 73 *Register-Guard* readers who responded magnificently to my request for "bites of summer scenes," I've soaked up hundreds of such moments.

In my Jan. 29 column, I asked for favorite summer scenarios from five locales: readers' homes, Lane County, Oregon, the United States and the world. I not only got that — but short stories, poetry, photos, videos, websites, all sorts of stuff designed to help sweep away our midwinter malaise.

"Breitenbush Hot Springs, immersed in the silence of a pool at dawn." (Michael Ireland, Eugene.)

"Walking through my garden, listening to the bees while picking vegetables I will serve at dinner." (Rebecca Harshbarger, Walterville.)

"Strolling down the dusty path in the warm coolness of late August dusk, swatting mosquitoes and swinging a bucket of fresh blackberries." (Phoebe Penix, Junction City.)

What did I learn?

That we are amazingly diverse in the ways we love summer. One man's "silence of a pool at dawn" is another man's high-rev all-terrain-vehicle kicking up dust near Christmas Valley.

Sometimes the diversity came from the same contributor. "Nothing beats finding a nice, shady spot just off Chela Mela Meadow at the Oregon Country Fair and dedicating the day to regarding the wonderful wacky world of humanity at play," wrote Ronald Duber of Eugene. But Duber also dreamed of "sitting at night, legs dangling off a pier at Key West (Fla.) under a star-glittered sky and watching July Fourth fireworks while Kate Smith's 'God Bless America' courses over on balmy breezes."

I learned that summer and simplicity go together like hot dogs and buns. "Yet another evening match of badminton with my ever-improving and competitive daughter," wrote Randy Sangder of Eugene.

"Inviting friends over for backyard lawn chair movie viewing," wrote the appropriately named Debbie Summers. "We project a DVD movie onto a big white sheet and if need be, after popcorn is served, curl up under blankets as the movie unfolds."

Oh, sure, with the world offered as their oyster, readers went far and wide — to more than 25 states and 27 countries. They listened to "Shakespeare float over the soft Central Park night" (Katherine Hlebakos-Paiva, Eugene), scuba-dived in the Philippines (Jan Schamp, Eugene) and helped build a school in Haiti (Roger Austin, Bend).

But what rushed to the forefront of readers' summer sweetness was the stuff of Oregon — and I don't say that just because I'm so well Oregon-ized myself. "How can you beat the beauty of Oregon?" wrote Molly Bannister of Eugene, who exalted hiking a 10-falls, 10-mile trail at Silver Falls State Park.

"Sitting in a camp chair in an ocean of sagebrush, the last of the ice melting into the whiskey, watching the evening sky on fire over Warner Peak in Hart Mountain National Antelope Refuge," wrote Tim Baxter of Eugene.

"Diving into the cool, clear water at a swimming hole on Fall Creek, followed closely by the family black Lab," wrote Whitney Donielson of Eugene.

In a random drawing, June Miller of Eugene won a $50 gift certificate for Johnny Ocean's Grille at the Oakway Center after offering her two-cents' worth, which included runs along the Willamette, hikes in the Coast Range and bike rides in Vancouver, B.C.'s Stanley Park.

Readers' offerings dipped deeply into the five senses; you could practically taste the "bodacious corn-on-the-cob, vine-ripe tomatoes, coleslaw and barbecued chicken — with wipe-your-chin local peaches for dessert," offered by Lee Darling of Eugene.

And smell the mint fields near Coburg suggested by Rick Doyle of Eugene.

"The feel of my summer dress softly brushing bare legs," wrote Candyce Rappaport of Eugene. "The welcome coolness of water on my feet."

The Bach Festival, Hayward Field and gardens emerged as clear summer favorites.

Interestingly, for many, so did the idea of going back in time.

"Someday as I drive on Highway 224, maybe five miles north of Trail, I want to catch a small glimpse of yesterday," wrote Dennis Anderson of Sutherlin. "When I pass my house, maybe just maybe, I will see my big brother and me, outside playing catch, our dog Toby watching. ... I can smell cookies and fresh-baked bread and, occasionally, I can almost make out the clinks and clanks of horseshoes hitting iron pipes."

Ah, summer.

Stay right there; we're comin'.

Letting go of summer

Sept. 5, 2010

The other morning about 6 o'clock, I peered out of my sleeping bag from a small sailboat on Fern Ridge Lake.

In the distance, a still-backstage sun pinkened the sky above the Coburg Hills before making its appearance. Two dozen geese flew south over the glassy water. And a lone white pelican, the first I've seen at Fern Ridge, paddled by not far from the on-anchor boat.

How do you let go of a summer like this?

For me, not easily.

I understand the pull of autumn. I heard a couple of young mothers the other night all but counting down the days until the kids are back in school. I'm all for leaf-covered paths, dried cornstalks and Autzen ablaze in green and yellow.

But I'm like my 5-year-old grandson, who, told by his folks that it's time to go, will say: "Just a few more minutes, just a few more minutes ... ."

We don't like saying goodbye to something or someone or someplace we love. And that resistance is the very sign of how much that something or someone or someplace means to us.

This was my 57th summer and maybe my best: a medley of journeys on land and water and sand and rails and trails; music at dusk; and magical moments, not the least of which was hearing, outside the door of a room at Sacred Heart Medical Center at RiverBend, the first cry of a grandson.

Never mind the soggy June, the sub-par blackberry season, the fence you and your neighbor were going to replace but never got around to. Summer, I've always believed, is meant for total immersion.

You eat outside whenever you can because you're an Oregonian and know your window of opportunity is limited. You notice the windless perfection of the late-August morning as you go to get the paper because you'll soon be doing it in the rain. You talk yourself into another trip to the lake because even though you've unfurled the sails aplenty, you know the lake will soon go dry.

I don't put away summer easily. In Dylan Thomas' words, I quietly "rage, rage against the dying of the light."

If I'm an equal-opportunity seasons guy and love a good three-day rain, nevertheless I am, at my core, a summer guy. In the Monopoly game of life, summer is the Park Place/Boardwalk side of the board: the same size and structure as the other three sides, just a touch more valuable.

We remember summers in a way we don't remember other seasons. We smell sun block or taste a fresh-off-the-vine tomato or feel the leather of the same baseball mitt we used when you were 12, and we're 12 forever.

We mark time with summers. In relation to our lives. And in relation to the passing of years.

We remember the moment it began — long after June 21 this year — and the moment we realized it was ending: on Thursday, noticing the blackberries have come and gone.

It was a short, late season for blackberries, and most that finally mustered themselves into shape weren't their zesty selves. But summer isn't about perfection.

Some of my summer's best memories involve imperfection, notably the night in Yachats last July when the damp, year-old briquettes were so slow to light that I got carried away with the charcoal lighter fluid.

Midway through the dinner, a son passing the plate of gassy-flavored chicken was asking guests if they wanted regular or unleaded. And after my failure became the seagulls' Chicken Surprise, he couldn't resist. "Look," he said, "a gull just exploded in mid-air."

In the summer of 2010, I went to two parades (Eugene Celebration and the Yachats La-De-Da) and two Eugene Emeralds games. I ate corn on the cob while an upstart trio of high schoolers named 3 Way Street soothed a summer night in Coburg with the sound of electric guitars and drums.

I completed an Albany-to-Eugene round trip train trip that I began as an 8-year-old Cub Scout in 1962, making the Eugene-to-Albany return trip with 5- and 3-year-old grandchildren.

I tried my first jumbo-marshmallow s'more, saw a falling star while 6,000 feet up in the Cascades and totally redeemed myself in the eyes of the chicken-dinner group by catching my first steelhead on a fly rod and grilling it to perfection. (Using propane.)

If I'd only experienced a smidgen of all this, it would have been enough. Still, I think of that morning on the boat, the lake completely still, the world at peace, the temperature perfect, and I think what I always think as the last of summer slips away.

Just a few more minutes.

3.

State of mine

A river runs through him

April 20, 2010

It will probably be told around the fire Saturday at Eagle Rock Lodge on the McKenzie River; like leaves in eddies, fish stories have a habit of circling round and round. And what better time to tell it than on the opening day of trout season when dozens will gather at Eagle Rock for the fifth annual McKenzie Wooden Boat Festival.

It's the story about how Greg Hatten, then chief merchandising officer at Bi-Mart, was, while at work, cajoling a co-worker to show him his special steelhead-filleting technique.

"All we need is a fresh fish," said the company's renowned "fish surgeon," Dennis Down, "and I'll show you."

"Deal," Hatten said.

Before anyone knew it, Hatten was out the door — it was noon — with the promise of a fish for a 1 p.m. demonstration.

With his fly rod already in his 1983 Toyota Land Cruiser FJ40 — never know when you're going to need a fresh fish — he drove to a spot on the Willamette River 10 minutes away. Pulled on his waders over his business outfit. And, an hour later, returned with a 32-inch, 12-pound fish that he kept under his desk in a plastic bag until show-time.

"Don't you love Oregon?" says Hatten.

Folks, there's a reason Hatten's homemade drift boat is named "Obsession."

He has one. With fly-fishing. With the McKenzie and Willamette Rivers — heck, with individual pools and riffles, which he names in his journal. ("May Tag," "Dire Straits," "Upper Homeless," etc.) And with the 16-foot wooden McKenzie-style boat, made from mahogany and Alaskan yellow cedar, that he spent 600 hours building.

"About 2 a.m., my wife would flip the garage lights on and off to remind me it was time for bed," Hatten says.

Janet Hatten has seen worse. There was the time Greg made *Epoxy News* magazine for his ingenuity in getting his glue to set up amid Oregon's 45-degree days: He moved the boat's two 16-foot panels into the house's foyer to dry.

Blog sites refer to Hatten, 52, as the "king of the town run," the Eugene stretch of the Willamette, and he and guide Lou Verdugo won the 2008 McKenzie River two-fly tournament. But what makes Hatten particularly interesting isn't just that he's good at catching fish.

It's his passion for the sport, the river, the experience. He is part artist, part (mad) scientist and part lighthearted ambassador for the fishing wonders of Oregon. (Did we tell you he once drove his Land Cruiser in the Rhododendron Festival Parade, a rhododendron-festooned replica of a "McKenzie Redside" trout mounted to the front — being "caught" by a fly rod mounted to a trailer he was pulling)

Naturally, when Hatten heard that Monty Python's *Spamalot* was coming to the Hult Center last April — and learned that the lead, John O'Hurley, likes to fish — he did something every bit as practical as slipping waders over his Dockers.

He invited O'Hurley, who played J. Peterman on Seinfeld, for a day of fishing on the McKenzie.

"I knew he had a week to kill while he was here," Hatten says. "I promised him a retro experience: wooden boat, classic river, bamboo rod and silk line. He said yes."

The two hit if off. O'Hurley caught a couple of fish. Invited Hatten and his family backstage. Even insisted that Greg and Janet stay in his Vermont home when the two were heading back to Boston in a few weeks, though it didn't work out.

"Five years ago, fly-fishing for me was about that charge, that jolt when you feel that fish hit," Hatten says. "Now, however, I get a bigger kick out of helping other people catch fish."

Which begins with knowing where the fish are. He flips out his journal, which shows sketches of different holes on the Willamette.

With each catch, he marks a red dot on his self-made river map. (More than 200 dots in the past five years.) He names nearby features and makes notes about the weather, air temperature, water temperature, fly and leader used — even on what part of the mouth the fish was hooked.

"It is," he says, "a natural progression of an obsessive fisherman."

Not that the fish itself is what this is all about. The deeper "catches," he says, aren't found in a creel, but in the face of his son Daniel, now 26, when he landed his first steelhead last year. In the way maneuvering his boat amid rapids is, he says, "almost like a dance, an impromptu, unchoreographed lovely river dance." And in the stories that will be told Saturday night around the fire at Eagle Rock.

"On some of my best days," says Hatten, "I don't catch a thing."

Songs of a state

Feb. 14, 2012

The sound of the surf, the silence of a high Cascades lake, the touchdown roar of an Autzen crowd — that's what I hear when I listen for Oregon, which turns 153 today.

But what is it that the songwriters hear?

Traditionally, I commemorate our great state's birthday with a column; this year's theme is songs about — and musical references to — Oregon.

Not that we're particularly known for either.

Face it. Nobody east of Ontario, north of Portland or south of Ashland has heard our songs. It's not like we have a single iconic "New York! New York!" or "Oklahoma!" or handfuls of "California Dreamin'" songs that are worn into the national psyche like grooves in a vinyl record.

Our songs, like the state itself, are more subtle in their bravado, more mysterious and, of course, more quirky.

Nobody's going to turn Shawn Mullins'"Twin Rocks, Oregon" into a Broadway musical. ("I met him on the cliffs/of Twin Rocks, Oregon/he was sittin' on his bedroll/lookin' just like Richard Brautigan.")

Oh, we've got our musty chest-beaters from decades past, including the state song, "Oregon, My Oregon," whose title alone very few Oregonians could probably name. ("Land of the Empire Builders, Land of the Golden West; Conquered and held by free men, Fairest and the best.")

And in perhaps the oddest business arrangement ever — given how dams tamed the river — the Bonneville Power Administration commissioned folk musician Woody Guthrie to write "Roll on, Columbia."

Me? I favor songs that give us a glimpse of the state's less obvious nooks and crannies, such as Yachats singer Richard Sharpless'"The Devil's Churn Song": ("Big sky above, big sea below/Five dollar parking for a heck of a show/Beauty abounds everywhere you turn/ And you can have a cup of coffee at the Devil's Churn.")

Sometimes it takes outsiders to remind us of our allurements. Greg Brown's "Eugene" offers back-to-nature with a fisher-poet's twist:

"I think I'll drive out to Eugene, get a slide-in camper for my truck, pack a bamboo rod ... I'll park by some rivers, cook up some rice and beans, read Ferlinghetti out loud ... ."

Some Oregon-esque music celebrates our, uh, less-outdoorsy side, such as Loretta Lynn singing, "Well Portland Oregon and slow gin fizz/If that ain't love then tell me what is/Well I lost my heart it didn't take no time/But that ain't all. I lost my mind in Oregon."

On the other hand, in the early 1970s, a sick-while-touring Dolly Parton — at the time, a rookie — apologized to her Eugene crowd for her lack of energy. But she got such a warm response, including two standing ovations, that after the show she wrote, "Eugene, Oregon," whose lyrics include: "Eugene, Oregon, I'll remember you for the rest of my life/I won't forget how good you were to me/No and I won't be forgettin' all the kindness that you showed/To a homesick country girl a long, long way from Tennessee."

Speaking of Elvis' home state, cowboy singer Dan Roberts, a former Eugene resident who opened for two years for Garth Brooks and lived outside Nashville, wrote a song called "Don't Bury Me in Tennessee": "So when my soul's glory bound/Plant me deep in the sandy ground/Overlooking Silver Creek in Oregon ... ."

Roberts, 57, couldn't shake the beauty of a place he'd fallen in love with while deer hunting west of Burns.

Some songs speak of an Oregon that once was but no longer is, musical versions of Ken Kesey's *Sometimes a Great Notion*. Among them, Johnny Cash's "Lumberjack" (1960):

"Well, you work in the woods from morning to night/You laugh and sing and you cuss and you fight/On a Saturday night you go to Eugene/And on a Sunday morning your pockets are clean."

But even if Grammy Award nominee Meredith Brooks might not find Corvallis quite as bucolic as she presumably remembers it in "My Little Town," she captures the pull many of us feel of a place we once left: "Spend half your life trying to make a change/And the other half trying to get back again."

It's true today. And it was true in 1916 when Bert Grant (music) and Sam Lewis and Joe Young (words) wrote, "Arrah Go on, I'm Gonna Go Back to Oregon."

Beyond Roberts' "Don't Bury Me ... " — and he's disqualified because he's a friend — my favorite Oregon song is one that enjoyed a meteoric burst in 1974.

It's called "Oregon (I can't go home)" by a Monmouth-based

group, Black Hawk County, and rose to No. 16 on Billboard Charts and No. 1 in the Northwest.

It was written about an on-sabbatical University of Oregon student, Joann McDaniels, who'd been thrown in a Turkish prison and been sentenced first to death, then life in prison, for drug smuggling.

And it is a hauntingly beautiful song.

"They say the Oregon rain will get you down,/But I hunger for the freshness of its sound/The wind, the sun, the things that I have known before,/Now seem like faded ghosts, like shadows on the floor ... ."

More on the McDaniels story in a subsequent column. For now, happy birthday, Oregon, though I'll spare you all the song.

Saving Oregon's beaches

June 22, 2010

Once I was talking to a class of high schoolers and, as an example of risk-taking, mentioned Olympic gold medalist Dick Fosbury. I got two dozen blank stares.

Fosbury was the Medford High and Oregon State high jumper who, in the tumultuous '60s, literally turned his back on the establishment to invent a new way of going over the bar.

But when I asked for a show of hands, I realized not a single student knew of him. All assumed athletes had just always flipped backward over the high-jump bar.

Nope.

So, when I saw Monday's Associated Press story about how folks in New Jersey, Florida and California are wrestling with private beach ownership, I imagined some readers being reminded that we shouldn't take our public shoreline for granted.

But I also imagined ho-hums from those unfamiliar with the likes of Oregon Govs. Oswald West and Tom McCall.

They're the two guys most responsible for our 320 miles of beaches being unfenced. The two guys you can thank when you, say, walk unimpeded for eight miles from Yachats to Waldport. Or note that Oregon, along with Hawaii, is one of only two states in the union where the public owns all the beaches.

McCall, a Republican, in 1967 spearheaded passage of one of the most far-reaching measures of its kind in the nation: a beach bill that established public ownership of the land along the coast.

"The beach bill is more than just a piece of legislation, it is a fundamental part of what makes Oregon a place we love to call home," former Secretary of State Bill Bradbury once said.

Even if McCall successfully overcame a small rip tide of opposition, you can't tell his success story without first telling West's. Both are splendidly twined in Brent Walth's *Fire at Eden's Gate* (Oregon Historical Society), a book on McCall that doubles as the finest post-World War II portrait of Oregon available.

In 1909, West defeated Republican Jay Bowerman, future father of future track and field guru Bill Bowerman, for governor. A land-fraud investigator, West had a passion to keep public lands public. Although by the turn of the century only 23 miles of the Oregon coast had been sold to private parties — and, unlike California, nobody was fencing off beaches — he worried about land speculators changing that.

Ah, but to run a campaign to give the coastline public designation risked alarming the Legislature and triggering a land grab. So, as he later wrote: "I drafted a simple short bill declaring the seashore from the Washington line to the California line a public highway. I pointed out that thus we would come into miles and miles of highway without cost to the taxpayer."

The 1913 legislature passed the bill without fanfare. The Highway Commission never made any pretense of building roads on the shore. And, in 1947, the legislature changed the designation of the sands from "highway" to "recreation area."

But as the decades passed, a flaw in West's bill made it a ticking time bomb. The bill said public ownership extended from low tide to high. Thus, over the years, 112 miles of dry sands had been bought by private parties, even if the state considered it belonging to everyone.

In 1967, the time bomb exploded. William Hay, a Portland real estate broker who owned the Surfsand Motel at then-sleepy Cannon Beach, fenced off a private beach from the motel to the high-tide mark.

The Highway Department quickly drafted a new bill that would give the state ownership of the coast's entire beach line, up to the vegetation line above the dry sands. That hit some like a tsunami.

Enter Gov. McCall, a six-foot-five maverick who — as his famous "visit-but-don't-stay" comment suggests — could be ferocious on land use issues. To gain public support for the bill, he got the press involved, first with a leaked letter and then with a high-profile visit to the Surfsand Motel.

His entourage, including reporters, scientists and surveyors, arrived in two helicopters. He grumbled to motel guests about Hay's audacity to stick up no-trespassing signs. And at one point, literally drew a line in the sand, which, of course, the photographers loved.

Ultimately, a compromise was reached: The state wouldn't take property away from private owners; however, it would have the right to zone the land for what it thought was in the best interest of the people, which it decided was public ownership of everything from the low tide mark to 16 vertical feet above that. Essentially, all sand, wet or dry.

On July 6, 1967, the landmark beach bill passed, 57 to 3.

Never mind that McCall gladly basked in the spotlight. At the bill's signing, he deferred to a quote from Gov. Oswald West, who had died in 1960: "No local selfish interest should be permitted, through politics or otherwise, to destroy or even impair this great birthright of our people."

State's 10 prettiest drives

June 27, 2010

Oregon's summer finally arrives with the reluctance of a teenager told to be home by 9 — on a weekend.

Sailboaters are heeling, children cartwheeling, motorists automobiling, drinking in sights from around the state.

Summer begs us to explore.

So, here's my Top 10 List of scenic highway stretches, with two qualifiers: I only chose those stretches I've been on. And I admit that emotion colored my picks. (The scenery from a road on which you've built feel-good memories is going to resonate more deeply than on a road with no such memories.)

So, the top scenic stretches of Oregon highways, saving the best for last:

10. Corvallis to McMinnville on Highway 99W (46 miles). Farms. Fields. Barns. A few wineries. Rolling hills of grass. A great swath of rural America, even if it also looks a bit like the back roads of France and Belgium.

9. Newport to Taft on Highway 101 (20 miles). Diversity galore: the Yaquina Lighthouse, 500-foot Cape Foulweather and one-of-a-kind Depoe Bay, through which I can't pass without thinking of that wonderful gone-fishin' scene in *One Flew Over the Cuckoo's Nest*. Includes one of the most beautiful scenes on the Oregon Coast: Whale Cove, two miles south of Depoe Bay, best viewed on a south-to-north drive. Stretch culminates with a sea-level view of Siletz Bay, with those water-locked stumps and trees that, given a foggy day, conjure the start of a good mystery novel.

8. Wallowa to Enterprise to Flora on highways 82 and 3 (62 miles). Wonderful views of Oregon's most-overlooked mountains, the Wallowas, which look like mini-Alps. Tiny towns offering that other-world feel. And, heading up Highway 3 to the state's far northeast corner, giant ponderosa pines on a high plateau — 4,683 feet — that make you think of the start of TV's "Bonanza," though without your road map bursting into flames. Two bonuses: the view of Joseph Canyon and the chance to literally be in Paradise, a former town that's now nothing more than a sign with its name.

7. Crown Point to Biggs Junction on Interstate 84 (76 miles). With morning or evening light, the chiseled walls of the Columbia Gorge, contrasted with the blue of the Columbia River, are awesome. Until you're in the gorge, you forget its immensity, given perspective by locomotives on the Washington side that look as if from a child's train set. Bonuses: Multnomah Falls. And, just before Biggs Junction, the Maryhill Museum of Art, perched dramatically on the gorge's northern edge.

6. Port Orford to Brookings on Highway 101 (59 miles). With its bay, Port Orford exudes a rare East Coast feel. Great ocean views are available most of the way until Oregon gives way to California, the sea sprinkled with those offshore rocks that remind you of ghost ships.

5. Bend to Highway 58 Junction on Cascade Lakes Highway (73 miles). Trees, mountains (The South Sister, Broken Top and Mount Bachelor) and lakes, including that impossibly green northeast corner of Devils Lake. One of those stretches that grabs me emotionally every time, my father having camped and fished here on Dutchman Flat in the 1930s, and me having done the same with my two boys in the 1980s.

4. Harrisburg to Corvallis on Peoria Road (22 miles). Though folks with allergies won't agree, particularly nice after a summer sunset when the grass fields are being cut. Mennonite country. Stretches of road uncluttered by telephone lines. And, for me at least, one of those iconic smells of an Oregon summer.

3. Frenchglen to Fields to East Steens Road/Route 78 junction (121 miles). Want to feel lonesome? Drive this remote stretch in the state's southeast corner. Because the route makes a "V" around the southern end of Steens Mountain, you get east, north and west views of Steens, plus a chance to drive on the Alvord Desert. (Note: Do not drive this stretch — it's gravel from Fields to the junction — without taking food, water and at least one good spare tire. And don't plan on cell service.)

2. Springfield to Sisters on highways 126 and 242 (92 miles). The McKenzie Valley, the McKenzie River, a twisting forest road into the high Cascades and reach-out-and-touch views of the Three Sisters from lava land. Nothing like it anywhere else.

1. Florence to Yachats on Highway 101 (26 miles). Even accounting for my Yachats bias, I can't not place this No. 1. As you climb 101 to meet the ocean at the foot of Cape Mountain, the Utah Beach look of the grass and dunes surrounding Lily Lake. The postcard-favorite Heceta Head Lighthouse and the adjacent light keeper's cottage, about which many have probably thought: Oh, I'll take that one. Ocean views from Sea Lion Point to sea level and back up to Cape Perpetua. Creeks bubbling to their final destinations. Cook's Chasm spewing frothy splash on the Lane-Lincoln County line.

Never mind that my sons, as teenagers, would roll their eyes when I'd say it each trip: "If you're a kid from Kansas, you may never see this kind of beauty. We're blessed."

It's corny but true.

4.

Outdoors

Hiking the Muir

Aug. 30, 2014

L ONE PINE, Calif. — When I first saw the Sierra Nevada from the east, the mountains rose ominously, like a frozen tsunami. Thunderclouds brooded amid peaks that looked like the jagged teeth of a 14,000-foot-high, upside-down buck saw.

Forget six months of training, research and planning. One look at those mountains and I felt completely out of my league for believing that, at 60, I could hike the 210-mile John Muir Trail south from Yosemite National Park to the top of 14,505-foot Mt. Whitney, the highest point in the contiguous United States.

"Excuse me," said a woman after I'd walked across Lone Pine's main drag, "but it looks like you have some toilet paper or something stuck on the back of your sandal."

Thus further bolstered with confidence, I began the adventure. We left my brother-in-law Glenn Petersen's Isuzu Trooper in our motel parking lot, paid a shuttle-driver $220 to drive us to a trailhead two hours north and, the next morning, began hiking. It was a Monday, July 28.

Hopes for doing the entire trail had been dashed by a forest fire near the entrance of the national park, which forced evacuations and led us to downscale our trip to 190 miles, starting from the Rush Creek Trailhead just north of Mammoth Lakes.

But what unfolded in the next two weeks was the most beautiful, most brutal, most mind-boggling backpacking trip I'll probably ever experience.

To hike the JMT is to see what many believe to be the most scenic trail in the United States: rugged beauty that's new and different on nearly every twist in the trail, as if you're on some Disneyland ride designed to thrill you at every turn of your head.

You'd sometimes camp in places — Thousand Island Lake comes to mind — that felt like an amphitheater of visual music being played on top of the world, the lake at nearly 10,000 feet and mountains jutting up beyond like a 3,000-foot band shell.

Streams pounded down canyons carved in granite and cascaded off cliffs. In flower-speckled meadows, trout swayed in pools of water that were neither blue nor green, but translucent. Thousand-year-old trees — junipers, sequoias and pine among them — jutted from mountain sides as if rooted not in soil or even in rock, but in time itself.

On Oregon's Pacific Crest Trail, classic views are subtle and sparse; much of the 452-mile trail winds its way like a green tunnel through thick forests. On Oregon's PCT, you're almost never above the tree line; on the JMT you're rarely below it. More than a third of the trail, which duplicates the PCT for most of its length, is at or above 10,000 feet.

Roughly 1,500 people, including PCT hikers, attempt the entire JMT each year. We met folks from Japan, Russia, Poland and Italy, though the only time you sensed you didn't have the place all to yourself was atop passes and in camp areas each night.

The price for this smorgasbord of stunning views was paid in weariness, blisters and having to subsist on food that, by park regulations, must be crammed inside a 2.5-gallon bear canister. In fact, anything that smells must go in the canisters, which explains why jerky, power bars, practically all my food wound up tasting like foot powder or toothpaste.

Whenever you needed something, you had to pry that sleeping-bag-sized canister out of your pack, a procedure I imagine to be no easier than helping give birth to a stubborn calf.

But we saw no bears. The steepness of the terrain was far more worrisome.

"There are four directions on the JMT," said a fellow hiker at our second, and final, food-supply-pickup-spot, Muir Trail Ranch. "Up, upper, down and downer."

Each day, you basically tackled one of nearly a dozen major passes, some of which were like doing three or four Mt. Pisgahs, only over trails that might be made of granite ranging in size from golf balls to school buses; that might reach from 10,000 to 13,000 feet in elevation; and that might, at their summits, twist their ways precariously along rocky pinnacles not much wider than a bike path.

Beyond beauty and the beastly passes, a third element we encountered was weather. Afternoon thundershowers weren't surprising; hail and all-day rain while crossing 11,991-foot Muir Pass certainly were. On the way down LeConte Canyon, winds gusted and the trail, in spots, became a virtual creek.

By early afternoon, we were so chilled we pitched our tents beneath the first flat spot we could find — and one protected by a giant pine. I shivered in my sleeping bag for 90 minutes before I was able to stop. (No fires allowed.)

Above, despite thick clouds, a helicopter raced toward Muir Pass, presumably on a rescue mission.

"We're heading home," said a Redmond, Ore., woman we saw with her husband and two children the next day. "We've been in a tent for three days. Snow fell last night at 12,000 feet. Lots of people are leaving."

The Oregon Boys plodded on, our impetus often becoming the courage of others. Heading up the Golden Staircase's 50 steep switchbacks on a prelude to 12,100-foot Mather Pass, my emotions reached low ebb.

Then I saw them: half a dozen Boy Scouts, high above me, one of them carrying an American flag through a wisp of fog.

That was inspiring. So was reminding ourselves of the north-bound PCT hikers who come through this area each May or June and do all this in snow — and with creeks and rivers whose crossings were far more dangerous than what we were experiencing. Unfathomable.

We crawled over Mather, on whose upper flanks teams of young workers were, like mountain goats, rebuilding the rocky trail that dates to 1938.

On the last leg of our two-week journey, our food supply was dwindling; we had to carry seven days' worth in those blasted canisters. But we got over 12,086-foot Pinchot Pass, then, with the encouragement of a 20-something couple from Santa Cruz, over 11,924-foot Glen Pass.

At the top, Nina and Dennis Murphy — they were doing a four-day loop — honored us with a cube of mozzarella cheese and a bunch of homemade jerky they didn't need.

That was among my favorite moments, eating that cheese and jerky atop Glen Pass while a Boy Scout nearby strummed a ukulele.

By now, our confidence was higher and we got over the last pass — Forester, at 13,118 feet, the highest point on the PCT — with less difficulty than expected.

All that remained was to summit Whitney from the west with a 3,000-foot climb, then exit the Sierra Nevada to the east with a 6,000-foot drop.

The afternoon before the finale, I swam in Guitar Lake — yep, it's shaped like one — that, at 11,488 feet, is higher than Mt. Hood. I expect to thaw any day.

After a rumbling thunderstorm, we caught five hours of sleep, awakened at 12:50 a.m. and, just before 2 a.m., hit the trail, aided by head lamps and a near-full moon.

It's not a technical climb and we had no snow to contend with, but drop-offs east and west left me weak-kneed a few times when we were on the "dinosaur's neck."

We arrived on top at 5:29 a.m., just in time to watch — with a dozen others — an orange sun rise in the east and bring life to jagged 12,000-foot peaks that we were looking down on as if from a jet.

It was 25 degrees with a chilly breeze. Outside the warming hut, after seeing the register, I wrapped my fingers around a pen.

"The Oregon Boys," I wrote, "made it here."

Peace like a river

April 25, 2013

IDLEYLD PARK — In the early days of the Normandy Invasion, seeing a fish and rod lying next to a French stream brought a 21-year-old soldier back to his simpler days in Oregon.

To fishing with his father in the Cascades. To life before the landing at France's Utah Beach. To a world he knew before men were killing each other.

So, that's one reason Frank Moore, now 90, is leaving his log cabin above the North Umpqua River next month to go fly-fishing in Normandy: to experience what he longed for on that June day in 1944 as soldiers' boots thrummed across a stone bridge near Saint-Lô.

The other is having learned that at a recent memorial service at the Luxembourg American Cemetery in Europe, not a single U.S. World War II veteran was on hand to honor his fallen buddies.

"I told my wife: 'I'm still young enough. I can do that.'"

Jeanne, Frank's wife for 70 of her 87 years, plans to join him when he makes his own trip to pay homage to those men.

"This may sound crazy," says Moore, a sergeant in World War II whose main job was protecting majors, "but to me, paying that tribute is really more important than the fishing."

The journey will include a documentary film crew from Portland.

Moore wants not only to honor his fellow soldiers who died in Europe — "it was hell" — but to honor the people in France and

Luxembourg who opened their homes during the war to "all these American kids."

In particular, he remembers Thanksgiving 1944, not far from that Luxembourg cemetery.

"I remember Mrs. Braun," he says. "Her family didn't have anything, but we were all invited to her home. How, my wife asked, was she able to feed us all? Because she and her family didn't eat the rest of the week."

His eyes grow glassy, as they often did in our 90-minute conversation on Wednesday.

Jeanne is off to prepare for this weekend's Glide Wildflower Show.

She is, Moore says, "as close to an angel as any person I've seen. I'm so glad she's coming, too."

Her thing is flowers. His thing is fish.

Moore is an Oregon legend, twining the dogged passion of University of Oregon track coach Bill Bowerman with the soul of author Norman Maclean (*A River Runs Through It*).

On his home's wood-paneled walls hang hundreds of photos, most involving fly rods and fish. Here and there: plaques for his conservation efforts and, along with Ernest Hemingway and Teddy Roosevelt, for having been inducted into the Freshwater Fishing Hall of Fame.

Above us, across two log beams, stretch more than a dozen fly rods.

In 1957, Frank and Jeanne opened the Steamboat Inn, about 30 miles east of Roseburg on the North Umpqua.

As the years rolled on, Frank realized that unregulated timber practices were ruining the waters he loved — and led a fight to right that wrong.

"The North Umpqua is the classic, traditional fly-fishing river that it is because of one person's dogged determination: Frank Moore," says John Shewey, editor-in-chief of Northwest Fly Fishing magazine. "He's not anti-logging, but his mantra has always been: 'We can do better.'"

Even when he went toe-to-toe with an opponent, Moore remained ever the gentleman.

"He's one of those rare people where you can't help but be a better person by just being around him," Shewey says.

Frank and Jeanne made scores of friends through their years at the inn.

In 1975, they sold it and bought 80 acres on a nearby hillside, where they built the log cabin they still live in. As nature lovers, they are, quite literally, in their element.

Frank need only walk 60 feet to show you the nuances of the roll cast — on his own private pond.

This is a guy whose line feathers onto the water with less commotion than a falling leaf — and yet has the handshake of a longshoreman.

"Everybody says I'm in pretty good shape," he says. "I've been blessed in so many respects."

And so when the Normandy idea arose, he didn't hesitate long.

John Waller, founder of Uncage the Soul Video Production in Portland — and a 1994 graduate of Glide High School — spent four days with Moore last summer for a couple of short documentaries.

"At one point I asked him: 'Frank, is there anything you haven't done in your life that you still want to do?'" Waller says.

Moore told him about seeing the salmon and stream near Saint Lô — and how he'd like to spend time in Normandy fishing, not fighting.

Thus will Waller and his crew — with financial backing from people who believe in Moore's story — leave May 23 for a 16-day trip. The Moores' son, Frank Jr., a 66-year-old doctor in Alaska, will go, too.

Moore will be the honored guest at a World War II commemorative event May 25 at Luxembourg American Cemetery, will fish the rivers and streams of Normandy and will be honored at Utah Beach on June 6, the 69th anniversary of the landings.

"I never was a hero," Moore says, "but I saw a lot of them. The kids in the rifle platoons — they were the heroes."

Soon he'll have the chance to honor those heroes. And to fish the waters of Normandy that he has never forgotten.

Sea to summit: Part 1

Aug. 9, 2009

FLORENCE — The foghorn on the North Jetty goes off about every 42 seconds during the night. I know this because when you can't sleep, you do things like count the time between foghorn blasts.

And I couldn't sleep because I had created this Frankensteinian outdoor adventure called Sea to Summit which, the nearer to our 6:11

a.m. Friday start time we got, the more I feared might go down as one of those "seemed like a good idea at the time" ventures.

The idea came late last year when I was thinking about the following paragraph I'd written for visitors in town for the Olympic Track & Field Trials to illustrate how amazing Lane County is:

"If you really hustle, you can walk the beach at sunrise; stop at the back-to-the-'60s Glenwood restaurant in Eugene for granola, yogurt and fruit; catch the last of the morning rise with your fly rod on the McKenzie River, play a quick nine at Tokatee Golf Course and climb to the top of the South Sister — elevation 10,358 feet — by dark."

I decided to see if it could be done. And to do so, enlisted a son, Ryan, and brother-in-law, Glenn Petersen, to be my partners in climb.

I was naive in picturing how this would all unfold. I'd been to the top of the South Sister twice, both on warm, clear August days, both with early morning departures. But we wouldn't be hitting the trail until about 2 p.m. And weather forecasts were calling for severe thunderstorms and 8,000-foot snow levels.

I consulted with hiking guru/author Bill Sullivan and former KVAL weatherman Tim Chuey. Should we cancel this thing?

Finally, we decided on a one-day postponement. Still, as the fog-horn moaned early Friday, I mentally moaned. What had I gotten myself into? Would bad weather waste eight months of training? Would our plan to have Ryan send photos and Twitter updates via his iPhone work? Would we flat-out fail in front of an Internet audience?

Just before our 6:11 a.m. departure time — sunup in Florence — I scooped some Pacific Ocean saltwater in a pill box, destined, I hoped, for the benchmark atop the South Sister — Lane County's highest point — 14 hours later. When I looked back toward shore I couldn't believe it: Sea to Summit fans were pouring onto the beach to see us off.

Both of them — Rachel Pearson and Debbie Olsen — had arrived as the unofficial Florence send-off delegation.

My watch hit 6:11 and I started running for the car a half-mile away. Road-construction stops cost us 7 minutes and 28 seconds, an unexpected potty stop another 3:30. (I was committed to success, but I'm no trucker with a bottle by his side.)

But the real time-killer on this cloudy morning had nothing to do with flaggers or bladders, just ineptness on my part.

The previous night, I had carefully rigged my four-piece fly rod to save time for the post-breakfast fishing segment. But after downing my fruit, granola and yogurt at the Glenwood — when I arrived, the staff had it on a table, ready to go — disaster hit: I realized I'd somehow aligned the second or third segment of the pole — can't remember which one — backwards. Don't me ask me how. All I know is that when I went to put the pole together, two pieces wouldn't fit together, meaning, with the clock ticking, I had to bust off the fly and start over. It was the equivalent of a monkey trying to defuse a ticking bomb.

Such time wasters — and an unexpected stop for gas — left me 23 minutes off pace. If anything, we wanted to be ahead of schedule so we could do less of our descending from the South summit in absolute darkness.

In the backseat, I wrestled into my chest waders without taking off my seat belt, a feat that makes David Copperfield's Statue of Liberty disappearance look humdrum in comparison.

I fished a caddis fly near the McKenzie's Silver Creek Landing for nine minutes as rain fell. (No fish, not even a strike.) OK, so I wasn't Hemingway's *Old Man and the Sea* fighting a fish for days. But did Santiago have to hike up a 10,000-foot mountain when he was finished?

We did, which is why, using electric carts, we zipped around Tokatee's back nine in a brisk 55 minutes and 55 seconds. Scores weren't important. (OK, 54, including an opening drive that bored into the soggy turf an inch in front of my tee.) What mattered was time.

Because of the speedy golf — most nine-hole rounds take two hours or more — and no more road construction, we arrived at the trail head at 1:35, 25 minutes ahead of schedule.

Of course, breakfast, fishing and golf were mere preliminary bouts to the featured match. We had gained about 5,000 feet in elevation by car. Now we needed to gain roughly the same elevation by foot, then return to base camp at Devils Lake, some of that trek in darkness.

Otherwise, Frankenstein would win.

Sea to summit: Part 2

Aug. 11, 2009

SOUTH SISTER — At the trailhead, I finished filling out our permit — after "destination" I scrawled "South Sister summit" — and left it in the box.

A reader, after seeing Sunday's opening piece on our three-man team's quest to go from Lane County's lowest point to its highest — stopping for breakfast, fishing and golf along the way — said it didn't sound as if we were having much fun.

The fun part began once I finished filling out that permit. Once we started up the mountain. Once all the preliminary steps, dating back to January when we started training, were done and we could concentrate on the hike.

Oh, we'd had some good times since gathering at my brother-in-law Glenn Petersen's cabin in Florence Thursday night before leaving from the North Jetty at sunrise — 6:11 a.m. — the next morning.

We'd laughed at 57-year-old Glenn's old-school, low-tech ways, his snowmobile pants and how he puzzled endlessly over how his pack could weigh so much, then pulled out binoculars and a flashlight about as thick as a pop can. Laughed at my 30-year-old son Ryan's high-tech ways, how he'd downloaded — and learned — a Global Positioning System program for his iPhone by the time he'd finished his grilled salmon at Mo's. And laughed at my obsessive-compulsive ways, how I'd gotten only two hours of sleep in Florence because of my mind polishing trip details like a rock tumbler. (About 3:30 a.m., I suddenly realized our postponing the trip a day meant a slightly later sunrise, meaning we'd need to start two minutes later to accurately fulfill my sunrise-at-the-coast and top-of-the-South-Sister-by-dark statement I'd made in print last year.)

We'd had fun cramming down breakfast at the campus Glenwood, fly-fishing on the McKenzie River and playing nine holes of golf in under an hour at Tokatee Golf Club.

But there was a constant edge of panic to these preliminary hoops I needed to jump through, knowing that every second lost was another second we'd be in darkness while going up and/or down the 10,358-foot mountain.

Once we hit the trail, however, our destiny was in our own feet, the final obstacles being weather and Oregon's third-tallest mountain, its summit 6.2 rocky, twisting miles away.

As we started, 1:33 p.m., skies were slightly overcast, the temperature 57 degrees. We were nearly half an hour ahead of our 2 p.m. scheduled start time and hoped to be on top by 8 p.m., then return by the light of head lamps.

Our moods were upbeat. We zigzagged upward through a thick forest on switchbacks chiseled into the flanks of Devils Hill and Kaleetan Butte. We reached the plateau in an hour, faster than I'd figured.

We were supposed to be rewarded by a glorious view of the mountain, which, I'd remembered from the previous year's hike, stands out like a castle atop a faraway hill. Instead, we found ourselves in thick cloud cover, visibility maybe a mile.

The words of Oregon hiking expert Bill Sullivan whipped into my ear on the 10-20 mph winds: "If you can't see the top of South Sister, it's probably snowing up there, even in August."

Great. All we'd wanted was a chance, a window of decent weather at the tail end of a week in which thundershowers had rocked the mountain and freezing levels plummeted to 8,000 feet. That's why we'd postponed the journey a day.

We trudged on, nobody saying much but all of us, I think, worried. A second downer: Ryan's iPhone — his carrier is AT&T — wasn't getting service. For months, Ryan and *Register-Guard* Web monkey Micky Hulse had been concocting ways to, in essence, take readers along on the trip.

On a specially created Web site we would feed readers Twitter comments, photos and location updates from sea to summit.

But though my Verizon phone got cell coverage from the top last year, Ry's AT&T service wasn't connecting, meaning our elaborate system was all dressed up with nowhere to go.

Then, within minutes — near the cutoff trail to Moraine Lake — two things happened: Ry's phone connected. And the cloud cover lifted. There, in the distance, stood the mountain, the Lewis Glacier carving what looked like a quarter-moon just below the lava-red summit.

We were heading due north near the crest of the Cascades. To the west — our left — valley clouds bumped up to the mountains like whipping cream in a pie tin. To the east — our right — blue skies prevailed.

My mood lifted like the cloud cover. I remember thinking: Home free.

The three of us were working well together, Glenn content with his slow-but steady pace and I appreciating the hiking-friendly temperature and new boots that weighed less than half of those I'd worn the previous year.

Meanwhile, jack-of-all-trades Ry seemed to be hiking effortlessly while taking pictures and sending photos and Tweets. Readers, through their own Tweets, were offering encouragement, asking questions, making for a harmonic convergence of good vibes.

By 4 p.m., we were at 8,218 feet. (Ry's iPhone, of course, gives elevation.) I was growing tired and had donned a stocking cap and gloves as the wind increased, but I felt as if I could almost touch the top.

At 6:26 p.m., after a few hundred more zigs and zags through the scree, I did, a full 90 minutes before we expected. The sun blazed above the blanket of valley clouds, but the temperature was 35 degrees with winds from the north that stung your face liked iced needles.

By dark, we would be down to the safety of the plateau and, at 10:10 p.m — the trail lighted by our head lamps — back at Devils Lake, a near-full moon peeking through the trees for the first time.

But for now, our mission completed, we took a group photo as we perched precisely on the Lane-Deschutes county line on the crater's jagged east edge.

Then it was time: I pulled out a pill box. I took off my gloves and poured a little Pacific Ocean saltwater, Glenwood restaurant salt, McKenzie River water and Tokatee bunker sand onto the summit bench mark.

One county. One day. One amazing landscape — stretching from sea level to nearly two miles into the sky — that we Lane County folks are blessed to call our own.

5.

Coast & country

I'll take Oregon's coast

Jan. 31, 2010

Thanks to book research, a mandatory furlough and 500-mph jets, I recently woke up one day in Lighthouse Point, Fla., and fell asleep in Yachats.

You know which I prefer.

I love seeing other places, meeting other people, experiencing other cultures. But they almost always make me pine for the places I know better.

In Lighthouse Point, just north of Fort Lauderdale, I'd turn my rental car down a neighborhood street and see a row of 30- to 100-foot cabin cruisers lining one of the man-made lagoons that wind along the coastline for six miles.

Though Yachats' many well-heeled retirees make it one of the state's wealthiest communities, per capita, its median family income is only a little more than half of Lighthouse Points' $72,418.

In Lighthouse Point, a guy shows up to wash someone's Hummer in his driveway. In Yachats, a volunteer group is helping ease the inconvenience of the only grocery store in town having closed.

Lighthouse Point is a retirement haven for the wealthy with an abundance of yachts — that's, uh, Yachats without the second "a" — sunshine, snowbirds and people in general: 4,695 per square mile compared with Yachats' 693.

And that's why, as She Who Picked Me Up at Portland International Airport and I wound our way south from Lincoln City to Yachats, I fell in love with this coast all over again.

So many people-less vistas. So many stretches of natural beauty, making Florida's seem like beauty on Botox. So much diversity — bluffs and flat stretches and coves, including what may be the most gorgeous one on the entire 363-mile coastline, Whale Cove, just south of Depoe Bay.

Look down at Florida's coastline from the air and it's impressive, but mainly for its expanse — five times the length of Oregon's. In essence, it is hotel after hotel after hotel, interrupted by neighborhoods like the one I frequented, looking, with monotonous sameness, like computer circuitry.

Florida's coast is sunscreen and swimsuits, riches and repetition;

Oregon's is Gore-Tex and sweatshirts, variety and the hidden riches that not everybody notices.

Florida's coast is a paved — and lagooned and hoteled — paradise, Oregon's a threatened-but-still wild strip of rock, sand and surf.

All of which made my week's beach reading — Bonnie Henderson's *Strand: An Odyssey of Pacific Ocean Debris* (Oregon State University Press, 2008) — the perfect choice.

Strand, an Oregon Book Award finalist, underscores the Oregon Coast essence as Henderson explores a coast's more subtle treasures: the stuff that washes ashore. The stories behind a grounded fishing boat, a Japanese float, heck, a Reebok running shoe.

Someone in Florida might see a book like this and think: how gauche. I see a book like this and think: Yes! A kindred spirit, a fellow Oregonian who notices the details. Who, like me, might wonder about the two dozen untreated "telephones poles" that washed ashore at Yachats a few years back, one of which has been heating my house the last few evenings.

Henderson asks the questions. And tracks down the answers. All based on stuff she found washed ashore on a one-mile strand about 12 miles north of Reedsport.

With the same kind of detail Sebastian Junger uses in *The Perfect Storm,* she takes us aboard the 62-foot fishing boat Sanak to recount the crew's final desperate moments before it runs aground in 1983 (my favorite chapter); travels to China to try to find which ship might have unleashed the Reebok she found in 2000; goes to Washington's San Juan Islands to track the mystery of a minke whale that washes ashore in 2004; and more.

Henderson's zeal to solve six washed-ashore mysteries is quintessential Oregon Coast. It's the idea that a "strand" — land bordering water — is, in essence, a place to which all sorts of subtle stories come to rest.

"Ultimately," she writes, "it was the stories I prized most. Everything on the beach — every discarded bottle, every dead seabird chick."

They help comprise the Oregon Coast, these nuances not often seen — along with the more obvious rough-hewn beauty, the brooding weather and ever-changing waves.

Every place has such stories and nuances, even Florida. But Oregon's draw me home, and at the end of a day that began 2,800 miles away, lull me to sleep like the surf.

Meat, American style

Feb. 9, 2010

B ELLFOUNTAIN — I know I'm not in Kansas anymore when I get out of the car.

"Be right back," says Romella Lee, the event organizer. "Got a bison in the oven."

That's a phrase a nonhunter from Eugene doesn't hear too often. But, hey, welcome to the fifth annual Bellfountain Wild Game Feed, where you will experience all sorts of new things, including tepid bites of Louisiana nutria chili and gut-hook knives given away as door prizes.

The feed is sponsored by the Bellfountain Community Church, which sits across from the old school where the event is held. (The school was once Bellfountain High, which, in 1937, with a student body of 27, stunned two Portland schools with nearly 4,000 students, combined, to win the state basketball title.)

The setting is beautiful, quintessential Americana, a white church steeple rising into the sky amid trees, fields and rolling hills about five miles northwest of Monroe.

The dress is primarily, well, camouflage.

And the décor is what I'd call country fish and game: guns, pelts, poles, antlers, traps, duck decoys and two giant elk mounts, including emcee Scott Ballard's world-record "8 by 9" Roosevelt elk — eight points on one side of the rack, nine on the other.

Lee blows a duck call to get our attention; dinner is near. "But first some trivia," she says. "True or false: Canada geese mate for life."

The response bounces back immediately. "True!"

Correct!

After a prayer, we head through the kitchen to go through the potluck line. As the speaker — admittedly an odd choice as I don't hunt — I am accorded the leadoff position.

Talk about pressure.

I'm a chicken, fish and occasional red-meat guy, but the spread is decidedly on the gamey side. I pass on bear and wild cow soup. Then come across lemon-pepper cougar.

Oh, why not? Elk? Sure. Nutria? Even I can't believe I sample that, but it is a columnist-gone-wild evening and, frankly, it's surprisingly not bad.

"Another trivia question," Lee says during the meal. "What percent of a bear's diet is vegetarian?" A hand shoots up. "Eighty-five."

"The answer is 80 to 90," Lee says. "Congrats."

Man, these folks know their animals, fish and fowl. Which makes it all the more intimidating that I am the after-dinner speaker. I don't know elk scat from black olives, wrote a column in 2002 about how "I don't get hunting" and, when joining an elk hunt to understand those who do, was bucked off a horse with the dude ranch name of Rusty.

"You have to understand, this is all new to me," I explain to the estimated 100 people crammed into the old schoolhouse. "The night before the 2007 hunt, we stayed at a guy's house in Pendleton, and until then I'd never slept in a den whose major decorative theme was 'modern animal scrotum.'"

Later, Lee asks the audience for the fastest-flying bird — "peregrine falcon," a man says (correct) — and gives out more door prizes: "whitetail deer" and "lures of the past" playing cards, shotgun-cleaning kits, waterproof Bibles.

Lee, who lives on a nearby farm but is a senior research faculty member in the University of Oregon's College of Education, is the driving force behind the event.

"A lot of the stuff at the church is designed for women, but there was nothing for men," she says.

With help from Ballard, whose "carnivore fest" Christmas party is legendary in these parts — folks still talk about his delicious porcupine — she launched the event in 2006.

Now it's so popular that, because of space limitations, it's an invitation-only affair.

"Early cave people gathered around a fire to eat deer, tell stories and worship their gods," Lee says. "Then later, aboriginal peoples in America hunted bison and partied all night with dancing and singing or told stories and shared food."

The folks in Bellfountain end with an open-mike for hunting stories. A handful of men and women tell about everything from sons being bequeathed guns from their fathers to inexperienced hunters resting their guns by cramming the barrels into the ground.

Everyone laughs about that one, so I guess that's a bad idea, one of the many things I learn at my first — and quite memorable — wild-game dinner.

Legacy made of wood

Aug. 15, 2010

ELKTON — Nobody can accuse the Elkton School District of trying to stop the hands of time. After all, it's now one of only a dozen rural Oregon districts to go the forward-thinking charter route. And it recently installed eco-friendly biomass boilers. But when it came to the bleachers in the 1953-built gymnasium, well, that was another matter.

Dean Gadda, CEO of Gladstone-based Northwest School Equipment, remembers it like this when, in 2009, he met with District Maintenance Supervisor Brian Kruse about replacing the gym's aging bleachers:

"I offered them fully automatic powered bleachers with colorful plastic seats," Gadda says.

"No," Kruse said. "No plastic."

OK, Gadda said, how about bleachers with wood benches made from Southern yellow pine?

"No," Kruse said. "No Southern pine."

Gadda, a former forestry student at Oregon State, got the drift. Elkton wanted something that echoed the area's fir-rooted history for its gym, which has the nostalgic feel of the one used in the movie *Hoosiers*.

And that's just what it got.

In late July, workers completed what Gadda claims is "arguably the prettiest bank of bleachers ever built."

How? By remilling the old growth fir bleachers that had been installed 57 years ago.

"Two school board members stopped by my house the other evening, having seen the finished product," Elkton School Superintendent Mike Hughes says. "They said, 'Unbelievable. You sit in bleachers like those and you think: I want my kids to go to school here.'"

"What it means is that our history lives on in that gym," Hughes says. "People look at it and their chests swell with pride."

Even though the more popular — and slightly less expensive route — would have been plastic, which is what nearly all schools have installed these days.

But Hughes had had a bad experience with the stuff in a previous district back in the 1990s.

"They had old growth bleachers like ours and put in new plastic bleachers," he says. "I told myself if I were ever a superintendent in a similar situation, I'd try to find a way to refurbish the wood we had. To Brian's credit, he found a vendor who could do it."

Gadda appreciated Elkton's desire to preserve the school's link to the land while bringing their bleachers up to safety — and Americans with Disabilities Act — standards.

On a whim, he had stopped at Elkton High while en route to a project his company was doing in Reedsport.

"They let me walk around the gym and here's this thick, beautiful, vertical-grain Douglas fir," he says. "You get this new and it's very expensive, if you can even find it. You wouldn't have any trouble selling this to furniture makers or woodworkers. One and nine-sixteen inches; never seen it so thick."

But the bleachers had no aisles and, thus, no intermediate steps between each row. What's more, they were "open deck" bleachers, meaning there was nothing to prevent, say, a small child from falling between rows. And, though they folded up, did so only with a cumbersome hand system.

So, the two parties hammered out a plan: the wood was removed, taken to Advanced Woodcraft in Eagle Creek, near Gresham, and re-milled. It was then returned to Elkton and affixed to a customized Interkal bleacher frame, the Kalamazoo, Mich., company creating a four-, instead of the typical three-, section setup to accommodate the extra heavy wood.

"When you look at it," Gadda says, "it looks like a piece of furniture. There's nothing else like it out there across the country."

True, the 500-seat, $62,000 project cost about 5 percent more than had the school gone the conventional route.

"But plastic just didn't seem right for us," says Kruse, a 1994 Elkton High graduate. "Quite a few of these boards came out of trees with a hundred years of growth in them."

The money for the bleachers came from savings left over from other projects — paid for by a 2008 maintenance bond — whose materials cost less because of the slumping economy.

Some of the bleacher wood not needed will be used to build a bench in honor of longtime school supporter Doris Tootie Dill (Elkton High, '49), who recently died. And the rest will be cut into two- or three-foot sections and sold for $25 each as part of a school fundraiser.

Oh, yes, the telescoping bleachers roll out and contract with the push of a button, giving Elkton the best of both worlds: The convenience of modern technology and the continuance of historic roots.

Oregon's best small towns

Feb. 13, 2013

Monday, Feb. 14, is that traditional day when we express our unequivocal love to — well, of course, the state born 152 years ago on that date: Oregon.

So, in keeping with my yearly tradition of honoring it at this time of year, here are my Top 20 Best Small Towns in Oregon (populations 10,000 or less).

My choices aren't based on crime statistics, economic viability or anything like that; instead, they're based on just basic coolness, my choices clouded by all sorts of emotional subjectivity:

20. Jacksonville (Jackson County, pop. 2,490). If Harper Lee had based *To Kill a Mockingbird* in Oregon, she would have chosen this tired old town west of Medford to be her Maycomb, Ala.

19. Dayville (Grant, pop. 160). It's a speck in a county that's the same size as Lane but has so few people it would meet the 10,000-or-less qualification all by itself. Wonderfully quiet — until a car zings by Highway 26, which happens less frequently than Oregon loses a football game. The Dayville Mercantile's floor has been worn smooth by 115 years of cowboy-booted history.

18. Fossil (Wheeler, pop. 460). Where else can you watch a parade where the most spectacular float is a tractor? Heavenly hills, homespun folks and Bill Bowerman stories abound.

17. Brownsville (Linn, pop. 1,530). Zipping off Interstate 5 and into Brownsville is the closest thing to backward time travel you'll find in Oregon. And give the yesterday-feeling town "brownie" points for having been the backdrop for *Stand by Me.*

16. Shaniko (Wasco, pop. 30). Every small-town list should include at least one ghost town; this is mine. Its heyday was a century ago, but as you drive north from Madras on Highway 97, there's still something eerily intriguing about the place.

15. Wallowa (Wallowa, pop. 870). Another one of those emeralds in the Eastern Oregon rough, a drive-through town surrounded by a surprising amount of head-shaking beauty.

14. Bandon (Coos, pop. 3,065). Named for the Bandon, Ireland, family that founded it, this coastal town has charm, offshore rocky islands, a lighthouse and, of course, a handful of world-class golf courses where the fairways are wonderful, I hear. (I wouldn't know, though I've played a handful of rounds in the Bandon gorse.)

13. Joseph (Wallowa, pop. 1,090). An off-the-beaten-track Sisters with fewer tourists and more antlers. Wallowa Lake and alpine mountains on its back porch; pine forests on its front; and Hell's Canyon as its intellectually deep neighbor.

12. Frenchglen (Harney, pop. 12, though it's not that crowded in the off-season). Not much here beyond the Frenchglen Hotel and a school where the principal has to warn hunters to stay off the playground. But a summer night on the hotel's porch, watching the sunlight fade on Steens Mountain, is a night to remember.

11. Cannon Beach (Clatsop, pop. 1,650). It's too upscale and too full of Portlanders to be among my leaders, but how can you ignore an artsy burg with iconic Haystack Rock sitting right on its beach?

10. Cottage Grove (Lane, pop. 9,110). It doesn't look like much from the freeway, but once you start poking around — and meet people — its charm escalates. Like Brownsville, its Main Street has been in pictures: the parade scene in *Animal House.*

9. Neskowin (Tillamook, pop. 169). Coasty and quaint, its beach is beautifully book-marked by Proposal Rock and Cascade Head.

8. Depoe Bay (Lincoln, pop. 1,275). Spectacular surf and sandstone coves, fishing boats, chowder, used-book stores and a smiling Jack Nicholson taking his friends deep-sea-fishing in *One Flew Over the Cuckoo's Nest.* What's to not like?

7. Elkton (Douglas, pop. 197). Coolest setting for a football field I've ever seen; a shanked punt almost lands in the Umpqua River. Plus a school-town bond that's like Superglue.

6. Florence (Lane, pop. 8,185). Nothing inspiring about the Lincoln City-like stretch of Highway 101, but its Old Town riverfront, beaches and glimpses of dunes more than compensate.

5. Coburg (Lane, pop. 1,070). I fell in love with this place after seeing my first Golden Years parade in 1978. Driving through Coburg on a warm summer evening is like a visual bite of watermelon.

4. Newport (Lincoln, pop. 9,925). True, it barely fits in our 10,000-limit category, but the bayfront is a rare blend of tourists and guys trying to shuttle forklifts of shrimp around. Worth it alone for the fishy smell — and the crab-line notches worn into the dock railings.

3. Sisters (Deschutes, pop. 1,600). Quilt stores, bookstores and a rodeo. Yes, and way too much tourist traffic, but it's flanked by the Three Sisters and studded with pines, so this town's rustic ambience — even if slightly contrived — works for me.

2. Camp Sherman (Jefferson, pop. about 200). Nothing gritty about this place; it was founded not by pioneers but vacationers, many of whom arrived in waders, ready to fish the Metolius River. Cabins, a *Golden Pond*-esque general store and acres of life-pondering woods. All with a river running through it.

1. Yachats (Lincoln, pop. 730). Surprise, surprise, huh? I've gushed for more than a decade about this place on the central Oregon coast, so I will spare you the details. But suffice it to say there's no place I'd rather be.

Another time and place

July 29, 2012

SEASIDE — Every now and then you have one of those are-we-really-in-Oregon? moments. My latest came Tuesday when, along the promenade here, I came across a sign that said: "Fire Wood, $10/box; Smores, $10/package; 4Roasting Sticks, $5."

It wasn't so much an "ah-ha" moment as a "huh" moment, as in: "Huh, in Oregon a s'mores package now goes for $25. Who knew?"

You wonder if maybe for another $10 you could have someone do the roasting for you and for an additional $10 someone would eat your s'more, lest you get that awful marshmallow goo on your hands.

But enough of my sardonic native Oregonian snobbery, let me climb down off my cultural lifeguard tower — yes, Seaside has those, too — and just say it:

Though I find Seaside curiously un-Oregon-ized in many ways, I like the place — weirdly, for that very reason. Because it's a little quirky, a little out of step with the rest of us, a true nonconformist instead of a pretender.

We think of Oregon independence as coming only in earth-tone hues, and yet here's a place that dares to wear fluorescent.

A place that's home to the Miss Oregon pageant.

A place to which teenagers flock on spring break, making it Daytona Beach with goose bumps.

A place where an inordinately high percentage of people you see are wearing shirts or hats from previous tourist spots they've visited.

Graceland. Mount Rushmore. Las Vegas.

They're all here.

They're the guy in the "I got crabs in Seaside" shirt and the young woman in the "Don't act like you're not impressed" T-shirt. They're the teens on the indoor Tilt-a-Whirl and the family burning a $20 bill in a video arcade.

When your usual beach experience means waves and books and s'mores with ingredients that cost a few bucks, the Seaside experience jolts you. One loop around the Broadway turnaround and you're reminded you're not in Yachats anymore.

Yes, those are beach volleyball nets.

Yes, that's a lifeguard tower.

Yes, that's a seven-story, 283-room WorldMark time-share hotel whose heated outdoor swimming pool and spa is separated from the beach by only Plexiglas.

If the Oregon Coast were a dinner party and most guests were talking quietly about dune erosion, Seaside would be up on the table, leading the Macarena.

Not that this is something particularly new. Seaside — where visitors can quintuple the population of 6,500 — has long been comfortable with being a touch zestier than its coastal counterparts.

At times, it has become a bit too zesty. In the early 1960s, youth riots rocked Seaside, instigated not by political issues but by teenage hormones and a tsunami of beer. I still remember older cousins at our grandparents' Cannon Beach cabin pleading to check out the scene, which included more than a few National Guardsmen.

Things still get can get hot when young people descend on Seaside.

The same carnival atmosphere that drew people 50 years ago draws people today. The same beach-side aquarium appears to be frozen in time, even as new hotels and beachfront vacation homes pop up like harbor seals.

Riots aside, what I like about the place is that it's not like anywhere else on the coast. It's a poor man's East Coast resort town, a shivering man's California beach.

On a coast known more for whale watching, Seaside is better for people watching. The half-mile-long promenade separates sand from city while connecting people with one another.

You don't go to Seaside to get away from it all. You go there to be part of it all.

It's ironic that its nearest neighbor, Cannon Beach, could not be more different. You look at the two places, only a few miles apart, and wonder if one was adopted.

But that's the glory of Seaside: It's happy not looking like its sea-front siblings, most of which eschew makeup of any kind.

Cannon Beach is Portland's seaside "village." People come to immerse themselves in coasty coziness, perhaps watch some glass-blowers, eat French or Italian at Newman's at 988 restaurant. Seaside is a miniature Coney Island. People come, immerse themselves in kitsch, perhaps win an arcade prize for their date and gobble down a giant stack at Pig 'n Pancake on Broadway.

It's not everybody's cup of Bud Lite and I prefer the quiet of Yach-ats to a pounding arcade. But since I first experienced Seaside in 1969 — I came for the eight-mile Seaside Beach Run — I have an odd affection for the place.

Though my body will be Pacific Ocean-cold before I ever pay $25 for a s'mores package.

Big stump

July 26, 2012

WALDPORT — Mike Anderson is smitten with a surf-side stump.

Who else on the planet is aware that 100 years ago Friday a Port-land newspaper published a story titled "The Legend of the Big Stump?"

Or has been studying the thing for the past 16 years?

Or has just launched a website about it (big-stump.com)?

"My wife calls it my obsession," says Anderson, a 63-year-old retired Eugene firefighter and paramedic.

The tree stump juts from the sand between Waldport and Yachats, about a mile south of Governor Patterson State Park and a mile north of Beachside State Park.

Anderson first saw it in 1996 while vacationing on the coast with his wife, Bonnie Miller.

"The tree was leaning slightly to starboard, like a sailing ship tacking into the wind," he writes on his blog. "I ran my hands over the smooth gunnels of my ship and tried to count the tree rings — clearly it had lived for hundreds of years. In my mind it became a time ship, sailing into a different age when the seas were lower and forests extended over the horizon."

I love his appreciation for what once was. Like him, I like a good natural mystery.

As a boy, when our family traveled to the coast, it was traditional for my mother to announce to us what motels had vacancies on Highway 101 and one of those motels was called Big Stump. So, though I don't recall seeing it when I was young, I grew up hearing stories of the stump.

Anderson's website refers to a 1959 memoir by Lenora Reynolds Strake. "When we lived there" — her family arrived in 1883 when she was 6 — "it was a really big stump," she wrote. "It is redwood and was standing in its own soil — a thick, black muck. My brother and I used to climb the big stump and look down inside — it was hollow and filled with shells."

In the 1960s, Strake, then in her 80s, lived at the end of the gravel road our family's cabin is on and would invite my sister and me to roast marshmallows in her rock fireplace.

So, as Anderson's story of the stump unfolded I was all eyes and ears. Just as he was back in the '90s when he first learned of it.

He pored through files at the Waldport Heritage Museum. Talked to the director of the Hatfield Marine Science Center. Found Strake's memoir. Even took a sample of the wood and sent it to the U.S. Forest Service's Center for Wood Anatomy Research in Madison, Wis.

It was, the center informed him, exactly what Strake said it was: redwood.

"The implications were immediately huge," Anderson says.

He figured only two options existed: The tree was part of a buried-in-the-sand redwood forest, even though today most redwoods grow only in a narrow strip along the northern California and extreme southern Oregon coast. Or the tree had once grown in that area and been displaced, floating north like the bow of the New Carissa, which was less than a mile from the stump in 1999.

While continuing his research, the newly retired Anderson —

keeping a vow he'd made long ago — returned to the University of Oregon and, in 2006, earned a degree in anthropology.

Meanwhile, he couldn't let go of the stump.

He learned that local Native Americans revered "Big Stump." "To the Alsea people, this stump marked the center of the world," he wrote.

He discovered a 1912 story in the *Oregon Semi-Weekly Journal,* which told of the gods using the stump to mark the resting place of two Indian lovers who drowned while fishing.

He got the interest of some University of Oregon geography and anthropology professors. The stump was tested for carbon dating. Ground penetrating radar was used to see what lay beneath.

Until such findings are published in a scientific journal — soon, he says — Anderson says he can offer only limited information.

"For now I can say that it was alive at the time of Christ and may have died when Trajan was Emperor of Rome," he says.

"It died about 1,750 to 1,850 years ago," says Dan Gavin, UO associate professor of geography. "That means it was preserved very well for a long time before we see it where it is today."

Some written reports suggest the tree died in a 1700 earthquake/tsunami. Anderson disagrees.

"Carbon 14 dates show this tree 'witnessed' several earthquakes and tsunamis. And if it is driftwood, it may have been deposited by a previous tsunami."

Some 12 to 14 feet of the stump was showing in the winter of 2008 though, with summer sand buildup, roughly half of that is now showing. It is about 7 feet wide.

Meanwhile, the Big Stump Motel no longer exists, the cabins sold to individuals. The stump itself continues to weather the years, however, sitting about 200 feet from the bank, near the Edgewater Cottages and Cape Cod Cottages.

"If it is driftwood, how did it come to be in an upright position?" Anderson asks. "How has it been preserved for hundreds of years, pounded by ocean waves and winter storms?"

His time ship may soon offer answers. For now, Anderson remains happily stumped.

Editor's note: In August 2015, much of the stump was burned, apparently by someone with little appreciation for history.

Character-building coast

Aug. 14, 2012

YACHATS — Saturday afternoon. Temperature: 58 degrees. Winds: Blasting from the north like a beachfront bullet train at a steady 15 mph, with gusts to 25. Visibility: Put it this way; people's kites were, if not out of mind, out of sight.

Meanwhile, three grown men — guys old enough to know better — were on the beach playing whiffle ball. Strangers whom I watched from a cabin window. One guy was wearing gloves — and I don't mean the baseball kind.

Boys of Summer? These were Lions in Winter, the central coast's August version.

Wildest curve balls you've ever seen, shaped like boomerangs. A batter fouled one up onto a bluff, deep into the salal, a souvenir ball for the ages.

But here's what I love about Oregon: These guys spent 15 minutes looking for it.

If ever there was an excuse to end this misery, here it was. And yet when I fished an old whiffle ball out from the garage for them, they said thanks but no thanks.

Not because they were going to quit. But because they said they had two backup balls on their way.

Meanwhile, they looked for Ball No. 1 like firefighters trying to save a child from a burning building, one guy stretched out in the thick leaves, another guy making sure his pal didn't fall over the edge.

You don't see that happening in Seaside, which I wrote about a few weeks back. Up north, a guy fouls one into the brush and it's happy hour. Same with California. Or Cape Cod.

You see, while folks around the country were working on their tans over the weekend, we coasties — even we adjunct residents — were building character.

Yachats looked like something from an Emily Brontë novel, the strip of fog giving the coast the feel of the Yorkshire moors in northern England. You half-expected the guy serving you your fish 'n' chips to be wearing a name badge that said "Heathcliff." Only around here, restaurants are too laid back to require name badges.

It's hard to explain how different from the valley — or the entire country — the coast's weather can get this time of summer. Inland Florence's high on Saturday was 67, but the unofficial high on our Yachats thermometer was 59.

For perspective, the lowest high temperature of major U.S. cities on Saturday was 69 in Minneapolis. Yachats may have been the coolest spot in the nation — in more ways than one.

The Register-Guard's weather map Sunday morning was a fiery orange. Here? It's Monday and I haven't seen color since Friday night, just shades of gray — and no, not 50 shades of gray; that would suggest a diversity that we could only dream of.

There was no ocean. No sky. At times, no beach.

Looking outside was like looking at the world though a frosted shower door.

"Hey, was that someone on the beach?" I asked She Who Sees Dimly on a Weekend Like This.

Indeed, not one, but four people, packing beach chairs on their backs. As they walked, they leaned forward into the wind like Olympic ski jumpers after takeoff.

They huddled up in a notch of bluff-protecting rip-rap and, near as I could tell, did not move for two solid hours, like actors in a movie called *Killer Winds*, their faces saying: *Is this the fun part?*

This is the saving grace of August weekends on the Oregon Coast: They harden us. Humble us. Chisel our character. And the character of visitors.

Up and down Highway 101, we saw out-of-state license plates everywhere. Texas. Utah. California. New York. Washington. Idaho. British Columbia. People embracing the Oregon Spirit, even as their RVs' fold-out awnings were buffeted so hard you half-expected some TV reporter to be nearby saying, "reporting live from the eye of Hurricane Florence ..."

At Beachside Campground, the "full" sign proudly shown all weekend, folks in gum-drop tents perhaps wishing that instead of sunblock they'd brought concrete blocks.

On Yachats' 804 Trail, people walked and talked. The stretch from the Adobe to Smelt Sands Beach took about five minutes into the wind and five seconds with the wind.

Down the beach, a young boy braved the chill to wade in the surf up to his waist. There's a kid who's going to be president someday.

On Sunday night, four people withstood the elements to build a beach fire. And while they did not last long, it was a symbolic marshmallow stick in the sand that said: I am Oregon, hear me roar.

But of course, we couldn't hear that roar, the wind howling as it was.

6.

Immersion

A sailor's lament

July 10, 2012

G iven the sailing season I'd had, I should have expected something like what happened Saturday night.

It was a splash of prophecy come to fruition straight from Henry Beard and Roy McKie's definition of the sport in their book *Sailing*: "The fine art of getting wet ... while going nowhere slowly at great expense."

But let me digress — considerably, but with "log book" brevity — so you have some context for this incident:

On May 25, at storage place near Fern Ridge Lake to pick up boat, realize trailer lights not working. Take to Springfield auto electric place for repair.

Drive to Fern Ridge's Richardson Park. After weathering half-hour downpour, rig 22-foot Catalina and launch it, a five-hour process.

Let the season begin!

Not quite. Bracket for 8-mph motor is stuck, meaning motor can't be lowered into water and, thus, boat difficult to get from moorage to heavier winds beyond.

Moot point because notice quarter-inch split in fuel line, meaning motor won't run anyway. Paddle 2,500-pound boat a few hundred yards to moorage slip.

Two days later, return to boat and attach new fuel line. Fellow sailor who happens by figures out motor bracket won't release because safety arm — I didn't even know we had one — is locked. Unlock it.

Another moot point because, even when lowered in water and connected with new fuel line, motor won't start. Electrical ignition system on fritz.

To alleviate frustration, turn attention to rigging mast. Realize one end of internal jib halyard — line inside the mast that raises the smaller sail on the front of the boat — is lost somewhere inside that mast.

Best way to get at halyard is to pull boat out, place on trailer and take down 25-foot mast in parking lot. Not an easy one-person job.

When cranking boat onto trailer, notice chunk of wood floating in lake. One of two braces for 35-year-old trailer had broken off. Wonder if millions of locusts might soon descend to, say, chew my sails apart.

Take down mast. Drive boat home on trailer. Use fish tape — similar to 25-foot tape measure — to rerun jib halyard through mast, though have to first remove light atop mast to get line through, a job that takes an hour itself because of balky screws. Re-secure light with epoxy.

Take boat to auto electric shop to have battery system repaired. Next morning, work day, leave at 5:08 a.m. to put boat, with fixed electrical system and jib halyard, back in lake.

Raise mast. Realize an inconvenient truth: Now, end of halyard for the mainsail (the large sail) has slipped inside mast like jib halyard had. What are the chances?

Drive back to Eugene, get fish wire, return, break off mast light I just glued on, run halyard through mast and reattach mast light — this time with duct tape. (No time for glue to set.)

Raise mast for third time of season without actually having sailed.

While raising mast, front pin on forestay — wire from top of mast that secures it to bow of boat — falls to ground. Find self in precarious position of holding up mast with one hand on the forestay while desperately trying to reach the pin on the ground with foot. Nobody in parking lot to help. Finally cajole pin over with foot, pick up and secure forestay.

Back boat into water. Engine starts. Heavenly chorus bursts into song. Electrical system works, too. U2 bursts into "It's a Beautiful Day."

Halfway to moorage, engine quits. Smokes. Will not start. I say words I didn't know I knew how to say.

Paddle toward slip. Wind blows me into wrong dock. Learn that paddling 2,500-pound boat stern-first against wind not easy. Finally get boat moored in slip.

Drive home. Wonder how much dynamite it would take to sink 22-foot sailboat, then chide myself for such thinking. Smarter to save money and chop hole in bottom with splitting maul.

Return with handtruck I normally use to carry books. Turn boat around so I can remove motor while standing on dock. Place engine on handtruck. Roll 150 yards to pickup.

Local marine store says it can fix — in three weeks. *Three weeks?* I've already lost much of summer. Desperate, do something never done before: offer monetary incentive for one-week fix. Get motor in one week.

Place engine on handtruck, roll to dock, attach. Works.

Estimated hours spent getting boat ready? Forty-five in one month's span. Expense? $700.

But Saturday night, as I anchored in a cove to enjoy dinner and a good book, I realized it was all worthwhile.

Until a sudden wind gust caught the unfurled jib. The sail blew into me as I walked along the rail, knocking me backward and into the lake.

Saved Olympic Trials hat. Lost sunglasses.

Make that $719.99.

And, hey, summer just began.

Olympic pedal to the mettle

July 1, 2012

The U.S. Olympic Track & Field Trials means pushing yourself to the physical limits. The thrill of victory. And, of course, the agony of de seat.

If, like me, you're a pedicab driver pedaling people to and from Hayward Field on a bicycle taxi.

On Thursday, I made 10 trips with people from 10 states: Ohio, New York, Washington, Michigan, Arizona, South Dakota, Delaware, Colorado, California and Oregon.

I transported coaches, parents of competitors, fathers and daughters, moms and sons — even a guy who claimed to have come back from the dead.

"Hey, rickshaw!" my first customer yelled to me near the Agate Street entrance to the University of Oregon campus.

He was a pole vault official from Ohio whose parents were at the Duck Shop and needed a lift to Track Town Pizza.

"I'm your man," I said.

The idea for this undertaking was to learn about some of the out-of-towners who are here for the Olympic Trials and what they thought of Eugene and Oregon.

Wayne Whiting, owner of Eugene Pedicabs, was more than happy to give me an afternoon shift on one of his five three-wheeled cabs, of which I'm an unabashed fan.

That said, I had not ridden a bicycle since 2008 when I set an

Olympic Trials record pedaling from Autzen Stadium to inside the gates of Hayward Field (7:59.75). And I had fallen far from my 2011 conditioning that I'd honed for hiking.

Under the watchful eye of Whiting, I'd gone through intensive training — OK, five minutes of riding in circles — and thought: Hey, this isn't so bad.

Later, I picked up Sue and Harry Newsome of Clyde, Ohio, at the Duck Store. This was bad.

I couldn't get the pedicab to budge. It wasn't the Newsomes' fault, though they had roughly tripled the 200 pounds of the yellow-and-green pedicab. I had the thing in the wrong gear.

Once I made the adjustment, I was off with a couple from the same small town where author Sherwood Anderson had grown up.

In only two days, the couple had been to Nike in Beaverton, Crater Lake and the Oregon Coast. "We've seen five waterfalls and a whale!" said Sue Newsome, 62. "But Crater Lake was scary. I was afraid I'd fall in."

"Find anything quirky about Oregon?" I asked.

"Yeah, that you can't pump your own gas," said Harry Newsome, 64.

Next up were Mitch and Vicki Merber of Long Island, N.Y. Their son, Kyle, a recent Columbia University graduate, would be running the 1,500 prelims.

Nice folks, the Merbers, none of that New York "attitude" you hear about. They were staying at the C'est La Vie Inn Bed and Breakfast on Taylor Street, and had just gotten into Eugene the previous night.

"Loved flying in over the mountains," said Vicki Merber, 54.

I next gave a lift to Cathy Goins, 43, of Spokane and her 17-year-old son, Kyler, a runner at Lewis and Clark High School.

"I want him to be inspired," she said. "His team has a chance to compete at the national level, and I thought this might light a fire for him."

Also, as a former Eugene resident, she wanted to show him the hospital where he was born and the house where he was conceived.

"I was a little grossed out by that," Kyler said.

Patrick Theut, 60, of Manistique, Mich., was in Eugene because he's a coach who has worked with pole vaulter Jeremy Scott, who would be in the finals of that event.

"Love Eugene," he said. "People are smiling. Lots of bikes. It's a people-friendly place. Reminds me of Los Gatos, Calif., in the 1970s or Key West, Fla."

"And the rain isn't bugging you?" I asked.

"I'm from Michigan," he said. "At least you don't have to shovel it."

Dan Schaller, 53, and his daughter, Bella, 7, of Phoenix, Ariz., were my next ride. He's a track and field enthusiast who's been to every Olympic Trials since 1992. She's a new Voodoo Doughnut enthusiast.

Places on their "to-do" list: Prince Puckler's, Mezza Luna Pizzeria, Sweet Life, and Beppe and Gianni's Trattoria.

By my sixth ride, my legs were starting to feel it; even though my route was short, mostly from the Duck Store to Hayward Field, 500 to 600 pounds makes even the slightest hill seem steep — and it was slightly uphill. In distance-running lingo, I was soon "sucking eggs."

But that's not why I stopped in mid-route with Mary Ginsbach, 17, and her father Pat, 56, of Hot Springs, S.D. I stopped because Mary, a discus thrower considering attending UO, mentioned she was also going to visit the University of Washington.

"Seriously?" I said after hitting the brakes. "Why would you go there when you could be here in the track mecca of the universe where people give you free pedicab rides?"

It didn't help my recruiting efforts that, less than a minute later, a Eugene police car, lights flashing, zipped down closed-to-traffic 13th Avenue and up a sidewalk near Villard Hall.

"Hey, I've been on this campus since 1972 and that was the first time I've ever seen something like that," I said.

My next ride was Harold Serkin, 66, of Willits, Calif, and Doug Van Rheen, 61, of West Linn, friends who met only weeks before Serkin died — or says he died. They'd played a round of golf just before Serkin had a heart attack.

"They did the paddle thing on me six times," Serkin said. "I was dead."

So was I, figuratively speaking. Sweat ran down my face as if I'd eaten a pound of red peppers. And my tush was toast. It felt as if I'd sat on Barbara Bowerman's waffle iron. But I gamely shuttled Rachel McCulley, 23, and her fiance, Kevin Kemmerle, 25, of Bear, Del., who had rented a beach house near Tillamook.

After three hours of near-constant pedaling, I decided to call it quits after one more ride: pole vault enthusiasts Sherry Young, 55, and her mother, Marilyn Sherman, 77, of Eugene.

But just as I was heading for the barn, Tim Harder, 50, of Denver, rushed up to me. Quick, he had to get some stuff from his car; could I take him to "19th and something?" My legs shouted no — in fact, went into a two-minute filibuster akin to Jimmy Stewart in *Mr. Smith Goes to Washington* — but my pride said yes.

Harder's trip to Eugene was a three-generation gig with his father and his son; I could enhance his stay.

But on the slight hill on University Street by Mac Court, my legs started balking. When the pitch increased between 18th and 19th, my Gumby-esque legs went on a sit-down strike. I reached for something extra, something deeper, something that so many athletes at the Olympic Trials seem to find.

I couldn't find it.

"Sorry," I told Harder. "I'm a columnist, not a professional pedicab driver. We're going to have to walk to the corner."

"Hey, I totally understand," he said as I pushed the pedicab.

I was ashamed. I'd tarnished the can-do reputation of Eugene Pedicabs, let down the city of Eugene's reputation for its healthy citizenry, and sullied the strive-for-excellence spirit that underlies the entire Olympic movement.

But after completing the mission, Harder reminded me that what's more important than quitting is being willing to start again, which I had. Reluctantly.

He handed me a $20 tip, which, along with another $15 in tips, I gave to Whiting.

Harder's tip took away some of the sting, but not all.

At Hayward Field that night, at times I watched the Olympic Trials the only way I could find comfort: while lying on my side.

My own private marathon

May 3, 2011

By the 15-mile mark of Sunday's Eugene Marathon, my walking buddy Rod Hanson and I were resorting to some pretty obscure trivia to stave off boredom.

"First song you ever heard on a pair of headphones," I said.

We were going west toward Autzen Stadium on Centennial Boulevard, just short of the Interstate 5 overpass. A couple of volunteers were beside us in a four-wheel gator, readying to pick up cones.

Just then, a blue BMW station wagon slowed down.

"Hey," the driver asked the volunteers, "are these the last two competitors?"

The words were salve to my aching body — and ego.

"Did you hear that?" I said to Rod. "He called us 'competitors!'" Our spirits thus buoyed, we ripped off a couple of sub-13-minute miles and were never seriously threatened en route to finishing dead last — 80th and 81st — in the men's 55-to-59 marathon division.

My time of 6 hours, 36 minutes and 56 seconds — somehow, it felt faster, like 6:30 — meant that out of 2,291 marathon runners and walkers, I had finished 2,267th.

What I'm telling you, folks, is that this "competitor" pretty much smoked 24 other people — or .01 of the field.

In the last 40 years, I've completed dozens of races, including two other marathons.

I've never had as much fun as I did Sunday.

Four reasons: First, walking a race — this was my first such effort, done to get in shape for summer backpacking — doesn't hurt as much as running. It hurts longer but less intensely, like taking out a 30-year mortgage instead of having to make a lump-sum payment.

Second, walking allows you to notice more than if you were running, such as the guy on Amazon Parkway with the "Just remember: Right, left, right, left. Repeat" sign.

You can talk to your walking pal, in my case Hanson, a Bend man who, since I wrote about him in 2009, has beaten tongue cancer. And who is a trivia expert, a guy who one moment is pointing out the joys of the Marx Brothers' *A Night at the Opera* (category: "Best Comedies") and the next is telling you about how, in a 1959 visit to

America, Soviet premiere Nikita Khruschev was denied entrance to Disneyland (category: "Best Recent Books Read.")

You can talk to other people, get Red Sox game updates on your iPhone, even record voice memos on that same device. ("Felt something squishy in right pocket. Realized I'd left a banana peel in there for three miles.")

Third, it was a glorious day, the course lathered in buttery sunshine, the Willamette River vibrant, the cherry blossoms gushing, the air crisp.

"I love Eugene," said a fellow walker from Vancouver, B.C., who told us about a running event in Canada that's part race, part wine tasting, appropriately called the Half-Corked Marathon.

Finally, the volunteers, musicians and residents along the way were simply incredible.

Where do I even start? The kid standing on his porch on East 21st Avenue, playing his trombone in our honor at 7:35 a.m. The man riding his stereo-affixed bike up and down Hilyard Street, pumping us up with hip-hop. The drummers adding that Country Fair feel.

Alas, in East Alton Baker Park just after the 11-mile mark, the half-marathoners headed for the finish line while we marathoners — far fewer — headed for Springfield. Suddenly, Rod and I were virtually alone going through Island Park. My spirits sagged.

But then a Springfield woman, who'd been out in front of her house on 10th Street encouraging runners since the first ones had come through two hours earlier, said, "Looking great!"

It was, of course, a lie — we were actually looking like a couple of lost soldiers trying to find our way home after the Civil War — but I believed it.

I believed the folks on the deck at McMenamins North Bank who looked up from their smoked salmon cakes and IPAs to clap for us.

And the Red Cross volunteer at Mile 19 who denied my request for morphine but did offer me two ibuprofen and words of encouragement.

From the 14-mile mark on, the course seemed to be closing behind us as if were fleeing falling buildings in a disaster movie; the guys in the gator, rolling along beside us, might have been vultures over our shoulders, but I envisioned them as angels on our wings, guiding us home.

I believed the "way-to-go" encouragement from the cluster of folks near Marist High School.

I believed the nursing mother at Skinner Butte Park who yelled, "Almost there!" I even believed when Rod threw out the "Famous-Lines-from-Movies" category, and we were both too tired to think of one.

Then, suddenly, we were there: entering hallowed Hayward Field. We'd started at 7:15 a.m. It was now almost 2 p.m. The temperature had gone from 35 degrees to 60. I was now 81 years old.

The crowd erupted in wild applause.

OK, so about 11 people were on hand, eight of whom were blood relatives. When I crossed that finish line — how cool that race organizers waited for us, allowing a guy in 2,267th place to finish where Olympians have finished! — it seemed as if all those encouragers along the way were packed into the (actually vacant) stands.

And I had a future trivia category:

"Best. Race. Ever."

Hoosiers' hoop heaven

May 24, 2011

KNIGHTSTOWN, Ind. — To the east, a basketball-orange sun rose above farmland that was flatter than a cookie sheet.

It was 6:35 a.m. Saturday when I came to the sign and arrow just off Interstate 70, about 25 miles east of Indianapolis:

"Hoosier Gym," it said in foot-high letters, as unassuming as you'd expect in these parts.

I took the exit, my hopes hampered by the thought that my only available slice of time was going to be far too early in the day to actually get inside the gym used in the 1986 movie *Hoosiers*, about unlikely, and fictitious, Hickory High winning a state basketball championship in 1952.

But if anything, *Hoosiers* is about believing against the odds. In the rental car, I turned up the movie's theme song on my iPhone — am I pathetic or what? — and continued my spontaneous pilgrimage.

It had begun two days before when, while here for book research on an unrelated subject, my host took me to a cemetery just down the street from Butler University's Hinkle Fieldhouse.

"Hey," I asked, "isn't that where they filmed the championship game in *Hoosiers*?"

Yup.

Five minutes later, I was standing in the middle of the court.

"You know," he said, "the gym they used for Hickory High is still around if you don't mind a drive."

And so here I was, alone in an Indiana town of 2,000 people before most folks had rolled out of bed.

I found the gym, a nondescript brick box with an arched entryway next to what used to be Knightstown High School. Might it simply be unlocked?

I walked toward it, immersed in the story based on a team from Milan High School (enrollment 161) that had finished first among 751 Indiana schools that began the 1953-54 basketball season. The story that, adapted to film, readers of *USA Today* chose as the best sports movie ever. The story that includes all sorts of inspiration, including a forced-to-play manager, Ollie, who hits a game-winning free throw that bounces high off the rim and drops through the net.

The door was locked. Nobody was around.

I headed to Main Street and chowed down at a Veterans of Foreign Wars community breakfast.

"You know, Rev. Kilmer — he's the head of the gym's board — has keys, and he usually shows up at the breakfast," a man said over his biscuits and gravy.

But the Quaker pastor didn't show, and I had an appointment back in Indianapolis. On my way out of town, I swung by for one last look.

"Hey," said a guy coming out of one of the neighborhood's many flag-draped homes, "weren't you here earlier?"

I nodded yes. Was he going to bust me for waking him up with a slammed car door?

"Want a peek inside?" he said. "I've got keys."

And so Glenn Orr, a retired drama teacher at Knightstown High, gave me a personal tour of the "Hickory High" gym.

It looks and feels amazingly as it did in the movie, a sort of miniature McArthur Court, which it predates by five years. It seats 660 people, 730 if they set up chairs on the old stage.

"We did 'Finian's Rainbow' on that stage when I was in high school," said Natalie Beckler, a volunteer member of the Hoosier Gym board who soon showed up.

The gray, wooden stands hug the court like the walls of a hallway; six rows on each side.

The basement locker rooms smell like the 1950s; a pair of high-top Converse hang on the wall.

The gym rents for $25 an hour. Coaches bring their high school teams here for inspiration. People have gotten married here. Last June, people came from 28 states and three foreign countries.

But mainly, the Hoosier Gym is a place for kids from the community to play basketball. And for gawkers like me who find a certain magic in the movie.

"I was an extra in the crowd," said Orr, "though I can't seem to ever find myself when watching it. The cast was great. Common as old shoes."

A volunteer tries to be on hand for folks who want a look. No charge for a peek, though you're welcome to donate a few bills in the basketball with the slit in the top. Or buy a Hoosier Gym T-shirt or pen.

The atmosphere is blessedly noncommercial, which fits the simpler times the movie depicts.

Meanwhile, the Knightstown people are as warm as fresh pancakes. They kept thanking me for coming.

Thank *me*?

I signed the guest book — "Go Hickory! Go Ducks!" — and was readying to leave when the Rev. Kilmer, who'd swung by after hearing from folks at breakfast, tossed me a basketball.

"Can't leave without taking a few shots, can you?" he said.

Want to know how that turned out? You'll just have to watch my three-minute movie at http://bit.ly/1Muzibr.

It's no *Hoosiers*. But Ollie the manager would love the ending.

Closing the generation gap

June 8, 2014

I just finished the exploration of a culture that, for a 60-year-old guy like me, might as well have been the anthropological study of a forgotten jungle tribe.

I taught college students.

The short-term summary: I spent nine months trying to figure them out and they spent 20 minutes in my second-to-last class teaching me a lesson that I'd overlooked for three terms: never judge an iBook by its cover.

Indeed, the technological gap alone had me fairly petrified as, back in September, I walked into Allen Hall to teach an Art of Writing class at the University of Oregon School of Journalism and Communication.

I knew something about writing — and had taught years ago — but trying to run computer-based slide presentations in front of techno-savvy students was like a Kidsports soccer player putting on a clinic for a World Cup team.

Beyond our 40-year gap in age — when I trudged these Allen Hall steps as a student in the 1970s dinosaurs nibbled on nearby firs — we were divided by technological and social changes that further distanced us.

I was a Baby Boomer; hard-copy newspapers. They were Generation Z; digital everything.

Goodness, these kids' *parents* were 10 to 20 years younger than me. And since I'd last taught — 2007 — the future of hard-copy newspapers had grown perilous and the entire social media scene had exploded. I was teaching some kids who'd been using cell phones since they were 12 and were now thumbing 200-plus text messages per day. (Yup, I interviewed them.)

Thus did I invite one of *The Register-Guard*'s interns — and a student in my fall-term class — to lunch before my first class to see if I could better understand his tribe. Midway through our conversation, I was talking when I realized his attention had exited the Welch Freeway at Cell Phone Road.

"I'll just wait till you're through," I said as he ignored me and remained fixed on the screen.

"Keep talking," he said. "I can multi-task."

In the ensuing school year, I learned much about college students. But their ability to successfully multi-task was not one of them.

"If you insist on focusing on your phones or surfing the web while I'm talking," I told my classes, "then certainly you won't mind if, during a one-on-one meeting you set up with me, I chat with another student or gaze outside at the rain and say: 'Keep talking. I can multi-task.'"

Most students — I had 40, total, in my three classes for the year — abided by that gentle warning. What concerned me more was how serious they were. I teach writers workshops — the average attendee is 50-ish — and laughter is a mainstay. So are questions from students hungry to learn.

But stories that triggered laughter in such workshops left my UO students less animated than the Pioneer Mother statue. I would finish a scintillating discussion of author Jon Krakauer's mastery of action verbs and the eyes in the room looked up at me like those of tired farm dogs on hot summer afternoons.

Where was the passion?

"Any questions?" I'd say. "Comments? Pulses?"

I even wrote it in my syllabus, this idea that learning should be fun. But nobody seemed to be having any. What we needed, I realized, was pizza, but these were labs with computers; no food or drink.

I would reach for a metaphor and realize, mid-sentence, that what I thought was a hip example was from a movie that came out 10 years before these folks were born; they were first- and second-graders on 9/11.

We seemed to be in two different worlds, that fact underscored when I assigned them to read a few hard copies of *The Register-Guard* and be prepared for a quiz. The day before the test, a student e-mailed with a question: "Professor Welch, where could I find a copy of this newspaper?"

Sigh.

I tried everything, included home-baked brownies as a reward for improvement, but nothing seemed to stir any latent passion for writing.

Then, over coffee, a mentor friend of mine asked: "Have you asked them about *their* expectations for the class? What *they're* interested in? What worries them about *their* futures?"

Humbling questions, these. Instead of trying to see life through their eyes, I had been trying to drag them into seeing it through mine. I was Professor Higgins in *My Fair Lady* — it's a musical from 1964, dear students — singing "Why Can't a Woman Be More Like a Man?"

Why can't your generation be more like mine?

That was no more fair than my pipe-smoking profs in the '70s expecting the same of me and my generation instead of respecting that the world was changing.

So, on the first day of spring term, my Reporting I class might have expected me to drone on about the syllabus. Instead, I listened to students: where they were from, why they'd chosen journalism and what they hoped for regarding futures that were far less certain than my post-Watergate college days, when we all wanted to get jobs at newspapers and most of us did.

The next class, to see how well they could write, I assigned them to fast-forward five years and imagine themselves working at their dream jobs. It was enlightening; suddenly, instead of just students they became photographers flying over Africa doing documentaries on endangered animals and covering the San Francisco Giants for FOX Sports and even hosting "The Today Show."

"That was cool," one said.

But none of this compared to our second-to-last class Monday. After discussing the importance of being vulnerable as a columnist, I asked them to do exactly that. "Give me your opening three or four paragraphs to a first-person column. You have just under half an hour. And then I'd like you to read it out loud, to the class."

Finally, I'd provoked passion — passion bordering on mutiny. *Half an hour with no idea in place? Read aloud? Are you kidding me?*

Half an hour later a young woman volunteered to read her piece. It was about her love for "Sarge," a puggle pup therapy dog that's helping her adjust to civilian life after her stint in Afghanistan with the army. When she broke down in tears and couldn't finish it, a classmate next to her stepped in to read us the rest.

In nearly 10 years of teaching over the last three decades, nothing has touched me more.

The pinch-hitting reader then offered her own piece, which began: "'America is the best country in the world!'" my mother exclaims. Her thick Peruvian accent makes it sound more like 'Ahhmerica is de best contry in da werld!'"

Her column was about how her mother's struggles growing up in Peru had made the student appreciate the educational system in our country.

I watched and listened in wonder.

A young woman read a teary lament about a friend back in California who had taken his life.

A soon-to-graduate senior read about he and his buddies going their separate ways and how much he was going to miss what had become "home."

Finally, a young woman read about what it's like being a fiancee to a soldier in Afghanistan, "not being able to count down the days because you don't know when you're going to see him again."

I was so stunned by the vulnerability, emotion and eloquence of these columns that I could only utter a few feeble words between each offering.

For nine months, I realized, I'd been subconsciously looking upon these students as projects, lab rats in my experiment to see if I could drag them into the glories of the written word.

What I'd forgotten along the way was their humanity. Their uniqueness. Their struggles.

Now, this exercise — their words — seemed to have galvanized us into a sense of oneness. As class wound up, students gathered around my laptop to see photos of my new grandson, McCoy, and I reminded them that Wednesday would be our last class.

"Pizza!" someone said.

Yes, pizza.

We had it outside, on the lawn, two days later — me and 13 students I'll always remember not for what I taught them, but for what they taught me.

7.
Icons

The Spandex Nun

June 30, 2013

The cranky man in Room 447 had already scared off a handful of nurses. Would Sister Aileen Trainor care to check on him?

"I'm Sister Aileen," she said to him. "I'm here to give you your pills."

He recommended they be placed elsewhere.

"I won't take the pills," he said.

She grabbed his catheter.

"You won't what?" she said with a fiendish look that morphed into a smile.

A slight smile creased his own face. He took the pills.

Officially, the reason PeaceHealth honored Sister Aileen Trainor Saturday was to mark her golden jubilee: 50 years since she took her vows with the Sister of St. Joseph of Peace, the order that founded PeaceHealth.

But the reason she earned a prolonged standing ovation from more than 200 people at St. Jude Catholic Church was because most of them know what the guy in Room 447 learned that day: Sister Aileen Trainor has an amazing way with people.

"God's gift to me is that I can see people's fear," she told me earlier in an interview. "That man who didn't want to take his pills had just been told he had cancer of the bladder. He didn't have much time to live. He said they'd taken away everything that identified who he was: his watch, his rings ..."

So, understanding his fear of loss, she went for the funny bone. "Humor," she said, "has a way of deflecting unhappiness."

Sister Aileen is part grin. Part grit. All compassion.

She skis, does tai chi and has run the Butte to Butte so many times she's been dubbed "The Spandex Nun."

But what distinguishes her even more is her vision to give hope to the hurting.

"Mother Teresa once said, 'It is not how much we do, but how much love we put in the doing,'" Jack Courtemanche, a member of PeaceHealth's Oregon Region Board, said at Saturday's event. "That's Sister Aileen."

It is, say some, as if she sees people with CAT-scan vision, beyond the obvious, to discover how they're hurting and how she can help.

"She's the consummate listener," said Alan Yordy, chief mission officer and CEO of PeaceHealth. "Steadfast in prayer ... steadfast in humor — and an occasional prank."

Sister Aileen, who grew up in British Columbia, graduated from nursing school in 1962 and took her vows the next year with the Sisters of St. Joseph of Peace in Bellingham, Wash.

She started work at Eugene's Sacred Heart Hospital in 1972 and helped establish the risk management department in 1982.

She's still part of that team, serving as a patient liaison. Through it all, she's maintained eye-to-eye connections with patients and offered serve-by-example inspiration to her peers.

"I often hear staff say — and have been known to ask myself: 'What would Sister Aileen do?'" wrote a colleague, Alicia Beymer, as part of a paper for an MBA class at Northwest Christian University.

Then, of course, there's her lighter side.

Sister Aileen has been known to tap dance in the hallways, show up in a clown's suit or distract an audience by swirling a laser pointer behind a speaker's head.

Yordy remembers his first encounter with Sister Aileen in 1981, when she was head urology nurse.

"Welcome," she said, "to the plumbing department."

"I'd tell people I'm her parole officer," said Robert Lowry, an attorney who had worked with her. "Half of them believed me."

Sister Aileen's desire to be a nun, her quest to serve, her penchant for practical jokes — all came at an early age.

By 10, she realized she was part of a family that was part faith, part fun. "Church was the center of our life, but there was always room for water fights, scaring altar boys and dressing up like the bishop."

By 13, she'd mastered the art of fooling neighborhood boys by ringing the eyepiece of a kaleidoscope with shoe polish — and laughing after they'd taken a peek, the boys not realizing they each had a prominent circle around one eye.

By 15, she'd decided to give up her plans to be a champion ice skater and commit her life to God and join a convent. She was visiting her father's childhood home on Prince Edward Island. While looking across miles of farmland, she felt "a call from God."

She's never regretted the decision. "I have never *not* wanted to be here," she told me.

And to the crowd gathered Saturday: "I was so nervous when I took my vows that I forgot the word 'obedience.' 'Don't worry,' another sister said to me. 'I was so nervous I forgot the word 'celibacy.'"

Sister Aileen has served through 10 administrators and seen hundreds of employees — and thousands of patients — come and go.

At Saturday's celebration, dozens of people in person and on video praised and lightly roasted her, some sporting red clown noses in honor of her penchant for humor. But amid the laughter rose unmistakable reverence for the serious work she's done:

Showing up in the middle of the night to comfort grieving families.

Leading morning prayers at the hospital.

Heading up a group of patients recovering from heart surgery.

Fighting for a neonatal unit back in the 1980s even though it looked as if it was a financial bridge too far.

"Because of her support then, and the support of the other sisters, the last three decades have seen thousands of babies saved who would otherwise have languished or been sent away," said Dr. Igore Gladstone, chief of medicine at PeaceHealth Sacred Heart Medical Center at RiverBend.

Beymer, a colleague, said she once asked Sister Aileen how she knew she wanted to be a nun. She turned the question around to Beymer, asking her how she knew she wanted to marry her husband, Aaron.

"I told her I just knew," Beymer said.

"That's what my calling to be a nun was like," Sister Aileen said.

"But," Beymer later wrote, "the difference in the vow I made and the vow the sister made is that I only have to wake up in the middle of the night for one person if they are sick or in need. Sister Aileen wakes up for all God's people. And she has done this for seven days a week, 24 hours a day, 52 weeks a year — for the last 50 years."

In honor of such, I place an exclamation mark of praise for the Spandex Nun.

Kesey's mom still his mom

Nov. 6, 2011

It seems impossible that so much time could have passed, but Ken Kesey died 10 years ago this Thursday.

His mother, Geneva Jolley, shakes her head — she can't believe it either — and tells you from across her dining room table that she still dreams of him, though the dreams pop like bubbles and she can't remember them.

"I keep thinking he'll come back from wherever he's been with lots of good stories and presents," says Kesey's 45-year-old daughter, Sunshine Kesey, who helps take care of her grandmother in Geneva's home off Hayden Bridge Road in Springfield.

Geneva Jolley, who remarried after her first husband died in 1969, turned 95 two weeks ago. She relies on a full-time helper, gets around with a walker and is, she says, "80 percent blind."

"But I'm a tough old broad," she says. "I don't cry easily."

The context is how difficult it was to lose her son, who died in 2001 at age 66 after complications from surgery to remove a tumor from his liver.

"I cried then," she says. "A lot. It's still your child, no matter how old he is."

She tells you of a poem he wrote her back when he was 11. At the time, the family was living at the corner of 5th and Q. The poem was called "Mother, Mine." Six decades later, she still has it:

> *All through the past ages of my eleven years*
> *My mother shared my trouble, my sorrows and my tears*
> *She corrected all my wrongs, and paid for all my duds*
> *She bought me all my play things and fed me all my spuds*
> *She tucked me in my covers and brought me up just right*
> *She wore out 15 razor straps to make me see the light*
> *She should be responsible for what I am today,*
> *And from now on what I do I'll do my mother's way.*

"He had a mind of his own," Geneva says.

She stares off into another time.

"He hypnotized his brother once. And got a little scared because he was afraid Chuck wasn't coming back."

Geneva gave birth to Ken in La Junta, Colo. The family came west after World War II when Geneva's husband, Fred, got a job here at a creamery.

"Ken was always attentive, always rebellious," she says.

He went to the old elementary school at what's now the Springfield School District office on Mill Street, then Springfield Junior High. In 1953, he graduated from Springfield High, where he had been a star wrestler, a decent football player and winner of the senior class's "Most Talented" award.

He attended the University of Oregon. Wrestled. And eloped with a girl he'd been in love with since junior high, Norma "Faye" Haxby.

"He didn't get off track until he went off to Stanford for graduate school," Geneva says.

Drugs. A faked suicide. A run from the law. Other indiscretions.

But, amid it, literary brilliance. After working night shifts at the Menlo Park Veterans' Hospital, he wrote *One Flew Over the Cuckoo's Nest* in 1962, now a standard on most best-novel lists.

Two years later, *Sometimes a Great Notion* was published.

"When the books came out, they were not red-letter days for me," Geneva says. "They should have been. But I didn't appreciate all that he had put into those books. I didn't appreciate how famous they were going to become."

She wonders if it was a mother's protective instincts. "Maybe I didn't want him to be a big turnip in a little turnip patch," she says. "He always liked a crowd."

But the Keseys were simple folk. And fame isn't simple — even if Geneva did come to accept him finding it.

She tells of her husband dying of amyotrophic lateral sclerosis (ALS) in the late 1960s and says, without skipping a beat, "At the time, Faye and Ken and the kids were over in London, doing some work with the Beatles ..."

She loves the downtown statue of Ken reading to the kids. "It's beautiful." Didn't mind, decades ago, when an occasional fan would show up on the front porch.

And yet, in a sense, that was about someone else's Ken.

Her Ken is the kid fishing off the stern of the family boat at Odell Lake. The man who brought her gifts from wherever he was in the world, her favorite a turquoise necklace from Egypt.

"He was always stopping by to say hi — and moms appreciate that."

She regrets not embracing his success. "I never gave him credit for all he accomplished," she says, "and he knew I didn't."

Not that it's ever too late to show your pride. The other day, when a doctor made reference to her turquoise necklace, she didn't hesitate with her response. "My son, Ken Kesey, brought this for me from Egypt."

Dozens of his books line her shelves, though her favorite Kesey writing, she says, isn't here. It's on the dining room table. A poem.

Hand-written by an 11-year-old.

Loss of a rare man

March 13, 2015

A few years ago, Dave Frohnmayer and I were speaking at Northwest Christian University on the subject of leadership when he shared an adage with students that I've never forgotten.

"Tell me," he said, "and I'll forget. Show me, I'll remember. Involve me, and I'll understand."

Now that he's gone — he died March 9 from prostate cancer at 74 — I realize that that's how Frohnmayer lived his life:

Showing. Involving. Partnering with people to some greater end, be it making a great university greater, spearheading a cure for the Fanconi anemia disease that claimed two of his five children or helping a freshman student in his leadership class understand the world better.

Showing. Involving. Partnering with people as opposed to the more common political ploys of finger-wagging, show-boating or sound-biting.

We live in a world where style often trumps substance, where tweets have supplanted face-to-face communication, where a public official's proud personal personna today lies tattered in the shame unearthed by a newspaper investigation the next.

The box score will show that Frohnmayer's 15 years as president of the University of Oregon represented nearly twice the current average stay for those in that position. His two successors managed only five — between them.

But Frohnmayer's legacy is more than his resiliency and determinedness against the odds: it's the reminder that nice guys don't always finish last.

Dave was Fred MacMurray on "My Three Sons," the protective father who watched over his state, his university, his family; a guy who drove a minivan as part of his unabashedly Old School approach; an unassuming guy who could just as easily have been a UO reference librarian.

And yet he was also a time-and-a-place guy — and when he felt something he loved was in danger, he would leave the Clark Kent personna in the phone booth. As state attorney general, he sued the Rajneeshee cult in 1983 on religion-and-state grounds for its take-over of Antelope in north-central Oregon — no small risk given that cult leaders later plotted to kill him and a handful of other government officials.

He was always quick with an op-ed piece when someone disparaged the UO.

And he took me to the woodshed once after taking exception to a column I wrote about UO athletics and money. But he did so with a style leavened with grace: he bought me a hot chocolate at the Oakway Starbucks and politely set me straight.

I've always thought character reveals itself the farther we get from the public eye and, in that respect, the behind-the-scenes Frohnmayer reminded me of another UO president who the two of us greatly admired: Robert Clark, president of the school from 1969 to 1975.

Years after he retired, Clark attended a book talk I gave at the Congregational Church; when looking for him so I could say good-bye, I found the former college president in the kitchen, doing the post-lunch dishes.

If it involved helping people, Frohnmayer was happy to get his hands in the dishwater, too.

Never mind that he and wife Lynn were honored in Atlanta in front of 20,000 scientists and physicians from around the world for their work with the Fanconi Anemia Research Fund. Dave loved teaching his freshman leadership class.

He would happily be a guinea pig, routinely coming to my journalism classes at the UO and allowing my students to interview him.

When driving to Salem with UO's student body president, to lobby a cause, Dave would insist they stop at Pioneer Villa Restaurant at the Brownsville exit to get vanilla sugar-frosted cookies with speckles.

My favorite moment with the man: because of our common love for Oregon's wilderness, I invited him to introduce me before a book event on *Cascade Summer* at Gerlinger Hall.

He was a busy guy; he could have mailed it in. Instead, he clearly spent time on his intro and talked of how in the decade before my family began camping at the west end of Cultus Lake, his family and the Bowermans had done the same. Never mind that the event drew about 12 people, I left feeling as if blessed by the pope himself.

Just recently, he had agreed to introduce me before my Nov. 6 "Evening With Bob Welch & Friends: My Oregon" event at the Hult. Instead, we'll dedicate the show to him and his love for this state.

Since his passing, I keep finding myself in disbelief, as if Oregon and Eugene and the UO are someone incomplete without him. I remember the beautiful words of his 27-year-old daughter, Amy, who has Fanconi anemia but lives a vibrant life in Bend.

"There are moments, especially when early fall days turn leaves fiery red, apples come into season, and the early morning chill calls for scarves and warm drinks, when I'm simply compelled to stop and breathe in the awe of being alive," she wrote.

In honor of her father, we should be compelled to do the same, thankful that Dave didn't just tell us or show us.

He *involved* us, as fellow heirs to the Oregon he loved so much.

Barbara was 'family'

June 6, 2010

In 34 years of journalism, you meet hundreds of interesting people. Few have been as gracious, humble and eloquent as Barbara Bowerman.

Bowerman, 96, died Saturday in a Fossil assisted-living home, not far from the family ranch on the John Day River that she called "my Picasso."

It was there, in Fossil, that I had the privilege of interviewing her in August 2005. Our conversation began in the Big Timber restaurant, shifted to the Haven House Retirement Home and concluded with us watching the Wheeler County Fair and Rodeo parade.

"Why, that looks just like Will Bowerman," she said about a young man riding a John Deere tractor. "That's my grandson!" (One of six grandchildren.)

She said it with a touch of earthy pride, as if he had just bent forward on a track-and-field victory stand to have a gold medal placed around his neck.

That's what impressed me about Bowerman: rather than get all ego-puffed about being the wife of track and running-shoe guru Bill Bowerman, she spent much of her life applauding those around her.

"She looked closely at everybody she knew, and whatever their role was, it counted with her," says son Jay, 67, the principal researcher at the Sunriver Nature Center & Observatory. "She felt great joy in seeing other people succeed."

In the past few months, she stewed about how best to thank the folks at Haven House who had taken such good care of her. And when Jay and his wife, Teresa, visited, spent a solid hour dictating a letter to them for a dear friend.

Which isn't to say she didn't relish being Bill Bowerman's wife. She clearly did.

"I always thought of Bill as that surfer who would pick the biggest wave and ride it better than anyone else," she told me, "and I got to go along for the ride. Because of him, I've had lots of adventures."

If that might sound like fingernails scraped against a feminist chalkboard, it was neither an "I'm-not-worthy" admission nor a "long-live-King-Bill" exaltation.

She freely admitted that Bill's passion for collegiate athletes, training programs, jogging, the University of Oregon and his new shoe designs cut into his time with her and their sons. But she had found a peace with life's rhythm.

"That was a role she filled extremely well and graciously, and I don't think she felt a need for anything else," says Jay. "I suspect that was consistent with her generation."

Whether it was attending one of five Olympic Games or seeing an evening sun slip behind the rimrocks west of the Bowerman ranch, she felt herself blessed.

She told me she had been so busy living her life that until Bill died in 1999, she hadn't time to put it in perspective.

"Thinking about it all has almost been like writing a book," she said. "And what I've learned is that my life has had all these segments, and each seemed to get better than the one before."

She was short on brag, long on eloquence. "She's magnificent," Kenny Moore, the author of *Bowerman and the Men of Oregon*, once wrote me. "She speaks in complete paragraphs that could stand unedited in *The New Yorker*."

In a rare public speaking appearance, she wowed a Nike crowd honoring husband Bill. "Blew everyone away," recalls Jay. "Everyone knew her as being this quiet, behind-the-scenes person, but she got up there for 10 spellbinding minutes and talked about Bill and her role in his life and how much she enjoyed it all."

She was a longtime member of the Christian Science Church in Eugene but, like with most things, did not trumpet the fact. "She didn't wear anything on her sleeve, including religion," said Jay. "She didn't offer too many opinions unless asked." (Though, on her 96th birthday last month, she did read the opening stanza of a Kipling poem to her family, memorized since her high school days in Medford, where she'd met Bill.)

True to form, she asked for no service upon her passing. Encouraged Jay and other family to not be sad. And died quietly in her room at Haven House.

After I heard the news, I pulled out a letter she had written me last March. In it, she made reference to a column I'd written about a daughter-in-law who'd met my son at a Young Life camp across the John Day River from the Bowerman Ranch that son Jon runs.

It connected us, she said; "made me feel like part of your family."

I thought about how the only other time I saw her was at the symphonic biography of Bill Bowerman at the Hult Center in 2008. And how warmly she'd greeted me and my wife, whom she'd met in Fossil.

I did not know her well. And yet that may be one of the hallmarks of Barbara Bowerman's legacy:

She left so many of us feeling as if we did.

8.

Call of duty

More than a parade

Aug. 22, 2013

Toward the end of the 2003 Lord of the Rings movie, *The Return of the King,* four hobbits are having a drink at the Green Dragon after pretty much having saved the world — though nobody else knows of that accomplishment.

Across the tavern, patrons have gathered to gawk over a huge pumpkin that a guy has brought in, showering him with attention as the four look at each other and say nothing, obviously feeling out of place.

Army Maj. Ben Van Meter knows the feeling.

The 32-year-old Eugene man has been back from war a handful of times now and says that's a little how it feels.

"These four go off on this epic adventure and come back and everyone's gathered around this pumpkin as if it's the biggest thing to ever happen in the village," he says. "It's this awkward moment. Their adventure is done. Now what?"

Don't take him wrong. Van Meter strikes me as a humble man who doesn't believe he and his buddies saved the world, nor that they deserve a parade.

"But we all have a story to tell," he says. "We're just looking for connections, so we can move forward."

He didn't come to me with a suggestion that I write about the disconnect between soldiers and the hometowns they return to.

Instead, I went to him.

I'd heard from someone else that Van Meter, a 2004 University of Oregon psychology major, was a hometown boy — born and raised in Eugene — who had some insights on trying to reconnect with the place you love after being off to war.

I wasn't disappointed.

We talked of how his returning-from-war experience has been nothing like the polar extremes of his grandfather's and his father's.

Van Meter's World War II era grandfather came home after a war in which American involvement was, with few exceptions, seen as necessary. A war that had a distinct end. A war that most young men were involved in. They returned as heroes.

Van Meter's father — a Navy medic who served Marine units

involved in Vietnam's ground campaign — came home during an unpopular war in which many who served bore the brunt of people's anti-war anger.

"It was definitely not a positive experience, his coming home," says Van Meter.

His wars — Iraq and Afghanistan — have left him as neither fish nor fowl, hero nor goat. The wars have been neither universally supported nor massively protested, his comings and goings quiet and, often, confusing.

"We come back like passing shadows," he says.

An Oregon Army National Guard unit might attract some media coverage when coming or going. But as "active army," Van Meter comes and goes on his own: four deployments since 2005, his rise to major coming last June in Afghanistan at a ceremony in which a Duck banner was held aloft.

He's gone long enough to feel disconnected but not so long that he can't keep apprised of a little news here and there.

"I feel a little like both newcomer and stranger," he says. "It's like I see everything about Eugene in snapshots. Because of the Internet, you hear this or that, but you don't have that pulse-check on the community when you're away from it."

And when he returns?

His family — he's single, but his parents still live here — connects with him.

"And 'thank-yous' from people are nice," he says of folks who will see him in uniform. But people seem hesitant to engage him further, ask a question.

"When you talk to someone, you get to know that someone," he says. "You make connections and can move forward."

As it is, he often feels stuck in the past.

"It's like seeing someone from a high school reunion," he says.

You recognize them — but sometimes just barely.

"You come back and the music is completely different," he says, "and people are talking about movies you don't even know exist."

Where do you start to reconnect? The civilian world he left has changed and the military world he's been in has little in common with the experiences of those at home.

"It's like describing something to someone that they've never seen before," he says. "Difficult."

The challenge, he says, isn't political. He remembers, as an ROTC student at the UO, that he'd stand out on days when he had to wear his uniform to classes. But he never felt ostracized or looked down on because of that.

And it's nothing unique about Eugene, he says. Sure, he's been to cities and towns where the military has a far larger presence. "But this isn't our community's fault," he says.

The challenge is finding a way to bridge that awkward chasm between soldier and civilian, between who he was then, a 1999 Willamette High School graduate, and who he is now, an army major.

"I don't blame anyone for that gap," he says. "It's not that I think I'm special. I'm just a hometown boy who's got a story to tell. Let's celebrate, OK? Drink a beer and have a good time."

Since it was Van Meter who brought up the movie scene, I asked him how he'd rewrite it to bring together community and soldier.

"Maybe we each need to make a more concerted effort," he says. "Maybe I need to go over and talk to those people who are admiring the pumpkin."

And maybe those of us gathered around the pumpkin need to pull up a chair at his table and ask him about his adventure. Listen to his story.

After all, as Van Meter says: "We'll always have one thing in common. We share a home."

Back to Marudu Bay

Sept. 27, 2011

You're a 23-year-old PT boat skipper when World War II ends.

In September 1945, on Samar, Philippines, you watch the farewell inferno: dozens of the wooden "patrol torpedo" boats, including yours, dragged together on the beach like so many logs on a fire and, after being stripped of any useful equipment, doused with diesel and set aflame.

This is a boat you lived on, fought on, watched men die on. Gone. You feel like a cowboy having to put down his horse.

You return home to Eugene, where your wife, Gloria, has clipped the articles from the local paper, *The Register-Guard*, about Lt. William H. Skade leading missions into "the mine-infested waters of Marudu Bay ..."

You and Gloria move to the house where you still live on Emerald Street, south of the University of Oregon.

Son Hank is born in 1948, daughters Dorothy in 1950 and Patricia in 1956. Thirty-seven years with Allstate Insurance. Retirement in 1987 at age 66.

You do a little fishing here and there, own a few boats. But nothing like that 78-foot wooden boat you piloted during the war, a craft with three 1½-ton Packard V-12 engines whose vibrations, if you close your eyes, you can still almost feel.

Not that you mention those years to anyone. You're like a lot of folks in your generation: just did what you needed to do, and got on with things when the war ended.

Still, when you find, in the attic, the tattered flag that once flew from the bridge of PT 143, you were honored that the kids had it framed. You hang it in your den, the edges frayed as much by time as by the way it once whipped above you in boat speeds of up to 40 knots.

Meanwhile, you haven't heard what some of your generational PT peers are up to 90 miles north, in Portland. How they've come across one of only 11 PT boats that survived the war, and trucked it from California to Oregon to restore it.

Never mind that, since the war, it had survived a fire and sunk twice. "You never tell a bunch of old PT boaters that it can't be done," one of them tells *The Oregonian*.

In 2004, 13 years of volunteer blood, sweat and tears after the project begins, the mainly 80-something guys and a few others proudly motor PT 658 up the Willamette River in a dedication ceremony.

It is the only authentically restored, operational U.S. Navy PT boat in the world. But of the 16 men who originally began working to restore it, eight don't live long enough to enjoy the day.

A thousand of your aging fellow World War II veterans are dying each day. A few months ago, Gloria reminds you that you'll soon be 90 yourself, which is a long way from that fresh-faced kid who'd heard the Navy wanted "athletic types" for PT boats so wore two extra sweaters beneath your coat for your interview.

In the same breath, Gloria mentions something about the PT boat in Portland. She and the "kids" — now 62, 61 and 55 — want you to see it Sept. 24 as part of your birthday celebration.

Oh, the grandchildren are coming, too, 13 family members in all, three generations, from Oklahoma, California and Seattle.

On Saturday morning, your heart quickens when you see PT 658, moored at Portland's Swan Island Pier; it's just like the Higgins boat you trained on in New Orleans in 1943.

The crew hands out life preservers. The whole family is seated on the boat. You're given an honorary medal.

Then up stands Jerry Gilmartin, a 50-year-old retired Navy man who's the PT project's curator. He still can't believe that, though only 36 boats of this class were made, there's an actual captain of one in his midst.

He welcomes the family, all decked out in their matching Bill Skade "90 Years and Going Strong" T-shirts, then tells you the bad news.

"The captain," he says, "has called in sick."

He looks at you. Everyone but you knows what he's going to say next.

"Lt. Skade," he says, "how would you feel about running the boat today?"

You're a bit confused here. "What, you're actually going to get under way?"

Gilmartin nods yes. Your daughter, Patricia, worries that you'll decline. *Please, dad, say you will.*

"It's been a long time," you say — 66 years to be exact — "but sure."

You're on the water for almost an hour, which, your children say, is about how long your smile lasted.

When you were at the helm, sometime before back-on-the-dock birthday cupcakes and before you donate your well-pressed captain's uniform to the nonprofit group that restored the boat, your son Hank asks the question.

"How does it feel, Dad?"

Your hands are wrapped around the mahogany wheel.

"Just like old times," you say, then return your gaze to the mine-infested waters of Marudu Bay.

Vietnam's first and last

Nov. 11, 2010

I've driven by the house on Tomahawk Street, off Harlow Road, dozens of times. But now that I know, it'll be different.

Now, I will always imagine that telegram from the secretary of the Army arriving in 1965, and the lives of the Shriver family inside being forever changed.

And next time I tee it up at RiverRidge, I'll think of that government vehicle pulling up in front of the Beglau family's farmhouse northeast of what's now the golf course, and of a father's anger, a sister's tears, a girlfriend's cold first encounter with death.

Robert Shriver Jr. and David Beglau were the first and last soldiers from Lane County to die in the Vietnam War. On this Veterans Day more than three decades later, I honor them as the bookends to the 75 lives of young men from Lane County whom that war claimed.

Shriver, 20, a 1963 graduate of North Eugene High School, died 45 years ago next week — Nov. 17, 1965. Beglau, 21, a 1967 graduate of Sheldon High School, died July 22, 1971.

They lived within four miles of each other. Hailed from middle-class families. Lived with a certain pedal-to-the-metal vibrancy. And had both enlisted in the Army.

"Bob was a fun-loving guy who always had a joke," says Mike Curtis, a classmate of Shriver's at North.

Shriver attended Cal Young Junior High School. At North, he served as a class president, helped the Highlanders win their only state golf championship — he made all-state — and dreamed of playing professional golf. But he also got kicked off the team for partying his senior year.

"Average student, above-average partier," says another classmate, Gary Draper. "He loved life."

"I always used to kid him that he looked like (singer) Ricky Nelson," says Nancy Collins Muhlheim, who was close friends with Bob's year-older sister, Pam. "He was a good-looking kid with amazing golf skills."

By November 1965, anti-war protests were heating up. Fifty thousand people marched on Washington, D.C. Two set themselves on fire to protest the United States' involvement in the war.

Meanwhile, Shriver, a private in the 1st Cavalry Division, was on a search-and-destroy mission when he was killed by hostile small-arms fire. His loss was among a single-week record — to that point — of 240 deaths.

He died in the Battle of the Ia Drang Valley, on which the book and movie *We Were Soldiers Once ... and Young* was based. Shriver is mentioned in the book.

His parents, Bob Sr. and Helen, are both deceased.

"A taxi cab driver brought the telegram," says sister Pam Shriver Claussen, who was attending Brigham Young University at the time. "I still remember the 6 a.m. phone call from my mom. It was horrible."

Nearly six years after Shriver's death, Beglau, a sergeant in the 101st Airborne Division, died when he stepped on a booby trap.

He had attended Colin Kelly Junior High School before going to Sheldon. Won numerous state fair awards for his sheep and chickens. And loved hunting, fishing and anything outdoors.

"He was Daniel-Boone-meets-Indiana-Jones," remembers Ann Gehrke Schar, who lived just across a bean field from him. "We'd just be finishing dinner and he'd show up. I'd grab my gun and we'd go do some target practicing."

Beglau had two brothers and a sister. "We weren't the Brady Bunch but we didn't kill each other, either," says Catherine Beglau, his sister, now 55. "He was the social one of the family and, like most teenage boys, could get himself into a little trouble."

David Beglau was a fixture on Willamette Street, where he'd often "drag the gut" in his red, souped-up Volkswagen Beetle. After graduating from Sheldon in 1967, he moved into an apartment with some buddies and fell in love with the girl next door, Pam Gesme Miller, a South Eugene grad.

She was at the Beglau home that summer night in 1971 when a military representative arrived with the news. What she remembers most was the scream-aloud anger in David's father, Rolland.

"David was the guy who lit up a room when he walked in, the glue that held everybody together," says Miller, now an assistant dean of engineering at University of California, Irvine. "When he died, everything fell apart."

"He was the best squad leader I had," an Army buddy wrote to David's mother, Lila.

Like Shriver's folks, Beglau's parents are both deceased.

Never mind that it's been nearly a half-century since his death; Catherine breaks down talking about the loss of her brother. "It just kind of sucks the air out of you," she says.

I leave her north Eugene home, reminded that time may heal, but with death from war, never completely. Family members who, decades ago, read those telegrams or saw those cars come up the driveway will never forget. And on this Veterans Day — and every day — neither should the rest of us.

Welcome home, flyboy

Jan. 9, 2010

COOS BAY — Today, an 82-year-old Marshfield High School dropout will be awarded an Oregon veterans' diploma.

Elgen Long's story is one of wings and roots. Of the lure of an endless sky and the pull of a hometown. Of dreams taking flight and memories calling him back to a house on 13th Court with an eerie twist of serendipity.

It begins, Long says, in Lincoln City in the early 1930s when, as a youngster, he and pal Joe DeJardin would watch airplanes buzz down the coastline. Someday, he told Joe, the two of them were going to buy a plane and fly together.

They never did. DeJardin became a priest and now lives in Spokane.

But Long — well, eight years ago, a Marshfield High teacher, Jeffery Eberwein, became intrigued with an autographed photo he saw in the principal's office of a man standing at McMurdo Sound in Antarctica. The signature? Elgen Long.

The photo's caption said he was a former Marshfield High student who, in 1971, became the first person to fly solo around the world over the north and south poles. Eberwein, a 48-year-old history instructor who teaches an elective on the history of aviation, was curious. Who was this guy?

He started to find out. On the Internet, he learned that Long had left Marshfield High in 1942 to enlist in the Navy as a 15-year-old sophomore, fibbing about his age.

Long flew patrol bombers in the Pacific. After the war, he earned a GED and an associate degree in aeronautics. Became a pilot for the

Flying Tiger Line that eventually became FedEx, his last 10 years as senior captain of a 747. And, in 1971, set 15 "firsts" during that North Pole/South Pole solo flight.

For that feat and others, he was awarded the Federation Aeronautique Internationale "Gold Air Medal" as the world's outstanding sports pilot. (Previous recipients included Charles Lindbergh and Chuck Yeager.)

There was more. Along with his wife, Marie, Long had written a book, *Amelia Earhart: The Mystery Solved,* that Simon & Schuster published in 1999.

Eberwein was amazed. "Here's a man who grew up here and accomplished these things and yet you'd ask people who he was and get blank stares."

Long was as obscure, Eberwein realized, as Marshfield's biggest hero, Steve Prefontaine, was famous. The teacher's Internet efforts to contact Long were proving fruitless. Eberwein kept digging. Month after month. Nothing.

Finally, he found a phone number for an Elgen Long in Reno, Nev. More than three years since starting the search, he placed the call. Bingo. It was the same Elgen Long. But, weirdly, Long wondered if Eberwein were contacting him about "the movie."

Movie? What movie? Turns out, the rights to the Longs' book had been bought by Fox Searchlight Studio; Elgen had been used as a technical consultant for *Amelia,*which would star Hilary Swank and Richard Gere. (The black-tie premiere was in October in New York, with Long — Marie passed away in 2003 — among the guests.)

Before the 15-minute conversation was over, Eberwein popped the question: Would Long be willing to return home to inspire the Marshfield High students? Long said he'd be honored.

"There's a disconnect between what kids think they can do and what they can actually do," Eberwein says. "I want them to sense Mr. Long's passion."

Under state law, a school district may issue diplomas to veterans who did not graduate from a high school because they were serving in the Armed Forces. Today, Long will receive such a degree in a 9:15 a.m. ceremony at the school and be recognized by the public at large at halftime of the 7 p.m. Marshfield-Thurston basketball game.

"It's wonderful," says Long, who left Coos Bay — then called Marshfield — for the Navy 68 years ago. "I want to let these students know that the world is your apple, now go out and get it. Just because you come from a small town doesn't mean you can't shake up the world a bit. If you can dream it, you can do it."

Long is staying at the home of Jeffery and his wife, Tracy. Listening to Eberwein's directions over the phone, he was curious to note that he was being guided to a familiar 13th Court neighborhood.

"You don't need to give me any more directions," Long said at one point. "You live in the house my late brother built and lived in for 15 years. I know it well."

And, soon, his hometown will know him well, too. At last.

The old soldiers

Dec. 1, 2011

For five days — eight hours a day — they walked, shuffled or were rolled in wheelchairs into *The Register-Guard* building to have their photos taken at our request.

To tell their stories. To don that sailor cap or squeeze into that Army uniform one last time. To reminisce about a period in their lives that, like an old newspaper, is yellowed by the years and yet — given the catch in a throat or a burst of laughter you'd hear from them — might as well have been yesterday.

World War II veterans — 130 of them. Mainly men, a handful of women. Ages 84 to 99.

A collective version of poet Oliver Wendell Holmes Sr.'s "last leaf on the tree."

Guys like retired Eugene architect George "Rusty" Mayer, a corporal in the Army Air Force who arrived in a flight jacket he wore in the South Pacific, proudly presenting us with a poem he'd written in the previous few days. One section reads:

> *And now with a tear running down my cheek*
> *I see the old soldiers coming for me*
> *I see the bend in that long, long road ...*

In part, that's why *Register-Guard* Director of Graphics Rob Romig proposed what will be a four-day special section starting in Sunday's paper: a photo-driven package on World War II vets, the images complemented by 16 stories.

Of 16.1 million Americans who served in the armed forces during

World War II, only about 2 million — or 12 percent — are still living. About a thousand are dying each day, their stories dying with them.

Beyond such urgency, next Wednesday marks the 70-year anniversary of the attack on Pearl Harbor, which drew the United States into a war that shattered the world, shaped America and defined a generation.

The timing for this last-call salute was ripe. Thus, we published a request for veterans to come in the week of Nov. 6 and have their photographs taken. The response, frankly, overwhelmed us.

For four straight days, all day long, Paul Carter photographed about four people per hour; by week's end, he'd snapped 3,400 digital photos, many of them with his subjects holding some memorabilia from the war: shrapnel, dog tags, knives, maps, medals, flags — even a spoon, the only thing Herb Fortner of Eugene still has from his days in a German prisoner of war camp.

Romig, meanwhile, plugged basic information on each person into a laptop and, using a microphone, recorded some of their most vivid memories. Comments from 70 vets will be available online.

Photographer Chris Pietsch took videos. Others scanned old photos the vets brought in. I prowled for subjects to interview in depth at a later time.

The hardest part of this project was realizing we couldn't include everybody; the demand far exceeded our supply of time and space.

The best part was watching the vets and hearing snippets of their conversations, sometimes with us, sometimes with each other: "I was paid $36 a month; I didn't know what to do with all the money" ... "You were on Okinawa, too?" ... "My brother's submarine was torpedoed; he's on eternal patrol in the South Pacific ... ."

Carter, who was in the Navy, talked with his subjects about their experiences as he shot photos. "Sometimes they could remember the date, the weather and other details," he says of those involved in the air war, "then, there would be a faraway look, and their eyes would well up. They would weep and apologize for showing emotion."

It was particularly interesting watching the vets be seated beneath the studio lights. I lost count of how many, at that point, said, "Now, you know I was no hero ... " — as if the spotlight made them feel as though they were, which brought a sense of guilt.

I wish *New York Times* columnist Maureen Dowd could have been there. Before the World War II memorial in Washington, D.C., was unveiled in 2004, she wrote that this generation "can't stop gushing and celebrating themselves," their latest alleged chest-thumping being "a kitschy memorial to honor themselves."

The fact is, Dowd and the rest of us have the freedom to spout such small-minded rubbish because men and women like these folks died on Omaha Beach and on Mount Suribachi and in Sicily.

"The real heroes," Alton Wheeler, 89, said, "never made it home."

Once, during the photo shoot, Nathan Fendrich, a World War II and Holocaust expert who was schmoozing with the local vets in a waiting area, pointed out an unassuming man being photographed.

"See that guy," he said. "Just a grunt. A GI. Carried an M1 across France and Germany. Did what he was told. He didn't do anything special, did he? Naw, all he did — with thousands just like him — was win the war."

We hope our series beginning Sunday gives readers a sense of the diverse people, places and experiences that comprise just one small sliver of that war. And, in so doing, pays tribute to those last leaves on the tree — and those already fallen.

Like Rusty Mayer, whose poem proved prophetic. Two weeks after he handed it to us, the old soldiers came for him. He was 88.

A sweet song of honor

June 2, 2013

Just before the "Heroes Among Us" Memorial Day Service began Monday at West Lawn Memorial Park and Funeral Home, he shuffled down the aisle to a spot in the front row reserved for him.

When 88-year-old William "Bill" Kunkle of Harrisburg was seated, Musgrove Family Mortuary Funeral Director Dee Harbison whispered to him: "Mr. Kunkle, at the end of the service, we'd like to honor you with the ceremonial flag."

Kunkle wondered if there had been some mistake, he said later. A guy who'd been sent home from Hawaii by the Navy because he'd been so emotionally wracked by war?

Kunkle looked at Harbison. His eyes glistened. His head nodded slightly.

To his right, tucked into the nook reserved for families during funerals, singers from Willamette High's Topnotchers musical ensemble noticed Kunkle.

"He had this sad lip quiver," said Jarom Jenkins, a 16-year-old sophomore. "He had this blank stare on his face, as if thinking of all the men he'd met back then who weren't here."

Later, during a song, Jenkins himself appeared on the verge of tears.

"Some of the singers were getting pretty choked up," Kunkle noticed.

As I sat beside him — I was one of the speakers — I'm not sure Bill understood why the teenagers were so emotional, that it was largely because of him.

This is a column about a bridge made of music, spanning the chasm between a generation leaving our world and a generation inheriting it.

Since 2007, the Topnotchers have sung at the three Memorial Day services each year that Musgrove puts on to honor vets. It's an eight-hour time commitment on a vacation day.

"I've never heard a single student complain about doing this," said Topnotchers Director Mike McCornack.

"It's personal for me," said senior Nicholas Silva, whose family tree has plenty of military leaves. "It's touching to see these men honored."

Earlier in the day, as a steady rain fell on the Springfield Memorial Gardens chapel, the 16-member group — eight girls, eight boys — had opened the first ceremony with *The Star Spangled Banner.*

When the group sang a military medley — a song for each major branch of service — vets were asked to stand during their respective anthems. A few stood up with uneasy looks chiseled on their faces.

"When I saw that, I just started crying," said senior Topnotcher Ellie Thompson. "I had to look away to compose myself. We're so young and haven't experienced anything like what they did."

"It was like you were looking not just at people but the stories in their eyes," Silva said.

At a second event, at Lane Memorial Gardens' much-smaller chapel on West 11th Avenue, the Topnotchers — the girls in sleeveless dresses — had to stand outside in a blustery wind until time for their three appearances.

"We could have renamed the group The Popsicles," McCornack said.

Again, no complaints from the singers.

Afterward, those helping put on the services — including Boy Scout Troop No. 60 — gathered at West Lawn Memorial Garden for a quick lunch before the final service. The Topnotchers serenaded with an impromptu trio of light songs.

"It was like we all needed an emotional release, to take a breath and lighten things up a bit," McCornack said.

But if the mood lightened, that soon changed when Bill Kunkle shuffled down the aisle and took his front-row seat for the finale.

He had been featured in *The Register-Guard*'s World War II series in December 2011. So anxious to serve, he'd altered his birth certificate before his interview with the Marines so it looked as if he were 18 instead of 16.

By the time he was found out, Kunkle had joined the Navy.

He became a medical corpsman at Pearl Harbor Naval Hospital, treating mainly burn victims of Japan's Dec. 7, 1941, surprise aerial attack.

After 16 months, he was so shell-shocked and guilt-ridden about not being able to save dying men that the Navy sent him home and honorably discharged him. By his own admission, he has never recovered.

"I would sit with these guys and watch them die," he said, "and there was nothing I could do for them."

When he saw an ad for the Memorial Day service, despite a fear of large gatherings — and concern from his wife — something drew him to West Lawn's chapel. And when Musgrove's Harbison learned who he was, she escorted him, his son and his daughter-in-law to the front, about 10 feet from the off-to-the-side Topnotchers.

"They were so professional," Kunkle said. "As good a group as I've heard — and just high school kids."

The emotions built as the Topnotchers sang.

"To us it's just songs," Jenkins said. "To them it's memories."

The group's final song was "America the Beautiful."

"Coming near the end of the service, that song is like putting on a blanket after shivering through some difficult spots," McCornack said.

Honor guards Adam Knutson and Jake Knutson, brothers with the Oregon Army National Guard, unfolded and refolded the American flag, then presented it to Kunkle.

He took it and held it to his chest like a mother might hold a newborn.

"It was one of the greatest days of my life," Kunkle later told me. "I am so grateful." Though unworthy, he added.

I disagreed.

With the service over, Kunkle was surrounded by well-wishers. Junior Kelsie Loomis, one of the Topnotchers, stepped in front of him.

"Sir," she said, eyes pleading, "can I get a hug?"

And on this Memorial Day, two disparate generations became one, melded by tears that neither should have felt ashamed to shed.

9.

Yesterday

The birth of jogging

Jan. 31, 2013

Women in flowered dresses. Men in suits and hats. Children in pedal pushers and winter coats.

Little did these 1963 Eugeneans know, as they rounded the practice track just west of the University of Oregon's Hayward Field, that they were making history.

The country's first joggers.

It was 50 years ago this Sunday that more than 200 men, women and children answered a call from UO track and field coach Bill Bowerman to explore a new concept that he had brought back from New Zealand: jogging.

No sweat pants. No water bottles. No swoosh-laden footwear, just wingtips, flats and tennis shoes.

"It was kind of fascinating," says Dyrol Burleson, a UO runner who was there. "Until that day you didn't see a bunch of older people — housewives, professors — jogging around a track. Suddenly, things changed."

Jogging's 50-year anniversary will be celebrated at 9 a.m. Sunday with a 5-mile run — or jog, if you will — from the Nike store at Oakway Center to Hayward Field and back to Oakway's Eugene Running Company Store. At Hayward, author/Olympian Kenny Moore will be among those making brief remarks.

To appreciate the cultural change that jogging represented, you have to understand what a nonrunning world it was.

"It may be hard for anyone born after 1960 to believe, but runners in those days were regarded as eccentric at best, subversive and dangerous at worst," Moore wrote in *Bowerman and the Men of Oregon.*

Burleson, now 72 and living in Turner outside Salem, says Moore exaggerated when he wrote that motorists would routinely swerve to coerce runners off the road. But he agrees that until that first "gathering," the only runners you might see on a sidewalk would be UO athletes — and male.

A Eugene woman, Cora Ross, tells of a friend who was a UO physical education teacher back when Bowerman suggested they all go for "a jog."

"They didn't know what the word meant and they didn't want to go 'running around' because 'somebody might see them,'" Ross said the teacher told her.

Bowerman, who died in 1999, never did any chest-beating about being the midwife for American jogging.

But, undeniably, he deserved to — though he imported the concept from New Zealand.

In 1962, Burleson and three teammates had just beaten the Kiwis' world record in the four-mile relay and were invited to a friendly rematch in New Zealand, where Bowerman looked forward to spending time with a friend, Arthur Lydiard, that country's track and field guru.

While there, Lydiard told Bowerman of having recently started the "Auckland Joggers Club" on the impetus of post-cardiac patients who were, he said, "pleading to exercise."

Soon, not only were heart patients jogging, but so was the citizenry at large. Bowerman, at Lydiard's coaxing, jogged in an event and found himself so out of shape — he was 51 — that he was shamed by a guy who'd had three coronaries.

Impressed by this "jogging," Bowerman vowed to continue doing it when he returned home. But he didn't stop there.

He talked the walk, er, jog. Spread the gospel. And people —lots of people — listened.

"Bowerman's friendships far transcended Hayward Field," says Jim Jaqua, whose family was tight with the Bowermans. "He knew three-fourths of the faculty. He knew business people. His athletes worked at mills."

So when he put out a call for joggers through *The Register-Guard*, people responded with gusto.

"While Bowerman was surprised to see so many people — 'I had no idea this many would turn out' — the big surprise was that so many girls were there," the newspaper wrote. About 25 percent, the paper estimated.

In subsequent weeks the turnouts mushroomed to between 2,000 and 5,000 people.

Egad, what had Bowerman begat?

Go home, he told them. Jog in your neighborhoods. Jog with your friends. But jog.

Meanwhile, through the Central Lane YMCA, he recruited 100 middle-aged subjects to be part of a study done by the UO Physical Education Department and overseen by Eugene cardiologist Waldo

Harris.

Members of Bowerman's track team were put in charge of helping people train.

The results? People lost weight. Felt better. And began singing the praises of jogging to others.

At the time, Moore writes, conventional wisdom was that "physical decline was inevitable as soon as one reached middle age, if not sooner, and that such decline was useless to resist beyond middle age."

Life magazine came to town to do a story on the phenomenon.

By then, Bowerman had been so barraged with questions that he and Harris put together an 18-page pamphlet on jogging.

The next year, 1967, it morphed into a book, *Jogging*, that would sell more than 1 million copies.

And America was off to the races — literally. Road runs began. A decade after the book came out, 8 million Americans were jogging. In 2011, more than half a million people finished a marathon.

"The energy all goes back to that original point with Bowerman," Jaqua says. "Those people who showed up that first day planted the seed for what became a worldwide phenomenon. It's an example of stuff that happens in Eugene — the perfect coinciding of the right guy in the right town at the right time."

Oregon's trail of tears

May 23, 2010

SPRINGFIELD — Mention around here that your great-great-grandmother's Oregon roots date back to the mid-1800s and you might imagine a woman freshly arrived from a wagon train.

Warren Brainard's great-great-grandmother, Jane, was already here.

The woman was part of the Miluuk Coos Indian tribe living on the coast.

Who knew that her great-great-grandson would one day wind up chief of the Confederated Tribes of the Coos, Lower Umpqua and Siuslaw?

Amid the spring primaries, in a separate election that generated little attention, the 70-year-old Springfield man won a 10-year term to represent the 960 people who are part of the tribe.

Brainard sees the job as a balance of preserving the past and providing for the future.

"You've got to know where you've come from to know where you're going," he says, sipping coffee in his comfortable home on Camp Creek Road.

The look back is often painful. Lane County, in fact, had its own "trail of tears." In the early 1860s, 800 members of Coos and Lower Umpqua tribes were forcibly marched from the southern coast, over Cape Perpetua, to a "subagency" in Yachats — all in the name of opening lands to white homesteaders who had flocked west. (Native American women married to white men were exempted, which is why Brainard's great-great grandmother, Jane, did not have to go.)

The Alsea Sub-Agency, across Highway 101 from what's now the Adobe Resort, was less reservation than prison camp.

Between the march, smallpox and starvation, about 300 Indians died in a decade's time.

In 1875, the subagency was eliminated, some of the Native Americans moving north to the Siletz Reservation, others staying in the Yachats area or scattering.

Brainard was born in Deadwood in 1939 and graduated from Mapleton High School in 1957.

His Indian blood has been passed down through women who all, since Jane, have been married to white men.

His grandmother, Abbie, and her husband owned the land that Eugene's Abbie Lane, south of Willagillespie School, now sits on.

"She was always reminding us that we were part of something, passing down the stories to us," he says.

Even though that "something" was often the scourge of the United States government. Beyond the broken treaties, beyond the forced marches, the U.S. government, in 1954, terminated all Western Oregon tribes.

Imagine someone showing up one day to tell you your family no longer exists.

"Terminated — that's the word they used," says Brainard of the Eisenhower administration's decision. "The U.S. government no longer considers you an entity."

That was among his life's lowest moments. Not that the high point was 30 years later when President Ronald Reagan restored the tribes'"federal recognition."

Even though Brainard advocated for the tribal restoration for four years before the decision, it's hard to rejoice when you're getting back something that was taken away to begin with, he says.

No, among the high points of his life is the tribe's annual salmon ceremony in Coos Bay; last year's drew 284 people. "It is," he says, "like a giant family reunion."

As tribal president, Brainard has already been to Washington, D.C., to, among other things, meet President Obama with 500 other tribal leaders.

"I'm not a Democrat, but I was impressed with how sincere he seemed," says Brainard, retired after owning a sheetmetal business for more than 35 years.

His goals as chief are lofty, nothing less than seeing the tribe become "completely self-sufficient" before his term ends in 2020.

"We're not looking for a handout," he says.

Just some consideration for the wrongs of the past.

The Three Rivers Casino, opened in Florence in 2004 on tribal land, was a step toward that but doesn't generate nearly enough to meet his goal of self-sufficiency. "It is," says Brainard, "a necessary evil for us."

But he'd like the government to return even 15,000 of the 1.9 million acres that the tribes lost when the government started forcing them onto reservations in the mid-1850s.

The Coos, Lower Umpqua and Siuslaw were the only Oregon tribes that, when "termination" was undone in 1984, did not have land restored to them.

Not that Brainard allows such wrongs to cloud his patriotism. He served in the U.S. Air Force. He and his wife of 48 years, Marjene, have a son, Warren Bradley Brainard, who's about to become a lieutenant colonel in the Air Force. And he serves as the tribe's veterans representative.

There he is in a photo, the chief in his long, silver ponytail, proudly waving the U.S. flag in a Veterans Day parade.

Disappointed by his country at times, but still believing in it.

UO in Corvallis?

July 20, 2010

W ere Sen. Wayne Morse still alive, he would have seen *The Register-Guard*'s top headline Monday and scoffed.

"Much ado about nothing," you can imagine him grumbling.

And given the part he played in a far more intense Oregon-Oregon State showdown, you'd have to agree.

The headline adorned a story about how the UO, after losing a battle with OSU to establish a branch campus in Bend in 2000, is now, a decade later, waving the white flag completely. The UO will not even offer the consolation-prize undergraduate classes it's been teaching, leaving Bend entirely to Beaverville.

"Small potatoes," says ex-UO Archivist Keith Richard.

Indeed, in the 1930s, what was on the line in an Oregon-Oregon State College faceoff was this: nothing less than UO's existence.

In short, the first chancellor of the Oregon State System of Higher Education — and, not incidentally, the previous president at Oregon State — was masterminding a plan to consolidate the two schools under one roof.

In, of course, Corvallis.

"It was certainly one of the most crucial periods in the history of the University of Oregon," Richard says.

It was late 1932. The Depression was on. And officials in Salem had slashed the higher-ed budgets, Oregon's more than OSC's.

"Oregon State had been under the strong hand of President William Jasper Kerr, who had spent nearly 25 years amassing influence in Salem," wrote Mason Drukman in his book *Wayne Morse: A Political Biography.* "Only in recent times had Eugene sought to catch up with Corvallis."

A Corvallis-based delegation was sent to Eugene to present the ultimatum.

"We told them to go to hell," *Register-Guard* Editor William Tugman responded, according to A. Robert Smith's book on Morse, *A Tiger in the Senate.*

So, the single-school backers fanned out across the state and gathered the necessary signatures to put what was called the Zorn-MacPherson initiative on the ballot, dramatizing their cause by having the petitions delivered to the state Capitol in an armored car.

Eight weeks prior to the vote on consolidating the schools, UO President Arnold Hall and OSC's Kerr resigned. But Kerr, it would later be shown, had a hidden agenda.

"As part of a pre-arranged deal, Kerr was then appointed chancellor of higher education," Drukman wrote, "a newly created office that would have authority over both campuses."

Voters soundly defeated the measure by a 6-to-1 ratio, but the real drama was just beginning. And much of it involved UO's Morse, who, at age 33, was the youngest law school dean in the country.

Kerr, 70, chose Eugene to establish his new chancellor's office and perhaps win back some political favor. Bad idea. Really bad.

"The faculty was openly hostile to the new chancellor, resisting and delaying Dr. Kerr's every suggestion for change," wrote Drukman. "Kerr, meanwhile, arbitrarily involved himself in administering the Eugene campus — much to the annoyance of senior faculty, who, unlike their counterparts in Corvallis, were used to a fair amount of self-governance."

At stake, in the eyes of UO's faculty, was academic freedom.

Tensions increased. In 1933, Roscoe Nelson, the newly appointed Board of Education chairman, emerged as an ardent Kerr supporter.

In a speech, he read from an anonymous letter appearing in the *Oregon Daily Emerald* to hint that Eugene was anti-Semitic. And, later speaking in Eugene, he blamed a small UO contingent on "sabotaging the chancellor's efforts" for unifying the education system.

When Nelson offered a similar speech in Corvallis to a cheering, pro-Kerr/Nelson audience, Morse was on hand with a few others from UO.

"(He) got so angry he could scarcely contain himself," wrote Smith. On his way home, he told a colleague, "I'm not going to take this."

And he didn't. At a homecoming luncheon at UO attended by 1,700 students and parents — and also by Kerr and Nelson — Morse unleashed a blistering attack on both men. He called Nelson's remarks "insulting, insinuating, unfair and vicious," saying the board president had been "duped" by a chancellor selected in a "plot so rotten that it stinks to high heaven."

The event turned into pandemonium. Dishes slid off tables. Some UO faculty were moved to tears. Kerr was moved to flee the room.

The speech made headlines around the state. A day later, Nelson resigned.

Kerr convinced the higher-ed board to charge Morse with insubordination. But after the American Association of University Professors sent a team to interview more than 100 people — state officials and people on both campuses — it ultimately called the elevation of Kerr to chancellor a "stupendous blunder."

On Jan. 14, 1934, the board voted to re-establish presidencies at UO and OSC. And bagged its investigation of Morse.

Kerr resigned on April 17, then retired. Morse went on to spend 24 years as a U.S. senator from Oregon.

And, other than football season, more tranquil days followed for Oregon and Oregon State.

Symphony's opening note

May 16, 2013

When the Eugene Symphony performs its season finale tonight at the Hult Center, it will be in honor of an 89-year-old woman in the front row.

Nearly a half-century ago, the city's symphony began in her living room.

You walk into a Hayward Field or a Silva Theater and you can easily overlook the idea that it hasn't always been this grand.

That long ago, people with inspiration and drive — and yep, bucks — blew on the embers of little dreams that later burst into flames.

When it comes to the symphony, Caroline Boekelheide is one of those people who helped start the fire.

"Since our founding in 1965, Caroline has been instrumental in our growth and all our successes," says Scott Freck, the symphony's executive director. "She has been with the orchestra through our entire history. We are eternally grateful for Caroline's passion for the Eugene Symphony and to her enduring belief that music is essential for a healthy community."

In honor of Boekelheide being a member of the orchestra at its inception — and soon retiring after 47 years on its board — tonight's concert (Dvorak Symphony No. 8) will be dedicated to her.

"She's absolutely deserving of it," says Karen Seidel, who also was involved in the symphony being started. "She was critical in the fundraising efforts."

When Boekelheide and her chemistry professor husband, Virgil, arrived in Eugene from Rochester, N.Y., in 1960, live classical music wasn't easily found.

"You had to go to the university and hear some student play," Boekelheide says.

Among those pining for more musical opportunities was Orval Etter, an attorney, anti-war activist, free-speech zealot and, not incidentally, a cellist. (He died in March at 97.)

"Orval started a list of musicians," Boekelheide says. "He had this card catalog that he'd keep the names in."

Here and there, trios and quartets and quintets began forming, many of them practicing at the Boekelheides' house near Hendricks Park.

"I remember it well," says Annie Boekelheide, a teenage daughter of Caroline's at the time and now 63. "They weren't that great. There was lots of squeaking and squawking and screeching. I had to either go visit a friend or hide in my room."

But, if nothing else, they were determined.

By 1965, a handful of musicians had become dozens of musicians. Time, they decided, to start a symphony.

The University of Oregon School of Music fed some faculty members into the group.

A flutist, Boekelheide shifted to the oboe just so there would be two.

"We had a string player who was too young to drive," says Boekelheide.

Annie Boekelheide started warming to the music. "I credit them for my lifelong appreciation of classical music," she says.

The symphony's first few concerts were held in the North Eugene High auditorium, which abuts the school's gym.

"On the night of a concert there was also a basketball game going on," remembers Seidel, 76, who played piano for the symphony in its early days. "You could hear the basketball being dribbled down the court — and it wasn't in the same rhythm as the music."

On the financial front, a musicians' union stepped in to help, paying symphony members $50 each for the opening concert. The musicians turned around and used the money to pay for conductor Lawrence Maves and for the music.

This, of course, was no way to run a symphony.

After a few years, Boekelheide set aside her oboe to help establish the Eugene Symphony Guild and start raising money.

"Caroline had contacts through the university and people she knew in the community and was extremely effective at that," says Seidel. "She was a very intelligent woman who was very good at people contacts and persuasion."

"They called her the 'Mother Superior of Fundraising,'" says daughter Annie Boekelheide.

She played bridge, belonged to theater groups, served on the PTA, took the "Hooky Bus" to go skiing, attended the UO's Faculty Women's Luncheon — in other words, regularly rubbed shoulders with lots of people in lots of different settings.

The Junior League began sponsoring the Guild.

Lumber companies stepped up to donate, says Boekelheide. So did folks such as Betty and John Soreng, and *The Register-Guard*.

Tickets were $10 — for four concerts. Early symphony programs were handwritten.

By the 1970s the symphony had come into its own. Members were paid modest sums for their services. Concerts at UO's Beall Hall had to be repeated because of seating demand.

In 1982, the Hult Center opened, launching the symphony into higher regions.

Now, the Eugene Symphony boasts more than 1,850 subscribers and often sells out concerts; attendance has reached 24,000 a year. Meanwhile, it has drawn such top-notch conductors as Marin Alsop — now with the Baltimore Symphony — and, as guest conductors, the likes of Hollywood icon John Williams.

Even if it all began in Caroline Boekelheide's living room.

"Every time I look up there at that stage, I think, my gosh," says Boekelheide, "this is a real orchestra."

Katy Perry in Junction City

Feb. 1, 2015

JUNCTION CITY — Long before Katy Perry agreed to perform at halftime of today's Super Bowl in Glendale, Ariz ...

Before she became the best-selling digital singles artist in the history of time ...

Before she amassed a world-record 64 million Twitter followers — more than the combined population of the Western United States.

Before "Billboard" magazine named her "Woman of the Year" for 2012 and "Men's Health" readers voted her the "Sexiest Woman of 2013" ...

Before she started doing concerts in such places as New York, London, Sydney and Zurich ...

Before all this there was Junction City.

On a warm July night in 2002, a year before she changed her name from Katy Hudson, Perry sang at a Christian music festival in a farmer's field south of Junction City.

It was organized by a guy who just thought it'd be fun to join with his teenage daughter to have a concert in what was essentially their back yard.

Afterward, Perry sold CDs — not many, frankly — from behind an eight-foot fold-up table.

I know. I was there. Friends, as it were, of "the promoter."

The 30-year-old singer who's now worth an estimated $55 million was paid $1,000, or roughly what four tickets to one of her concerts today fetch on the secondary market.

The event was free for those who attended. And Perry wasn't even the headline act. That distinction belonged to a now-defunct group named Superchic[k], which was paid $3,000.

"I don't even remember Katy Perry being there," says Misha Klein, 23, of Monroe, who attended the festival as an 11-year-old. "I came to hear Superchic[k]."

I have only the vaguest recollection of Katy alone on the stage, doing a handful of acoustical songs with her guitar while about 500 people listened.

Ex-Oregon quarterback Danny O'Neill offered spiritual inspiration. Shawn McDonald of Eugene played. So did a Junction City band named Speedshift, complete with a drummer who occasionally sprayed a fire extinguisher beneath his stool to give the stage that cool, foggy atmosphere.

So, how did the most famous female singer in the world today wind up playing in what was essentially the back yard of a "promoter" who had never put on a concert and never would again?

Because Tom Penix, and his teenager daughter, Maggie, began wondering if they could pull off such an event.

"We both enjoy music and we thought, 'Wouldn't it be cool to have someone come play in our field,'" said Maggie Penix, now 28, married and living in Helena, Mont.

Maggie was a junior-to-be at Junction City High and, at 17, the same age Katy Perry was at the time.

"Katy was an up-and-comer in the Christian music world," says Maggie. "Reasonably priced. West Coast. From Santa Barbara. And I liked her Jennifer Knapp sound."

"I heard her CD and thought, 'What a beautiful voice,'" says Tom Penix. "I wondered if we could pull it off and get her to Junction City."

The whole event was a leap of faith for Tom Penix, who was — and is — the assistant director graphics/design at *The Register-Guard*. (And — full disclosure — illustrator of the Keyboard Kitten children's book series I've written.)

More to the point: The guy didn't have a clue what he was doing.

On his first talk with Superchic[k]'s promoter, he introduced himself as "a 44-year-old dad with five kids who's interested in putting on a concert in my back yard."

"So you wanna be a promoter," the promoter said.

"Not really," said Penix. "I've got a real job."

Instead, Tom explained, he wanted to book Superchic[k] for a field behind his place south of Junction City. The band, it turned out, had summer gigs in Southern California and, a few days later, at the Gorge musical venue in George, Wash., so a stop near Eugene was on the way.

When Penix learned that insurance for the event would cost nearly as much as what Superchic[k] was charging, he wondered if the idea was feasible. But he learned that if the event were held on land designated as "farm-use-only" the cost would be only a fraction of the $2,600 it would have cost to hold it on his own property.

A neighbor, Bill Baker, happily offered a nearby three-acre field.

Penix rolled a few thousand dollars into the effort and did a little seat-of-his-pants fundraising to help pay for the event, which wound up costing about $17,000.

Katy Perry flew into Eugene Airport on the afternoon of the July 26, 2002, concert. She arrived with one piece of luggage and a guitar. The only people greeting her at the airport were Maggie, a friend and the friend's brother.

They were holding a cardboard sign that said, "Welcome, Katy."

"It's hilarious, thinking about the kind of crowd that she'd have now," says Maggie Penix. "She was surprised. She said she'd never had anyone awaiting her with a welcome sign before."

Maggie found Katy to be "a fairly normal teenager who'd gotten into the music world. She struck me as very laid back. Had an artsy flair to her. Even though we were the same age, she seemed older. She lived in Southern California and we were just a couple of Junction City country girls."

Perry had one interesting request: she wanted to swing by a thrift store before the concert.

"She loved thrift stores so we stopped by the St. Vincent dePaul in Santa Clara, near Fred Meyer," says Maggie Penix. "She took quite a long time — we gave her her space — and she bought a pair of earrings."

Once on site, Katy and the other musicians gathered in the Bakers' heavily shaded backyard for feta chicken and Sobe drinks before the evening concert.

Tom Penix asked if she might sing a song called "Spit" that he loved, but she politely declined, saying she would need her band for that.

Perry came on stage after rehearsing in an ant-infested 20-foot trailer that had bad upholstery.

As dusk turned to dark, she played a handful of songs.

Nobody recalls much about Katy Perry being on stage. "But I do remember that at one point she had this towel," says Maggie Penix, "and she threw it out to the audience."

Right, as if she were some sort of big star or something.

Of roses and thorns

Dec. 29, 2011

Seventy years ago, as Oregon State's football team departed for the first and only transplanted Rose Bowl game — in Durham, N.C. — the Beavers left one player home.

Chiaki "Jack" Yoshihara wasn't injured, hadn't broken team rules and hadn't failed to meet academic standards.

Instead, he was forced to stay home because the U.S. government considered him a threat to national security.

I came across his story while researching another, a piece on Roy Maeda for *The Register-Guard*'s recent series on World War II veterans.

Maeda and Yoshihara were among about 110,000 Japanese and Japanese-Americans who were shipped to relocation camps in the months after Japan's attack on Pearl Harbor.

Like Maeda, Yoshihara grew up in Portland and graduated from Benson High School.

In the fall of 1941, Yoshihara was a sophomore engineering student at Oregon State — and a reserve on the football team — when the Beavers, on Nov. 29, clinched their first trip to the Rose Bowl with a 12-7 victory over Oregon.

"Everyone was real happy the week after the game," Yoshihara told the Los Angeles Times in 2008. "All my friends wanted me to get them tickets."

But on Dec. 7 the Japanese bombed Pearl Harbor and the United States declared war on Japan the next day. In the eyes of many, anyone of Japanese ancestry was immediately suspect.

A few days later, at an Oregon State practice, two well-dressed men in overcoats and hats arrived and met with Coach Alonzo "Lon" Stiner.

"I will never forget that day," the late George Zellick, a teammate of Yoshihara's, told the Times. "It was late afternoon. It was drizzling. ... You could tell they were 'different' people. They met with the coach and, the next thing we knew, Jack left with them. It was the first indication that Jack had a problem."

He was told that he wasn't allowed to travel more than 35 miles from his home and, thus, would not be able to go to the game, which had been shifted to North Carolina because officials feared that the traditional Rose Bowl site, Pasadena, was at risk for a Japanese air attack.

Yoshihara remembered watching the train leave. "I just kind of walked away," he told PBS NewsHour in 2008. "That's all, one of my worst moments."

"Nobody felt that Jack was a subversive threat," teammate James Busch told the New Orleans *Times-Picayune* in 2005. "He was an American. My heritage was German. Nobody discriminated against me."

Times were different. Japanese and Japanese-Americans were temporarily placed in Portland's Pacific International Livestock exposition grounds behind barbed wire and armed guards.

Decades later, Yoshihara still remembered the smell of animal manure beneath the hastily built wooden floors.

Despite the prisonlike setup, some people in Portland decried the "special treatment" they thought the Japanese and Japanese-Americans were getting.

"Please help us to understand why the government is showing the Japanese aliens so much consideration," wrote a woman, "Mrs. F," to *The Oregonian's* "Mr. Fixit" column, headlined "That Jap Problem." "They are people who are used to hard work and simple living. Then why put them together where they can take life easy with plenty of time to visit, with shows, radios and ballparks?"

The Japanese and Japanese-Americans in Portland were slated to go to the Minidoka Relocation Center in Idaho.

Wrote "L. Brown" in a letter to the editor: "Why should they be sent inland to comparative safety and security, while the rest of us 'take it'? Work them for what they are getting, the same as the rest of us, so, if their 'relations' come over to attack our coast, they also may be in the 'fireworks.'"

Meanwhile, while Yoshihara stayed in Oregon, his teammates upset No. 2 Duke 20-16 on Jan. 1, 1942, in what many considered the biggest Rose Bowl upset to that point.

After the stint at the livestock grounds, Yoshihara and his family were sent to Minidoka, where he worked on farms, drove trucks and made deliveries for the duration of the war.

He never returned to Oregon State. Instead, when the war ended, he got into the refrigeration and air-conditioning business in Portland.

Yoshihara was married twice — to his first wife, Elsie, for 50 years — and was a father of two children, a grandfather to three and a great-grandfather to three.

In 1985, when his team was inducted into the OSU Hall of Fame, Yoshihara received a ring from the 1942 Rose Bowl game just like his teammates had been given.

Three years later, Yoshihara was among 42 Japanese-Americans who, because they'd been forced to leave school and sent to camps, were given honorary degrees by OSU during the school's June graduation ceremony at Reser Stadium.

OSU President Ed Ray briefly mentioned Yoshihara's story and asked him to show the crowd his Rose Bowl ring, which he held up as his eyes glistened with tears.

He died the following April, in 2009, a footnote to history that you wish you could forget but know you should not.

Nuclear plant on coast?

March 17, 2011

In light of Japan's earthquake, tsunami and subsequent teetering on nuclear disaster, imagine driving north on Highway 101 just beyond the Heceta Head Lighthouse.

You wind inland, dip down the long, straight stretch toward Big Creek and, suddenly, there it is: a nuclear power plant gouged into the beach.

A nightmare?

Perhaps, but one that, nearly 41 years ago, came perilously close to becoming a reality.

In 1970, Eugene came within less than a thousand votes of essentially green-lighting the Eugene Water & Electric Board's desire to build a $234 million nuclear power plant — and Big Creek was among a handful of preferred locations.

"Unless you're an old-timer and have lived in Lane County a long time, people don't know about it at all," says Daniel Pope, a University of Oregon history professor who's written about the issue.

The fact is, he says, if a grass-roots group from Eugene had not led a fight to place a local moratorium on building such a plant, it may well have happened.

"It was an incredible fight to overcome EWEB's plans," says Jane

Novick, then a 46-year-old activist who helped spearhead such efforts and now, at 86, is a resident of the Willamette Oaks apartments. "Many people joined the movement. And it took all of our energy."

Four decades removed, it seems inconceivable that such a plant, particularly at such a scenic — and seemingly dangerous — location, would have even been considered.

"With the Cascadia fault, we have records of 41 earthquakes in the last 10,000 years with an average of 240 years apart," Yumei Wang, the geohazards team leader at the state Department of Geology, told The Associated Press. "Our last one was 311 years ago, so we are overdue."

But remember, the environmental movement back then was in diapers (cloth, of course). And, with signs that the era of abundant energy was ending, Northwest's energy czars were giddy about going nuclear.

Armed with predictions that U.S. power needs were going to double every decade — it didn't happen — the Washington Public Power Supply System was launching a five-plant nuclear system.

EWEB wanted a piece of the nuclear pie, too.

"Many had come to see it as the best source of safe, cheap electricity," Pope wrote in a 1990 piece for *Pacific Historical Review*. "Some were predicting that nuclear reactors would generate half of the nation's electric power by the end of the century."

Bonneville Power Administration officials envisioned 20 nuclear plants in the Northwest by 1990.

Now, we have just one — at Hanford, the other four WPPSS plants having been quashed amid the project's financial meltdown. Meanwhile, the country's 104 nuclear reactors now produce only about one-fifth of our electrical power.

But attitudes were different back then. In November 1968, when EWEB placed a $225 million bond measure on the ballot to fund construction of a nuclear power plant, it passed by a whopping 79 percent to 21 percent.

Once voters OK'd the measure, however, some started second-guessing the decision. After Novick's League of Women Voters book group read a just-out exposé called *The Careless Atom* by Sheldon Novick (no relation to Jane), she started organizing opposition.

Others jumped on board, forming the Eugene Future Power Committee.

Meanwhile, EWEB identified about a dozen sites it was considering, from Oakridge to Florence, whose city officials welcomed the economic boost that the proposed plant would provide.

On the other hand, farmers voiced concerns about reactors raising river water temperatures that would hurt irrigation. The state got involved. EWEB brought in experts from nuclear plants to defend the decision. *The Register-Guard*, which favored the bond measure, hired an outside investigative reporter to do what turned into a 14-part series that, in Pope's view, didn't advocate a position but showed "evident sympathy" for those questioning EWEB's decision.

The Future Power Committee's stance was not in opposition to nuclear power, but in favor of studying the issue more. After going door to door to get the required number of signatures, it placed an initiative on the May 1970 ballot putting a four-year moratorium on EWEB building a nuclear plant.

By the time Eugene voters went to the ballot box — no mail-in voting back then — EWEB had narrowed its choices to six sites: Big Creek, about midway between Florence and Yachats; the south bank of the Siuslaw River, about two miles upstream from the Highway 101 Bridge; a second Siuslaw site nearby; a third Siuslaw site about nine miles up river; Poodle Creek near Noti; and High Prairie, north of Oakridge.

Big Creek was considered a front-runner because the engineer leading EWEB's site selection study preferred an "ocean water" location. Water would be drawn from the ocean to cool the plant generators, then returned after it became warmed.

But the site became a moot point. Voters approved the measure to halt the project, though by a mere 851 votes — 51.8 percent to 48.2 percent.

Still, the turn-down essentially killed EWEB's construction plans.

In hindsight, even Keith Parks, who took over as EWEB general manager three years later, had grudging respect for the Future Power Committee.

"They did a great favor for this community," he told Pope. "They saved its butt."

Not to mention a superb stretch of scenery.

The uncivil war

Nov. 28, 2010

Civil War week arrives and "civil" is the operative word.
      Oh, there'll be moments: the I-need-a-life folks on both sides who'll lose perspective and get nasty before, during and after Saturday's Oregon-Oregon State football game in Corvallis.

But history suggests that, as a whole, the rivalry, if not necessarily classy, isn't as trashy as it once was.

As evidence I could rewind us to 2000 when, after a Beaver win in Corvallis, some OSU students swung literal dead ducks around by their necks.

I could talk about how the Ducks celebrated a 30-3 win in Corvallis by ripping down the south goalposts — well before the game was even over (1972), UO abducting OSU's homecoming queen (1960) or the 2,000 Oregon State students who caravaned to Eugene to rub in a 14-0 Beaver win, only to be met with fire hoses, tossed in the Eugene Millrace and used as human paint brushes to turn the Skinner Butte "O" back to yellow from orange (1937).

But none of this stuff did what a post-game brawl did 100 years ago this month: cause the only cancellation of an Oregon-Oregon State game in history because of bad blood between the two schools.

It was Nov. 12, 1910, the two teams meeting for the 16th time since 1894.

On the night before the game, UO rallied around the largest pregame bonfire it had ever had: 48 feet high and fueled by 100 gallons of kerosene.

But the metaphorical fire that broke out following Oregon's 12-0 win over then-Oregon Agricultural College the next day in Corvallis made that look like little more than wienie-roasting flames.

According to the (Portland) *Morning Oregonian*, one UO student returned to Eugene "in a semi-conscious condition, another with his head sheared and many of the Oregon supporters, of both sexes, returned minus personal belongings which had been stolen."

What the newspaper called a "riot" broke out at the train station, where UO fans were starting to board for the return trip home.

The seeds had been sown earlier, the paper said, when: "The automobile bearing the injured (UO) quarterback, Earle Latourette, to the dressing room was intercepted by a crowd of (OAC) students led by Right Tackle May.

"The Oregon banners were torn from the machine and the lights and horn apparatus were badly damaged ... The only defense made for this performance by Corvallis students was that (UO was) flaunting their colors in our faces."

"Later a horde of Corvallis students or town boys gathered downtown and commenced a raid on all the visitors wearing Oregon colors. An attempt was made to steal every 'rooter's hat' in sight, and in some instances the colored armbands were torn from the clothes of the Varsity coeds."

Things intensified, according to the paper. OAC "ruffians" spit in the faces of UO students and "used clubs that were five or six inches in thickness." They knocked UO student Harold Bean unconscious. "They attacked Wallace Cooley, a (UO) freshman from Silverton, who has but one leg and who at the time of the assault was upon crutches."

Later, the "band of Corvallis boys" boarded the train, grabbed Herman Sigglin, a UO student who had attended OAC in years past, "and sheared his head."

When UO President Prince Lucien Campbell tried to restore order, he was "hissed and hooted by the Corvallis contingent."

Another *Oregonian* story said "the rioting ... started purely in fun and the visitors ... were as much to blame as the Corvallis students ... The Eugene boys were equally guilty."

Indeed, in the days to follow, OAC fans claimed the brawl was hardly the one-sided affair the *Morning Oregonian* — and *The Eugene Daily Guard* — had reported.

OAC witnesses said Cooley wasn't struck, but fainted. The town's chief of police said no punches were thrown. And it was "town boys," not OAC students, who hissed President Campbell, witnesses insisted.

Campbell himself said the hissing and hooting was "not done by Corvallis students; I do not think it could have been," and said he hoped the "good relations between the two institutions might not in any way become strained."

Alas, such wasn't the case.

While the UO faculty was investigating the incident, OAC students, on Nov. 22, voted unanimously to "sever all athletic relations with the University of Oregon."

In Eugene, many characterized the move as a ploy to avoid the embarrassment of having been found guilty as charged.

Regardless, the schools parted ways — at least temporarily.

No game was held in 1911. And in 1912 and 1913, the games were held at a neutral site, Albany, to lessen the chances of brawls.

(It apparently worked, the *Guard* reporting in 1913 that "the two rooters' sections repeatedly cheered each other and the men on the opposing teams.")

In 1914, the schools resumed their home-and-home series. And though the rivalry has had its black-eye moments since, a century after the Riot of 1910, the annual Oregon-Oregon State game is, indeed, a more civil war.

Without robbing the good fun rivalries can be, may it always remain so.

10.

Artists & authors

Shy Mr. Keillor

June 14, 2012

A rnold Ismach, former dean of the University of Oregon School of Journalism and Communication, remembers the incident whenever Garrison Keillor comes to town.

Which, with Keillor at the Cuthbert Amphitheater on Saturday to put on his "A Prairie Home Companion" show, means recently.

It was in the mid-1970s. Ismach was a journalism professor at the University of Minnesota and president of the Twin Cities chapter of the Society of Professional Journalists.

A speaker for the organization's monthly meeting got sick. Seeking a replacement, Ismach called an obscure young man who had done "The Morning Program" on a local public radio station, a guy named Keillor, then in his early 30s.

"Garrison stuttered for a moment, and then said no," recalls Ismach, now 81. "I asked him why, and he said he wasn't comfortable speaking before a live audience.

"I said, 'You can do it.' He said, 'No, no, no, it shakes me up.'"

"Sounds to me like an invented excuse for something I didn't want to do," Keillor said Wednesday when reminded of the exchange in a telephone interview. "In the Midwest, we always want to please but rather than talk to a bunch of journalists at lunch, we might feign illness or shyness."

Indeed, if you saw Keillor two years ago at the Cuthbert, you saw a performer who, if he's shy, certainly hides it well. He sauntered onto the stage like a stagehand, then, with cordless microphone in hand, walked down steps and through the audience, singing, making impromptu jokes, even acting as an usher — while nattily attired in a suit and red tennis shoes.

Still, the shy guy reputation lingers.

"I have met Keillor on several occasions since 1988, most recently about two years ago, and he remains generous in public settings, but yes, he is basically shy," wrote Judith Yaross Lee, author of *Garrison Keillor: A Voice of America*, in an e-mail.

Jennifer Levenson, now of Eugene, worked for Minnesota Public Radio and ushered at "A Prairie Home Companion" shows in the 1980s.

"The Garrison Keillor I knew was a very nice man and, I think, a bit shy," she said. "I was the first person one would see upon entering the executive offices, and I got a lot of the rollover phone calls for Bill Kling, the MPR president. (Keillor) would always say, 'Hi, this is Garrison' — like I didn't know — then usually politely ask, 'Is my president in?'"

Deeper into our phone interview, Keillor admitted that the stage did not come easily for him. He never performed in high school or college.

"That was simply a result of my family background, a fundamentalist Christian background," he said. "We wouldn't be inclined to any sort of showing off through performance."

So how did he break through his reticence?

Radio, he says, gave him a safe environment to tell his stories. "Then I started to feel there was a particular kind of show I could do that nobody else would do. And that inspiration gave me the courage to venture out. You come to a point in your life where you think: 'If I don't do it now I'll never do it and I'll always regret it.' So you hike up your shorts and get out on stage."

"A Prairie Home Companion" began in 1974, replete with commercial spots for "Powdermilk Biscuits" — "made from the whole wheat that gives shy persons the strength to get up and do what needs to be done."

"In the final analysis, Keillor's reputation for shyness (deserved or not) proves unequivocally how effectively the humorist exploited the pose," Lee wrote in her book on Keillor. "Like any other comic device, he used it as needed."

In 1985, *Time* magazine declared Keillor Minnesota's, if not America's, "Most Famous Shy Person."

Now, at 69, he's one of America's most famous people, period. And, of course, he's the only nonlocal person among the 130 featured in David Joyce's "Flying People" photo sculpture at the Eugene Airport.

Not that he's apparently noticed. "I've only been through that airport once," he said. "This week I'm coming down on the train from Seattle, making it a Father's Day weekend with my daughter, so I'll miss it again. But I remember being photographed. Was I lying on a mat?"

Yep.

But, no, he had to politely turn down my offer from two years ago to become an honorary Eugene citizen.

"I don't think I qualify," he said. "I'm not good enough to be an Oregonian. Oregon is one of those states where many Americans wish they were from. I think of my ideal Oregon heroes — writers like William Stafford, Ken Kesey and Gary Snyder. That would be overreaching on my part, and I'm afraid I would draw the inevitable sharp rebuke from Oregonians, and I'd feel bad."

Me? I think he really wanted to say yes.

He was just too shy.

Finding Thoreau

June 29, 2010

The Fourth of July is almost here, meaning it's time to tell the story.

About that day in downtown Boston last month when my wife and I stumbled across one of the oldest bookstores in America, the Brattle Book Shop, which began in 1825.

About author Henry David Thoreau.

And about finding the unexpected.

Since reading a copy of *The Portable Thoreau* in the summer of 1972 — just before leaving for college — I've always had a certain respect for the author, even if reading him can be like scrambling up a steep mountain in ankle-deep scree.

But I admire people who dare go their own ways, which Thoreau certainly did. "If a man does not keep pace with his companions," he famously wrote, "perhaps it is because he hears a different drummer."

In 1845 to 1847, his 27-month stay at the Walden Pond cabin he built was only one of many ways he expressed his independence. Thus, when I saw, in Brattle's open-air collection, *Thoreau*, a 1939 biography by Henry Seidel Canby, for a mere $5. I snatched it up, one of a dozen purchases I would make.

I had a speaking gig that evening, but, looking at my watch, deemed I had time to skim through it and other books. In so doing, I was interested to note that Thoreau once mused with friend and fellow author Ralph Waldo Emerson about going to see Oregon, though author Canby insists, "Oregon was just tall talk."

Compulsive about putting historical events in a broader context

— Eugene Skinner first arrived in Lane County as Thoreau was hunkering down in "the woods" — I was intrigued to learn, on page 217, that Thoreau "entered into residence on the fourth of July, 1845, to be reporter of Walden Pond for two years and three months."

So this Sunday marks the 165-year anniversary of Henry David's quest to live in the woods in Concord, Mass., to see what he could learn.

"I went to the woods because I wished to live deliberately," he wrote in *Walden; or, Life in the Woods*, "to front only the essential facts of life, and see if I could not learn what it had to teach, and not, when I came to die, discover that I had not lived."

Heady stuff for someone like me, whose life has been predicated by deadline after deadline. No wonder Walden's quest for enlightenment — imagine, two-plus years to just sit, think and write — had always held in me such wonder.

Later that day, when it came time to leave for the speaking engagement in Boxborough, 25 miles west of Boston, it was clearly the Thoreau influence that caused me to recommend to She Who that we bag the MapQuest directions.

MapQuest wanted us to take Interstate 93 north, then Interstate 495 south. *Boring.* We chose, instead, to wind our way along smaller, less traveled roads, a path which, in Frostian terms, would ultimately "make all the difference."

We were mesmerized by the Massachusetts countryside. Large, neat, shingled houses tucked amid trees, nearly all surrounded by unfenced grass and splashed with American flags.

Eventually, we segued onto a thickly forested, lightly trafficked area — we had little idea where we were — that reminded me a bit of the Old McKenzie Highway (242) before you break into the plateau of lava.

"Did you see that sign?" She Who ... said. "The Shop at Walden Pond."

Before I could react to whatever this sacrilegious setup was, I saw it through the trees: a glimmering lake. And a Forest Service-type wooden sign: Walden Pond.

"Oh. My. Gosh," I said. "This is it!"

We had accidentally found Thoreau's Walden Pond.

Never mind that in July and August, more than 100,000 people will visit the pond each month. On this weekday in early May, only a couple dozen people mingled around the pond.

It is a beautiful body of water, surrounded by mainly deciduous trees and, at 61 acres, about half the size of Cottage Grove Lake or Sutton Lake on Highway 101 north of Florence.

I walked to its edges, took some photos, splashed some Walden water in my face.

We poked around a replica of Thoreau's one-room cabin. (Given its java hut size, it's a good thing he was a loner.) And before leaving, stopped in the gift shop that the non-materialistic Thoreau may have frowned on but, tucked into the trees and full of rough-hewn timber, was tastefully done. (I passed on buying a "The mass of men lead lives of quiet desperation" T-shirt, but couldn't resist the "Simplify, Simplify" hot chocolate mug.)

"Every journey," the Austrian-born philosopher Martin Buber once wrote, "has a secret destination of which the traveler is unaware."

In a state with 35,782 miles of roads and with us having no clue about the pond's location, we had found one of those secret destinations.

How sad to miss such wonders. How sad to travel only life's freeways and discover — to paraphrase Thoreau's words written from Walden Pond — that when it came time to die, you had not lived.

I hear the people sing

July 30, 2013

Toward the end of Actors Cabaret of Eugene's *Les Misérables* Friday night, the eyes of the man next to me, Kenneth Van Dyken, began glistening.

He began mouthing the words Jean Valjean (Tony Joyner) was singing: "On this page I write my last confession ... "

And with the transition to "Do You Hear the People Sing" his forefingers became miniature batons, swinging back and forth like windshield wipers, as if Van Dyken were conducting an orchestra that didn't exist.

At this hole-in-the-wall theater at the corner of 10th Avenue and Willamette Street, a lot of stuff doesn't exist: a big budget, a spacious lobby, a sweeping stage upon which you might build a *Les Miz* street barricade that would rival fuel for a 1960s homecoming bonfire.

But here's what does exist: superb theater.

Drama so good it had Van Dyken enraptured and the rest of us close to it, judging by the standing ovation, which virtually all shows have earned since it opened July 5.

As a fan of the unabashed melodrama, I went to Vancouver, B.C., in June to see a *Les Miz* production spearheaded by original producer Cameron Mackintosh.

Given the grandeur of the B.C. production, it was with a touch of timidity that I took my seat in the back of the dinner theater Friday. Not that I expected a schlocky performance; though I'm a newcomer to Actors Cabaret, I knew of its reputation for doing first-class stuff.

But, goodness, the ticket office at Vancouver's Queen Elizabeth Theatre is larger than the Actors Cabaret stage, as are some family dinner tables.

Les Miz, about an ex-convict who turns around his life — and saves others — after grace shown to him by a bishop, became the world's longest-running musical, in part, because of an over-the-top set that often includes revolving stages.

Watching it in Eugene, I figured, would be like watching an Ems game after seeing the World Series.

But the bishop had barely forgiven Jean Valjean for stealing his silver before I was smitten with the show. More specifically, smitten with the way Actors Cabaret had downsized an expansive musical into theater-in-a-phone-booth, and made it work.

"(Director) Joe Zingo concentrated on the story itself," says Tom Grimsley, who plays a spot-on Javert, the police inspector who tries to drag Valjean back to his past. "He said the intimacy was going to give us more of a story about the interaction of people, not about grand, revolving stages."

The play succeeds in exactly that.

Acting on a dinner-theater stage is like being a live mannequin in a department-store window: (a) you can't move around a whole lot and (b) if you have flaws, folks are going to notice.

But, frankly, beyond Fantine's wig listing to port, I didn't see — or hear — any obvious flaws.

Les Miz is an all-sung musical, meaning added potential for lines to get lost. None were, though a few had to be rushed to keep pace with the piped-in "orchestra."

As you would expect, the sets lean toward the simplistic. One audience member actually guffawed when the barricade was "erected"; and true, as kids retrieving whiffle-ball homers, many of us scaled fences more daunting.

But good drama is about taking an audience from "here and now" to "there and then" — and Actors Cabaret did that splendidly.

The cast and crew put on a show as you imagine Sun Tzu, the Chinese general and strategist, might have fought a war, knowing he was outmanned so relying on creativity, quickness and savvy.

Not easy when you're dealing with 100 costumes, a cast of 35 and a backstage so tight that, while making a quick pit stop before show's start, you have to slip past three prisoners and a French soldier in the hallway.

"The stage-left entrance is one-person wide," Grimsley says. "There's no room for shyness back there."

While I was concerned that the production wouldn't be big enough, afterward I wondered if the 3,000-seat Queen Elizabeth Theatre had been small enough.

When Eponine (played by sweet-singing Sophie Mitchell) dies, the anguish from Marius (Anthony Coslett) is real and riveting, not only because the young man can flat-out sing and act but because he's doing so as if in your living room.

Indeed, if at times you worried that on an-stage tussle might spill an audience member's Pinot gris, the actor-to-audience intimacy did more to amplify "God-on-high" poignancy and "master-of-the-house" humor than reveal imperfections.

Finally, the coziness of it all filled some sort of latent emptiness within me that I've felt since the passing of Mac Court and Civic Stadium, venues where the stage was as alluring as the actors on it.

The charming clincher?

Mark VanBeever not only plays a superb Thénardier-the-tavern-owner and serves as vocal director, but is the guy taking your drink and dessert orders at intermission.

And, as you leave, the gentleman saying good-night to you is Joyner, who does the heavy lifting — and does it well — as Valjean.

"Thanks for supporting Actors Cabaret," he says.

My pleasure.

As a community, *our* pleasure.

Finding 'Touch of Oregon'

Aug. 4, 2013

The six-year search is over.
Thanks to Linda Wheatley, I finally found — and can publicly thank — the artist who painted "Touch of Oregon," one of those giant Ducks on Parade that infatuated my then-2-year-old grandson Cade.

But it took brain surgery to find her.

The story begins in 2007 when Cade and I would grab a hot chocolate and wander around Oakway Center's Heritage Courtyard. He liked the giant duck in front of Chapala Mexican Restaurant. But he loved the one that sits in the northwest corner of the courtyard, on the upper level.

"Touch of Oregon," its plaque says. Artist: Janet Roberts.

Cade loved it because it was so kid-friendly, featuring a whale, eagle, squirrel, ocean, lake, trees, mountains, starfish, frog — the works. And that each image was textured, as if the duck were a rounded and raised topographical map of Oregon's flora and fauna.

At the time, I remember thinking how public art enriches our community, but the artists themselves live in obscurity. Rarely do they get to hear how their work touches us.

I wanted Roberts to know that a 2-year-old kid and his grandfather loved "Touch of Oregon," but I couldn't get any traction finding her.

In 2002 and 2003, local artists created 50 such ducks — and 25 mini-quackers — that were auctioned to raise some $150,000 for area nonprofit agencies.

Linda and her husband, Steve, hatched the idea after seeing the "Belfast Bearfest" in Belfast, Maine.

The couple — she's 71, he's 72 — are like civic hummingbirds, flitting from one community project to the next.

I met Linda over the phone in 2008 when writing about a new mapping system for the Ruth Bascom Riverbank Path that she and Steve had spearheaded. For some reason, she mentioned that she'd been involved in the Ducks on Parade project.

"Maybe you can help me find one of the artists," I said.

Though she'd never met Roberts, Linda immediately knew the duck I mentioned.

"When we saw that design we were thinking, 'that is so cool,'" she said. "Janet textured it like that because she's legally blind and wanted those who were visually impaired to be able to appreciate it, too."

The Oakway Center paid $5,000 for it.

As I said, Linda is a do-er and didn't slough off my wish.

She dug through old notebooks and found a phone number. But it was no longer in service.

She had heard Roberts was a nurse at PeaceHealth's Sacred Heart Medical Center. She tried making inroads that way but, because of federal privacy regulations, the hospital wouldn't help make a connection.

She heard Roberts lived in Springfield, right across the street from then-Springfield Mayor Sid Leiken. But Leiken said she'd recently moved.

Said Linda: "I remember thinking, 'I'll find her, perhaps when I least expect it.'"

Four years passed. Last fall, tragedy hit: Steve was diagnosed with a brain tumor.

After the surgery in November — the tumor was benign — two nurses were wheeling Steve's gurney into the ICU at PeaceHealth Sacred Heart Medical Center at RiverBend. Jani Hoburg, a close friend of the couple's — and another Ducks on Parade artist — had joined the parade.

Linda introduced Jani to the two nurses.

"She's one of the Ducks on Parade artists," she pointed out.

One of the nurses perked up. "Interesting," she said. "So am I."

"You're Janet Roberts!" Linda said.

"I knew I was going to find her," she said later. "But I didn't think it was going to take brain surgery to bring us together."

Linda quickly had Roberts jot her name and phone number on a napkin, and the two went their separate ways.

For eight months, Linda's focus was on helping Steve recover — specifically, get back his memory, a process that's gone well.

The other day, she was rummaging through notes she'd been keeping at the hospital when she found it: the napkin with the phone number on it.

She called me. I called Janet and thanked her for her wonderful duck.

Now 56, she had lost most of her sight at 33 while pregnant with the last of six children. "My eyes hemorrhaged," she said. "I have only peripheral vision, no central vision. To me, people look like part of some witness-protection program on TV: blurry. When I read, I can see the first few letters and maybe the last letter of a word. It's like 'Wheel of Fortune.'"

She loves art; "You can create something from nothing." She started an art program for children at the old hospital and has never forgotten "Touch of Oregon," which depicts ocean, valley and desert.

She used 70 tubes of caulking for it. "I wanted the blind to be able to experience it," she said.

She worked eight hours a day on it for three months, but says "I don't even compare" to the other artists who did ducks.

The project, Roberts said, seared images of Oregon into her creative mind that had faded in her blindness.

"I'd forgotten that there are stars in the sky," she said.

Yes, and in the eyes of a now-8-year-old boy and his grandfather, she'll always be among them.

The Shakespeare conflict

March 9, 2013

ASHLAND — Like *My Fair Lady's* Professor Henry Higgins trying to enculturate Eliza Doolittle, each March the Oregon Shakespeare Festival strains to turn me into a proper man of the — ahem — thee-au-tah.

A daunting job when your subject is more familiar with the less-refined world of sports. And yet, now in Year 7 of the experiment, it's kind of working.

I continually marvel at how three hours in the Bowmer Theater can move me to laughter and throat lumps, gently confront me with old biases and nudge me to new perspectives.

But amid such transformation my Other Self occasionally whispers a question from Stage Left: What's the Duck score?

Because of the availability of a friend-provided cottage, we always go to Ashland amid March basketball madness. And this year, game-play conflicts loomed like never before.

Game One of the Pac-12 Tournament worked fine. With no play to see, we caught Oregon-Washington on TV, just after arriving.

But conquests can create conflicts. To wit: on Friday, an 8 p.m. start for *Fair Lady* and an 8:40 p.m. start for Oregon-Utah.

Recording the game wasn't an option; the cottage wasn't equipped for that.

Thus did I concoct a recording setup using my iPhone. In a house decorated primarily in Elizabethan themes, I put a chair in front of the TV and propped the iPhone atop *Shakespeare: The Complete Works* and *Uppity Women of Medieval Times*. Just before we left for the half-mile walk to the theater — if you're late, you're out of luck — I pressed the button to begin videotaping.

Alas, returning at 11:30 p.m. after a fantastic *Fair Lady*, I was dismayed to find the iPhone's memory had maxed out after 55 minutes.

When I learned Oregon had ripped Utah, it not only ramped up my regret for having missed the game but added another conflict: The UO-UCLA championship game Saturday would begin at 8 p.m., the exact time as *Taming of the Shrew*.

Friends had reported that this contemporary version of Shakespeare's *Shrew* — Padua, Italy, transformed to a boardwalk setting complete with corn dogs — was exceptional.

And yet how often did the Ducks play for a conference basketball title?

I wanted desperately to see both dramas.

Wait! What about that "Watch ESPN" app I'd seen? Could I download it on my iPhone, see the play without hearing a score, then watch the game?

All I needed to do, I learned, was provide ESPN with my Comcast account number. Alas, of 145 account numbers and passwords I keep secure on my iPhone, Comcast's was not among them.

"My kingdom for a horse." The line from *King Richard III* came to mind. I was a handful of digits away from a win-win.

On Comcast's website, I then saw one last option: Without my number, Comcast would link me to that account — trust me — if I could provide them with the last four digits of my Social security number and the name of where I'd spent my honeymoon.

I soon had an ESPN app on which to watch the replay.

I was so relaxed the rest of the day that I didn't even champ to get to the theater early, as is my usual obsessive way. We left at 7:42 p.m. and arrived at 7:52 p.m.

She Who is Usually Uber-Organized handed me my ticket. "Uh, this is for last night," I said.

"She Who" ripped through her purse like a dog digging for a bone. No bone. "Oh, no, I must have left tonight's on the table," she said.

I turned and ran. Out of shape and hampered by a lingering Turkey Bowl knee injury, I was wheezing within two blocks.

Nick Symmonds has run 1:42.95 for 800 meters, roughly the distance to the cottage. He could be back by 7:57 p.m.

I'm not Nick Symmonds. I'm a 59-year-old guy with a bad knee in a winter coat who's flailing down East Main Street in sweat-drenched desperation.

If ever there was an excuse to miss a play and settle for — I don't know, whatever might be on the tube — this was it.

I could just phone She Who, tell her I couldn't make it, and she'd certainly understand. Victory, in a sense, borne of defeat.

On the other hand, going to Ashland and missing your play is like going to Mecca and missing your prayer.

Besides, unless you regularly perform on the stages or courts of life, there are limited opportunities to be a hero these days.

I burst into the cottage, grabbed the tickets and turned around like Olympic swimmer Michael Phelps at pool's end — only slower and perhaps wetter.

Meanwhile, a kind but firm usher at the Bowmer told "She Who" that the doors would close in four minutes.

I lumbered back — did I really once run cross-country in high school? — and struggled up the hill.

"The door's closing in one minute," the usher announced just after I entered the lobby.

My chest heaved. I settled into my seat as inconspicuously as Phil Knight at a Beaver rally.

But the play was great. And the game was great.

It ended — for me at least — at 12:58 a.m., with a small fist pump to punctuate an observation from The Bard himself.

All's well that ends well.

Two deaths and a lesson

June 7, 2015

S ince we last met in this Sunday space, two writers I admire greatly have died, only three days apart.

One was famous, at least among writers: William Zinsser, 92,
whose 1976 book *On Writing Well* sold 1.5 million copies and, along
with *The Elements of Style*, is considered *the* essential book on basic
writing.

The other was obscure: LaVae Robertson, 82, whose book *Five
Years of Fridays*, about babysitting her great-granddaughter Madisen, arrived on her Creswell porch two weeks before she passed
away May 15. It hasn't sold at all, but LaVae did give away 59 of
the 60 copies she ordered before her unexpected death after a brief
illness of encephalitis.

What the two had in common, beyond a certain optimism about
life, was a sense that writing matters, that it needn't be pretentious
and that it's easier to have done than to do.

"I don't like to write," Zinsser told a dozen or so University of
Oregon journalism professors and adjuncts over lunch in 2003. "I
like to have written."

Robertson spent seven years on her book, the same amount of
time Laura Hillenbrand spent on *Unbroken*.

"For someone with two master's degrees, it didn't come easy for
her," said her son, Springfield dentist Lonn Robertson. "But she enjoyed the challenge."

On the surface, Zinsser and Robertson were as opposite as the
places they lived — he in a Manhattan high-rise, she in a house
tucked into the woods east of Creswell, along Bear Creek.

A Princeton grad and a Yale teacher, Zinsser wrote 19 books, Robertson just the one. But beyond their differences, they were bound
together by their craft.

"All of life is like a lake made up many stories, fed by many
streams," wrote author Jean Rhys. "Some of the streams are long
and mighty, like Tolstoy and Dostoevsky, and some are small, like
me. The size of the stream doesn't matter. What matters is the lake.
Feed the lake."

Ten years ago when, without much of a clue, I launched a writers workshop in Yachats, Robertson was among the 24 students who showed up. Since then, only one of our 1,009 students has attended more times than Robertson's 11.

She was a fixture, even if she never mastered our online registration system. I'd get an e-mail from her a few days before an event. "Have room for one more? My check's in the mail!"

On Saturday nights, our traditional read-aloud time in Yachats, she almost always read something from her Fridays-with-Madisen manuscript. Like the time her great-granddaughter came across a dead bird and insisted they have a funeral for it, with Madisen presiding.

"'Dear beautiful bird, you are dead. You used to fly into the sky and the tree. You used to sing beautiful songs. But you are dead now. I gave you flowers — beautiful flowers. I love you, birdie. You can sing in heaven now and then you can come back to your nest. Thank you, bird.' The prayer was more to the bird than to God, in my opinion, but I went along with it, as all good Grammys would. 'Amen,' I answered with my head bowed low, mainly in hopes that I wouldn't giggle and also to conceal a slightly irreverent smile."

What I liked about Robertson as a writer was that she *noticed*, which is where every good story begins. And what we notice depends on who we are as human beings.

"Ultimately, the product any writer has to sell is not the subject being written about, but who he or she is," Zinsser wrote in *On Writing Well.* "I often find myself reading with interest about a topic I never thought would interest me — some scientific quest, perhaps. What holds me is the enthusiasm of the writer for his field."

That writer, to get Zinsser's approval, presumably kept things simple. Wrote clearly. Didn't toss in a bunch of $500 words when he could find good ones for a nickel here and a dime there.

"There's no sentence that's too short in the eyes of God," Zinsser wrote.

He isn't my favorite writer, but he is among my favorite famous people. I count lunch with him in 2003 as one of my famous-people highlights. He was warm, humble and engaging, as opposed to other writers I've interviewed, such as George Plimpton, who was cold, egotistical and aloof.

Years later, after I'd written to Zinsser about endorsing a book I'd written, he sent a handwritten note so gracious that I hardly realized he was turning me down — like being gutshot while slow-dancing.

Zinsser and Robertson: Two good people. Two good writers, even if on far different literary trails.

"Every writer is starting from a different point and is bound for a different destination," Zinsser wrote. "Yet many writers are paralyzed by the thought that they are competing with everybody else who is trying to write and is presumably doing it better."

If you want to write, he said, write. "Don't be afraid to fail."

Zinsser was a guru to millions, Robertson simply wanting to forever freeze in time a bunch of Fridays with her great-granddaughter.

She reached her destination. Zinsser reached his.

Both fed the lake well.

11.

Games of life

The golf dilemma

May 17, 2011

This is a story of golf interrupted.
Of a young woman balancing academics and athletics.
Of time and tests and divots and stress.

We begin months ago when Churchill High School senior Erin Butler discovered an inconvenient truth: The second day of the Midwestern League golf tournament at Tokatee Golf Club near Blue River was going to fall smack on the date of a college prep test she could ill afford to miss.

No ordinary test, this. Instead, the International Baccalaureate, which is to International High School seniors what the Masters is to professional golfers: a test for which Butler had been preparing since her junior year and for which, if successfully completed, she'd be granted 12 credits to be used at any college in the world.

Did we mention that Butler, who already has accepted a Presidential Scholarship to the University of Oregon, wants to study abroad to become a forensic anthropologist?

The test would involve two hours of essay writing on two of three books Butler had read: *Balzac and the Little Chinese Seamstress* by Dai Sijie, *1984* by George Orwell and *Sula* by Toni Morrison.

"You miss this, and two years of work are down the drain," says Butler's mother, Julie.

Oh, yeah, did we also mention that the Lancers have only four players on their girls golf team and would need scores from all four if they were to have a chance at going to state for an unprecedented second straight year by finishing among the top two teams?

Wait. What if Erin played Sunday-Monday instead of Monday-Tuesday as the rest of the field was doing?

Churchill Coach Jim Nielsen proposed the idea to tournament director Barry Bokn. "The district gives each team some flexibility in determining their state qualifiers," says Bokn, the athletic director at Willamette High.

This, however, would be unfair flexibility, he said. Bokn wisely ruled out the Sunday idea because the course's pin placements, tee boxes and weather would be different from what the field would experience Tuesday.

Butler's test started at 1 p.m. Tuesday. It would be impractical for her to try to squeeze in a four- to five-hour round before the hourlong drive back to Eugene. And it would be equally impractical for her to play afterward because of darkness and because she'd delay the tournament finish by hours.

So it looked as if nothing was going to — wait a minute, Bokn said. What if she played part of her round in the morning, drove back for the test, then returned to Tokatee to complete her round?

A sort of golf sandwich — chips included — wrapped around the literary meat of Morrison & Co.

Erin and her mother liked the somewhat zany idea. Did we mention that besides having a 3.96 GPA, Butler also has a slightly zany side that includes devouring entire pints of Ben & Jerry's Phish Food ice cream?

Other coaches were fine with it. And when nobody else volunteered, Marist Coach Rick Nelson agreed to be Butler's "mark," a playing partner.

"I've been involved in tournament golf since I was 5, and I've never seen anything like this," Nelson says.

After Butler, who usually plays in the team's third or fourth spot, posted a so-so 101 in Monday's opening round, she teed off at 7 a.m. Tuesday with Coach Nelson, whose Marist team Churchill was trying to beat to win the title.

"We kept the conversation real light," Butler says. "I appreciated how he handled it."

At 10 a.m. — Mom's predetermined leave time — Butler completed her 12th hole, hopped into a golf cart and headed for the parking lot. She'd shot a 51 front side and was five over par on the back.

Mom drove to Eugene. Butler began mulling literary themes, the test-takers' equivalent of hitting a bucket of practice balls.

After a drive-through stop at Arby's for a roast beef sandwich and potato cakes, Butler nailed the test.

Mom and daughter zipped back up the McKenzie for the final six holes. The rest of the field was finished.

Butler didn't play stellar golf — she shot a 102 — but she did finish. Thus, the Lancers were going to state, even if Marist won the title by five strokes.

Afterward, nearly 12 hours since her day began, Butler was emotionally spent; she had spent so much time in a sand trap on No. 15 that she may forever be traumatized about going to the beach. She dropped her bag and slunk into the clubhouse restroom to compose herself for the awards ceremony.

That's when she heard it: the applause.

"The entire Marist team, the Churchill team, a smattering of other players, they were all applauding her," Bokn says. "People knew she'd put in a superhuman effort."

A smile replaced Butler's somberness. All things considered, maybe she hadn't done so badly after all.

And, thus, with a stop at Harbick's Country Store, Julie figured there was only one way to honor her daughter the true student-athlete:

Phish Food. A whole pint, gone by the time they'd arrived back in Eugene for the second time that day.

Vision beyond the field

July 14, 2013

It's just a baseball hat — or so it might appear to the untrained eye. But to the retired Eugene optometric physician holding it, the cap is far more.

Where do you even begin to tell a story about the Sheldon High hat with the initials "JA" inked in red just above the bill?

A story about baseball and fathers and sons and loss and, ultimately, connection.

About 80-year-old Rod Gillilan, a father who lost a son; a visionary who raises money for kids; a doctor who has helped numerous local athletes improve their eye-on-the-ball skills.

And, more so, about a young man, 18-year-old Cooper Stiles, who, as Sheldon zeroed in on the school's first-ever state baseball championship this past spring, displayed vision the likes of which Gillilan had never seen.

Never mind that the young man's vision had nothing to do with seeing a baseball.

It is 1981. Gillilan is 58. His son, John, is 21 and three years removed from a stellar football and track career at Sheldon. He lives in Colorado.

Or did.

The phone call brings the news: John has died in a motorcycle accident.

Amid his grief, Gillilan, to honor his son, launches a foundation to provide money for Sheldon students who can't afford the Eugene School District's sports participation fee.

"If I were to have to tell my son we couldn't afford to let him play sports, it would have been horrible," Gillilan says. "And so I didn't want other kids denied that joy."

In 2000, Gillilan merges his foundation with a similar one begun by Jim Torrey, the former Eugene mayor and current Eugene School Board member whose son Tim, a Sheldon High baseball player, died in 1978 after the car Jim was driving was hit by a driver who had been drinking.

By the time Cooper Stiles saunters into the Sheldon program as a freshman in 2010, the fund has raised well over $100,000.

Stiles is talented, well-traveled in summer baseball circles and the son of a volunteer coach at the University of Oregon, Dean Stiles.

"He had quite a bit of swagger," Sheldon Coach Stan Manley says. "That's not bad, but he struggled with the team concept."

"Cooper's a leader who doesn't like to lead," says Megan, his mother.

Manley thought Rod Gillilan could help. Not just to hone Stiles' eye-on-the-ball skills but to help the young man start seeing himself in a new light.

Manley has great respect for Rod Gillilan. In 1978, while playing baseball for Sheldon High, Manley went through Gillilan's eye-training program himself. "It was very helpful," he says.

Manley — he played football with Gillilan's son, John — was named *The Register-Guard*'s Senior Athlete of the year for 1977-78 and went on to play baseball at Linfield.

So, with Manley now coaching the program he once played for, Stiles, a sophomore, and teammate Ryan Land begin working with Gillilan in the team's makeshift "clubhouse" to sharpen how they track a baseball: exercise after exercise in which their eyes dart left and right like windshield wipers, following the erasers of two pencils as they're moved back and forth, sometimes while the players themselves are moving. Following letters written on a baseball that's swinging from the ceiling on a string. And more.

Stiles doesn't say much to anyone but believes he's starting to see the ball better — at the plate and in the field.

Midway through Stiles' junior year, Manley notices something about the shortstop: He's becoming more team-oriented.

"That's the best game you've played for us," Manley tells Stiles after he didn't even have a hit.

But, Manley says later, he had tried to hit the ball where it needed to be hit, played great defense and was at the top of the dugout rail the entire game, yelling for the other players.

Though the training has ended — the boys keep doing the exercises on their own — Gillilan shows up for most of the games. An amateur artist, he paints pictures of Stiles and Land in action, frames them and gives them to each player.

The Irish roll into the 2012 Class 6A semifinals but blow a one-run lead in the bottom of the seventh — and last inning — and lose to Thurston.

A new school year arrives. Last New Year's Eve, the Clackamas High baseball coach, John Arntson, is driving west on Interstate 84 with his 7-year-old son, Jacob. They're coming home from celebrating Christmas in Montana.

Arntson's pickup hits a patch of ice near Mosier, skids off the road, smashes through a guardrail and tumbles down a rocky embankment into the Columbia River. John Arntson survives.

His son does not.

Last spring, Stiles, a senior, emerges as one of the state's best baseball players — for lots of reasons. Among them, Rod Gillilan's eye-ball training.

"He definitely helped me," Stiles says. "You can see the ball sooner. It slows down the game."

At the time, Gillilan isn't so sure he has made any difference in Cooper's life. "We didn't really have much of a relationship," he says.

The Irish make the playoffs. In the semifinals, Sheldon is down 3-1 to Roseburg when the Irish explode for 10 runs in the sixth inning and win easily.

En route home on the bus, the guys hear who their opponent will be in the June 1 championship game at Keizer's Volcanoes Stadium: Clackamas.

On Twitter, Stiles keeps seeing messages such as "Go Clackamas! Let's do it for JA!"

As the bus rumbles home, he sends a text to his friend Austin Kelly, who plays for Clackamas and was a teammate of Stiles' on a Junior Olympic summer team. "Who is JA?" he asks.

Kelly tells him it's their coach's son, Jacob, who died in an accident that his father survived.

"It kind of touched me," says Stiles, looking back. He's heard the story of Mr. Gillilan losing a son, too.

Back home, the Irish are issued new hats in honor of their getting to play in the championship game. Stiles gets an idea.

"He has this sort of humanitarian empathy that I don't even think he understands," Megan Stiles says.

Cooper inks a "JA" onto his hat in red for Clackamas' school color, the letters no bigger than a fingernail. Then, out of respect, he e-mails a photo of it to Kelly to make sure he and his teammates are OK with this.

"Sure," Kelly writes. "Means a lot."

On game day, Stiles goes to his teammates with the red pen. Not one player balks at the idea.

On the bus, Manley notices all of his players have the "JA" on their hats. He nods his approval, even while wanting to keep the already-light mood light.

In the dugout, he tells the team that the last time — and only time — Sheldon played for a state championship, in 1966, assistant coach Jim Fryback was playing for the Irish — in fact, made the last out in the game.

"Fryback can't hit today," Manley tells the team, "so we've got that going for us."

No team from Eugene has won a state baseball title at the highest classification in 51 years.

During the National Anthem, Gillilan watches Manley, 53, and his 75-year-old father Gene, an assistant coach, remove their hats.

"I've known Stan and his dad since high school days," Gillilan says, "and to see them, father and son, standing there before a state championship game — well, I've been to millions of games, but never quite had that feeling. It was electric."

Cooper Stiles hits a double and a single, each time scoring David Bellamy. The Irish lead 6-5 in the bottom of the last inning. Two outs. Nobody on. An out away from a state title.

Up comes Stiles' friend, Austin Kelly, who's hitting .407 and will soon be named Gatorade State Player of the Year. He promptly doubles off the wall in left-center.

When pitcher Mike Ralston throws two balls to the next batter, the tension ratchets up. But after issuing a walk, Ralston strikes out the next batter, flings his mitt in the air and the dog pile begins. The Sheldon Irish are state champs. It's a one-run win, and Stiles' two

RBIs prove to be difference-makers.

The e-mail comes a few days later, to Manley from Arntson, the Clackamas coach.

Congrats, it says, and thanks for honoring my son with the hats.

Stiles is named the Oregon School Activities Association's Class 6A Player of the Year.

A week after the game, Gillilan comes home from running an errand. Anna, his wife — the woman who had to take that phone call about her son's death in 1981 — is holding up a Sheldon baseball hat.

"It's for you," she says. "A player dropped it by."

On the opposite side of the "JA," a message has been scrawled on the hat from a reluctant leader who has stepped up to the plate: "To Mr. Gillilan: Thank you for everything. Cooper J. Stiles #2."

Rod Gillilan is stunned. "He nearly cried," Anna says. "He didn't feel worthy of it."

Someone else thought otherwise. Someone whose eyes are firmly trained on the stuff that matters.

Days of misery

Oct. 21, 2010

For any Duck fan, Oregon going into tonight's nationally televised game against UCLA as the No. 1-ranked team in the country is heady stuff.

But the view from Mount Everest looks all the more amazing for those of us who remember the Death Valley days.

Let's put it this way: In 1975, I was sports editor of the *Oregon Daily Emerald* when head coach Don Read was carried triumphantly out of Autzen Stadium and plunked into the shower by his team — after Oregon, despite losing five fumbles, had beaten a 1-5 Utah team to snap a 14-game losing streak.

In front of 10,500 fans.

Last spring, Oregon drew more than twice that for its spring intrasquad game.

Back then, being charged with covering UO football for a newspaper was like being given the keys to a 1972 AMC Gremlin. Yeah, it was a car made by a major automobile manufacturer, but any connection to quality or coolness ended there.

Overall, the athletic program was strong; in 1975, the *Knoxville (Tenn.) Journal,* using national finishes for all collegiate sports, ranked UO the ninth-best program in the country. But the football team stunk worse than the burned chili at my 1997 Civil War tailgater.

Indeed, the difference between now and then — between worst and first — is more than 35 years; it's light-years.

As players were being introduced before that infamous win over Utah — UO's first victory in 393 days — *Oregonian* columnist Don McLeod shook his head in the press box. Beyond him: 30,000 empty seats.

"They should introduce the fans to the players," he said. "It'd be faster."

In 1975, the Ducks sold 6,457 season tickets. This year it was about 43,000.

From 1972 to 1979, Autzen failed to muster a single sellout. Now, even with the stadium having an additional 12,000 seats, it has sold out 71 straight games dating back to 1999.

Back then, Autzen was a bowl-shaped mausoleum that exuded less ambiance than a bathroom at a freeway rest stop.

"It was awful," says Art Marshall, chief operating officer of Tiffany Food Service, which handled concession sales starting in 1976. "Autzen was bare concrete walls, no running water for our concession stands and colder than a Norwegian's heart. And I swear it rained nearly every game."

Indeed, Autzen was like this concrete edifice to futility surrounded by a parking moat.

Since 1990, however, statistics show it has rained at Autzen roughly only once every two seasons.

Good teams and good weather equal good concession sales.

"We do in one game what they'd do in a season," says Eric Brandt, the athletic department's director of food and hospitality. "We'll do at one concession stand what they did in the entire stadium."

Likewise with UO sportswear.

Last year, the Duck Store made far more money on the sale of one football-related item — the "I Love My Ducks" shirts — than the bookstore made on all football-related sportswear in 1975.

Thirty-five years ago, the store did $300,000 worth of sales on football-related items, according to Jim Williams, then a 27-year-old assistant manager, now the general manager. "Now, we'll do that for a single weekend with a home game."

In 1975, a small portion of the bookstore's 10,000-square-foot first floor was devoted to sportswear. Now, most of the store is awash in green and yellow — and five Duck Stores have popped up across the state, with a sixth to open soon in the Clackamas Town Center.

Times change.

Were you bummed because Oregon didn't beat the spread against Washington State, winning only 43-23? In 1974-75, the Ducks went 51 weeks without leading in a game.

They were regulars in syndicated columnist Steve Harvey's "Bottom 10" feature, reaching No. 2 in 1975.

Near the end of the 1974 season that would end 2-9, an *Oregon Daily Emerald* headline sighed: "Only one more week of this."

The Ducks opened the next year with a 62-7 road loss to Oklahoma and a baseball-esque 5-0 home loss to San Jose State. The latter prompted new UO President William Boyd to publicly proclaim that "I'd rather be whipped in a public square than watch a football game like that."

Who could blame him?

Though it won't be easy, if this year's Ducks win their final six regular-season games, they will have won more games (12) than the teams won during my entire four years at school (11).

My college-day Ducks didn't do much for the school's image, nor for the athletic budget, which was about a tenth of today's $75 million and on life support.

The UO was so desperate to save money, it quit giving its coaches freebie tickets and quit feeding the media before kickoff.

Sportswriters grumbled. It was hard enough having to watch a team give up 66 to Washington or get the ball inside the 15-yard-line three times against Stanford without managing to score a point.

But on an empty stomach?

Cheesy Rose Bowl pickings

Jan. 1, 2012

I admit it. I like Wisconsin. The football team. The state. The people. I am married to a farm-bred woman who loves cows.

Madison and Eugene are basically sister-city "college towns," joined at the hippy hip. So, no, on the eve of the Oregon-Wisconsin Rose Bowl game, it's not easy making fun of the Badgers in my traditional here's-who-wins-based-on-nonfootball-factors column.

But UO Coach Chip Kelly talks of preparing for "faceless opponents." Meaning enough of this "On, Wisconsin" manure. The breakdown:

Initials — UO vs. UW. Enough said. TD, Ducks. (UO, 7-0.)

Cheese — Any way you slice it, Wisconsin scores here. (Tied, 7-all.)

Mosquitoes — Like their respective football teams, Oregon has speed and numbers, Wisconsin size. You don't slap a mosquito in Wisconsin, you bring it down with a shotgun. TD, Badgers. (UW, 14-7.)

Tacky roadside attractions — How can the Ducks compete against giant fiberglass fish, the National Mustard Museum and the world's largest six pack? TD, Badgers. (UW, 21-7.)

Water — Wisconsin is flanked by two Great Lakes and has 26,767 miles of streams and rivers. The UW campus even has its own lake. Unfortunately, all this water is frozen until the Fourth of July. And when it comes to geographic poker, one Pacific Ocean beats two Great-Lakes-of-a-kind. Field goal, Ducks. (UW, 21-10.)

Movies — Filmed-at-UW's *Back to School* (Rodney Dangerfield, 1986) is to UO's *Animal House* (John Belushi, 1978) what paint-by-numbers is to Van Gogh's *Starry Night*. TD, Ducks. (UW, 21-17.)

Seasons — Oregon has four, Wisconsin two: winter and summer, the latter defined as three months of bad sledding. Field goal, Ducks. (UW, 21-20.)

Elevation — Wisconsin's highest point is 1,941-foot Timms Hill. Lane Forest Products has bark dust mounds higher than that. Field goal, Ducks. (UO, 23-21.)

Rose Bowl rap videos — Let's let the people decide this one. Number of YouTube views of Wisconsin's 2010 and 2011 Rose Bowl raps: 280,453. Views of the two "I Love My Ducks" videos: 2.9 million. TD, Ducks. (UO, 30-21.)

Last-second heroics — Wisconsin lost two games this season in the last minute. Lost. Hey, with only seconds remaining, Oregon lineman Mark Asper saved the life of a guy choking on prime rib Wednesday night. In other words, won. Field goal, Ducks. (UO, 33-21.)

Shoveling stuff — In Wisconsin, people have more miles on their snow-blowers than on their cars. And don't get me going on cow dung. TD, Badgers. (UO, 33-28.)

Mascots — Are you kidding me? We're talking about a badger wearing a red-and-white striped sweater — the animal world's answers to a barber-shop pole — and struts around with a smirk on his face as if to say, "we produce a quarter of the nation's cheese." UO's duck, meanwhile, leads the team onto the field on the back of a Harley, is an ESPN favorite and exudes coolness. TD, Ducks. (UO, 40-28.)

College towns — *Sports Illustrated* ranked Madison first and Eugene seventh in the nation, the list obviously created by someone smitten by pre-game polkas and post-game cow-tipping. But fair is fair. TD, Badgers. (UO, 40-35.)

Place names — Wisconsin has big, lumbering offensive-lineman sort of towns: Sheboygan, Mukwonago, Oconomowoc ... Oregon counters with quick-darting, LaMichael James sorts of towns: Zigzag, Glide, Mist and Pistol River. Field goal, Ducks. (UO, 43-35.)

Weather — With 50 inches of snow per year, UW starts spring football whenever it can find its indoor practice facility. Field goal, Ducks. (UO, 46-35.)

Authors/naturalists — When I pitted John Muir (UW) against Barry Lopez (UO), things turned embarrassingly ugly when — arguing about the rare-breed swallowtail — the two began sparring, Zorro-esque, with butterfly nets. Offsetting penalties. No play.

Post-game traditions — The Badgers' "Fifth Quarter" celebration at Camp Randall Stadium — singing and dancing with the band — is legendary. TD, Badgers. (UO, 46-42.)

Political controversy — After last February's meltdown in Madison, Eugene's City Council meetings look like the Cleavers enjoying dinner chat. TD, Badgers. (UW, 49-46.)

School mottoes — UO's is Mens agitat molem ("Minds move mountains"). Wisconsin's is Commodo obduco caseus ("Please pass the cheese.") Field goal, Ducks. (Tied, 49-all.)

Cold — January's average high temperature in Madison: 25 degrees. Low: 9. For the Badgers, Pasadena isn't about football, it's about feeling their fingers again. TD, Badgers — plus a two-point wind-chill conversion. (UW, 57-49.)

Uniforms — Wisconsin updates its "Oshkosh B'gosh" look less often than John Deere upgrades its tractors. Meanwhile, the Ducks will debut a Nike-designed "integrated pro combat system," complete with "LiquidMetal" helmets. TD, Ducks, but a missed two-point conversion because, let's face it, folks, uniforms don't win games, players do. (UW 57-55.)

Karma — Wisconsin has already avenged its fluke loss to Michigan State so the Badgers' destiny bucket is empty. Monday, it's UO's turn to right the ("Missed-it-left!") wrong of the USC game — and the ("Field-goal-is-good!") Auburn game.

With a second left, UO kicker Alejandro Maldonado — his body air-cooled by an "enhanced thermoregulation" uniform — lines up for the potential game-winner.

And with a single swing of his leg — and a final cheesy Nike description — the Ducks soar into history on the "iridescent-sheen" of their redesigned "armored wings," 58-57.

Winter of Ducks' content

Jan. 3, 2012

Now is the winter of our Ducks' content.
  I know, bringing in Shakespeare to help put Oregon's Rose Bowl win in perspective may seem incomprehensible.

But no more incomprehensible than, say, those four previous words: "Oregon's Rose Bowl win."

No more incomprehensible than fireworks going off in our normally staid neighborhood as time ran out — literally — on Wisconsin's comeback attempt.

No more incomprehensible than a bunch of guys in mirror-hip helmets doing what last was done by an Oregon team wearing leather helmets.

And the Bard is right: UO's 45-38 victory over the Badgers on Monday night promises to warm Duck fans with the balmy pleasant-ry of Pasadena through the dark, wintry months ahead.

Perhaps even beyond for those of us old enough to remember when pain wasn't a last-second loss in a national championship game but a 14-game losing streak (1974-75) or shutting out Oregon State and still not winning (0-0 in 1983).

Still, Monday's triumph isn't rags to riches stuff. That story line came and went in 1994-95 when Kenny Wheaton and the Ducks snapped a 37-year Rose Bowl drought.

Oregon has played in bowl games 18 of the past 22 years, which is why younger fans aren't as likely to have the "I-can-now-die-in-peace" contentment of those of us who have "seen too much."

Oregon's fly-by-Knight wealth as a football program has been well-documented since the Joey Harrington banner was unfurled in New York in 2001. Two years later, the Ducks made the cover of *Sports Illustrated* with the headline "Rich, Cool and 4-0."

So, no, rags to riches doesn't work as a theme for this monumental victory.

It isn't quite a "reverse of the curse" vanquishing of some decades-old drought, either, a college football version of the curse of the Bambino, the Boston Red Sox's 86-year World Series futility ostensibly triggered by the sale of Babe Ruth — aka the Bambino — to the Yankees.

True, it's been 95 years since Oregon won a Rose Bowl, but the Ducks have had only five chances to play in the game since — and that's not enough at-bats to qualify for an official curse.

It isn't a Cinderella story either like, say, Boise State's 2007 Fiesta Bowl win over Oklahoma with all those trick plays and the postgame proposal of the running back to the cheerleader on national TV. Remember, UO is a team that played for the national championship just last year.

No, here's what it is — and I hope the Bard will forgive my step down in analytical sophistication:

It's Charlie Brown going to kick the football and, for once, Lucy not pulling it away at the last second.

With the exception of the 2002 Fiesta Bowl, that has happened in the four recent marquee bowl games the Ducks have played in: the 1995 Rose Bowl, the 2010 Rose Bowl and last year's BCS Championship.

The hoopla. The hype. The game. The loss. The cold winters that followed each.

And you could argue that Lucy pulled the same trick after the Ducks' win in that Fiesta Bowl since they were denied what many thought was a well-deserved spot in the title game.

Not now. Lucy's reign is over.

Now, it's sealing the deal, finishing strong, whatever cliché you want to choose.

But, above all, it's making history.

If 95 years between Rose Bowl wins doesn't make for a curse, it does represent — in the words of Crosby, Stills & Nash — a long time gone. The last surviving member of the 1917 team, John Parsons Sr., died 25 years ago.

When the Ducks won in 1917, the United States was three months away from entering World War I and Ford's advertising highlighted the superiority of cars to horses and buggies.

The UO's football "facilities" — they consisted of muddy Kincaid Field — were so bad that a football was once lost during a game. And Oregon was so poor that to fund the team's trip to Pasadena, the school's bookstore was sold to a private party to generate some quick cash.

On Jan. 1, 1917, fans filled the McDonald Theater to follow the game. A teletype machine reported the ebbs and flows of the 14-0 win.

Monday, Duck fans gathered around high definition, flat-screen televisions. (Some of us superstitiously clinging to certain viewing spots that coincided with good Duck plays.)

In the football mecca of Pasadena, fans shelled out $90 apiece to attend UO's official tailgater.

But whether you were at the game or watching from afar, what mattered for Ducks fans in the end wasn't your location.

What mattered wasn't the hype or the pinball helmets.

What mattered wasn't bragging rights.

What mattered was simply knowing that for one day, in a place that is to college football what Augusta is to golf, Oregon won the day.

Enabled some of us old-timers to check another item on our bucket list.

And staved off another winter of discontent.

Ramping up with class

Oct. 29, 2009

It happened 10 years ago this fall in a setting not unlike the one we'll see this weekend:

Southern California vs. Oregon at Autzen Stadium.

Night game.

Lots of potential for trouble, much of it caused by people so drunk on school pride and other stuff that civility gets sacrificed in the process.

Lots of potential for one person's pride to trump another person's right to enjoy a football game, especially if that other person is wearing the wrong school colors.

Lots of potential for overlooking the idea that getting to the top is pointless if you can't do it with a little class.

Which brings us to the evening of Sept. 25, 1999, an evening Steve Temple has never forgotten

Not because of Oregon's 33-30 triple-overtime win over USC which had been, in Steve's words, "the nuttiest game ever," secured only when a second-string field goal kicker booted the game winner after the first-stringer injured his knee while celebrating an earlier successful kick.

But because of a single moment just before the game.

Temple, a Eugene contractor and 46 at the time, was pushing his father-in-law in a wheelchair up the southwest ramp to a flat perch for those with disabilities.

Bob Hansen, then 70, was a diehard Duck, a native of Eugene who remembers seeing Norm Van Brocklin fling the football at Hayward Field, a plywood mill superintendent who had scraped together money to take 12 members of his family to Los Angeles for the 1990 Freedom Bowl.

He wasn't about to let a heart problem prevent him from seeing Oregon play the vaunted Trojans. "He could walk but not up an incline like that," Temple says. "He was on oxygen."

Hansen was a big fan in more ways than one. By the time he got Bob halfway up the incline, Steve was spent. "My legs were gone," he says.

But he had to get Bob to the top; goodness, he'd married the guy's daughter. If he failed, how does he explain this one back home — or in the waiting room of the emergency room?

Steve was like a green-and-yellow Sisyphus, pushing a green-and-yellow stone up the hill. But as he rolled the wheelchair, step by step, upward, he realized he couldn't go on. His legs were Jell-O.

He bent over and leaned on the chair to keep it from sliding back.

"I was totally out of steam," he said. "I had nothing left. But we had to either go up or down. There's no middle ground on a ramp."

Suddenly, a man rushed to Steve's side. "Here," said the stranger, hurriedly handing Steve a clipboard. "Take this."

"The guy was, like, 6-foot-2 or 6-foot-4 and really well-built, maybe in his mid-30s," Steve remembers.

And, not incidentally, wearing football shoes, khaki pants, a crimson top and a USC hat.

"Clearly he was a USC coach on his way up to the press box before the game," says Steve.

The guy gripped the wheelchair handles and powered Bob to the top in a matter of seconds. The stranger nodded to accept Steve's thanks, then raced off for the elevator.

"It helped me see the bigger picture to all this," says Steve. "I mean, here's a USC guy in the midst of preparing for this huge game, stopping to help a couple of guys in green and yellow."

Guys supporting the team that, if USC couldn't beat, could help cost a coach and their assistants jobs down the line. The bad guys. The enemy.

It humbled Steve. "I still think about it all these years later," he says. "It helps me keep things in perspective, that it's just a game and there are bigger things out there."

I showed Steve photos of USC assistant coaches from back then. "I'm pretty sure that's him," he said when seeing a picture of Ken O'Brien, then the USC quarterbacks coach and prior to that an All-Pro quarterback who played for the New York Jets and Philadelphia Eagles.

Nope. Though O'Brien told me any coach on any team would have done the same, he said it wasn't him. Nor, he said, could it have been Steve Greatwood, the Oregon offensive line coach who, as USC's line coach back then, was, like O'Brien, on the field and not in the press box.

Whoever it was, in a time when the magnificence of college football is increasingly tainted by selfish jerks, he showed us what getting to the top with class really looks like.

Graveyard Duck

March 7, 2010

Past the Pioneer Cemetery headstones, I was walking back to my car after Thursday's Oregon-Washington basketball game when I saw him: the Ghost of University of Oregon Athletics Past.

"Rough night?" he rasped, a tattered UO letterman's jacket hanging on him like swamp moss.

"Rough winter, period," I said. "Forget the Ernie Kent stuff. I'm talking about how one minute you're basking in Rose Bowl sunshine, thinking it doesn't get any better. The next minute reading another 'Duck Arrested' headline and wondering if we'll have enough guys to field an offense next fall."

He offered me a seat on a bench next to a Civil War soldier's grave. "Almost makes you pine for the good ol' days," he said.

"You mean like when Autzen was the tomb of the unknown players? Do you really want us to go back to obscurity, mediocrity and humiliation?"

"Well, you've already got back the humiliation, so you're one for three," he said, chuckling. "But you suggest it's an either-or proposition, like a team couldn't be classy on the field and off."

"OK, assuming it could, how did we get to where we've gotten?" I asked.

"Like a boiling frog: slowly, but inexorably. Nobody realizes the water is scalding until it's too late."

"And who's to blame for that?" I asked.

"It's not a case of blame," he said. "It's a case of lost perspective."

"Meaning?"

"You taste some success. You want more. Your swagger increases. So does your sense of entitlement; just ask Tiger Woods. Like Rick Telander wrote after an egocentric U.S. basketball team lost twice in the World Championships: 'Nobody kills the hero; the hero gorges himself at the trough of greed and indulgence.'"

"Easy there, Will Shakespeare," I said. "We're talking about a handful of 20-year-olds who simply made some bad choices."

"'Bad choices?' said the ghost. "I, sir, come from a time when 'shooting Ducks' referred to our 1939 NCAA championship basketball team, not what today's basketball players do at Alton Baker Park in the off-season. And, yes, had ESPN existed in 1937 as it did when Mr. Blount threw his punch last fall, Oregon and Oregon State's students would have been shamed for weeks for their infamous Millrace brawl."

"Don't forget the football team's little transcript-altering scandal in the early '80s," I said.

"OK, OK, so the past wasn't perfect," said the ghost. "But the present is getting downright scary. Don't you see? These recent player arrests are only pieces in a larger puzzle.

"It's not just players, it's the alleged adults at Autzen so drunk they can't see the world beyond their pickled noses," he continued. "And UO students making *Sports Illustrated* for their nasty treatment of UCLA's Kevin Love.

"It's giving bonuses to coaches based, in part, on their players' graduation rates but hiring an athletic director, Pat Kilkinney, who dropped out," the ghost said, on a roll. "And in a time when thousands of fans are reeling from a recession, having the audacity to bring out four sets of football helmets when one set would suffice."

"Goodness, are you going to also roast our Duck for attacking that Houston Cougar mascot?" I asked.

"You said it, not me. But don't you see? All these things suggest a certain 'we're-accountable-to-nobody' attitude. That works great for the group in power; not so great for, say, the fan who doesn't want to watch a game while peppered by — what do you call them these days? — 'f' bombs, or, more seriously, someone being physically attacked by a football player.

"Aren't we on our soapbox," I said.

"No, it's a headstone," he said, pointing a bony finger at me. "And don't underestimate skewed vision. If a player hadn't lost perspective on the big picture, would he really have risked losing a four-year scholarship — and going to jail — just so he could make his point with his fist?

"If a fan hadn't lost perspective, would a game — it is still a game, you know — mean so much to him that he'd boo his own quarterback?

"If an athletic department hadn't lost perspective, would it really have built a locker room that's really an entertainment center with showers?"

"OK," I said, "so maybe we've lost some perspective."

"Oh, you're losing more than perspective. You're losing connectedness. To each other."

"Oh, please," I said, grimacing. "For a guy from the day of leather helmets and set shots, you're starting to sound positively New Age."

"Sports," he said, "was never intended to wall off the elite from the others. It was meant to bring people together to compete and celebrate the effort of striving for excellence.

"In the '60s, Bowerman's track guys worked in the mills with community folk. In the '70s, Pre pumped beer at the Pad and school kids followed Ronnie Lee around playgrounds as if he were the Pied Piper. Players felt a certain accountability to the community, a certain standard to live up to — and that's obviously waned.

"Now, you build buildings so your athletes don't even have to study with non-athletes, which only adds to the divide between these athletes and the 'real community' beyond."

"So — what? — you're saying it's wrong to want the best for our athletes?" I asked.

"I'm saying it's time you took stock. It doesn't have to be 'either-or'; you can shine on the field and off.

"For now, it's getting late," he concluded. "Best be on your way."

With that, he drifted away, leaving only two words hanging in the darkness: "Go, Ducks."

A sportier approach

April 1, 2010

When Lorraine Davis was named the University of Oregon's interim athletic director last week, some people cringed.

Some wondered whether it was an early April Fool's joke that, like a lot of stuff in the athletic department lately, got leaked to the press.

The same athletic department that hangs its helmet on cutting-edge thinking — that outsources its basketball search to Nike and changes its football uniform styles with the same frequency most of us change our oil — was hiring a 66-year-old former health professor who seemingly knew more about field hockey than football. (What's field hockey?)

Who, when hearing the news that she was a finalist, wasn't hobnobbing with the NCAA hoops crowd in St. Louis or Syracuse but crossing Zumwalt Prairie in Eastern Oregon.

In short, who didn't exactly fit the description of a Division I athletic director or coach.

Goodness, the woman has a college degree!

She lives full-time in Eugene!

There's even talk that her contract will be signed on UO letterhead, instead of having been penciled out on the back of a Kowloon's napkin sometime between the egg flower soup and the kung pao chicken.

I mean, seriously: Is this someone we want representing the university?

But after meeting with Davis for some organic espresso at the Divine Cupcake, my doubts about her vanished like a frat-house laptop.

Not that I was so sure about her thinking at first.

"For years," Davis began, "I've noticed this divide between how the athletic department operates and how the academic side of the university operates. I intend to realign things so we become one team."

I gulped. My worst fears were coming true.

"It is high time we recognize that the Willamette River divides this institute, often in ways counterproductive to our educational goals."

I coughed into my hand. Was she pulling some sort of April Fool's prank on me?

"Yes, Bob, it's my goal to transform the academic side of the university to more closely align with the athletic side. In short, to get our English Department deans, biology profs and Peace Studies students to start playing — as my predecessor used to say — 'one inch out of control.'"

Any apprehension I'd had drained out of me like the fruity flow from the juice bar dispenser in the $8 million sports treatment center.

"You know," I said. "Just when I thought you couldn't possibly be any more worrisome, you go and do something like this — and totally redeem yourself!"

She smiled. "Would you like your espresso freshened? You know, they use reusable bamboo coffee filters here. Helps reduce the waste."

"Uh, thanks, I'll pass. But I am interested in hearing more about your vision."

"Consider it a sort of duck-lipped perestroika, Bob, a restructuring of a broken system," she said. "I see a day when a geography major needn't trudge 300 feet on a smooth concrete path to the library and wrestle with ordinary students for the latest copy of *Map* magazine. Why? Because the geography department will have its own swanky study center, preferably with surrounding water and moat to keep out the ordinary students.

"I see a day when we stop this ticky-tack legalism that suggests the head of a department should have at least an undergraduate degree. What do people think we are — a comprehensive research university that serves the world through the creation and transfer of knowledge?

"I see a day when every dean has a country club membership. History, Medieval Studies, all professors will get lavish bonuses based, in part, on how many of their students compete on our school's athletic teams. And associate profs who need only wink at the host to get the best seat in the house at Marché."

"Interesting, I said.

"We're calling the shift in thinking 'Serf and Artificial Turf: Bridging the River.' We've already ordered the 10-story banner of Katey Gries for the Times Square building."

"Huh? Who's Katey Gries?"

"A UO student who earned a master's in literary nonfiction — at age 51, while caring for her elderly parents and working at a retirement home. And who has nearly $100,000 in student loan debt."

"I imagine President Lariviere is excited about this new emphasis," I said. "I'm going to head to Johnson Hall and —."

"Oh, he's gone," Davis said. "We renegotiated his contract so he doesn't have to live in Eugene more than seven months a year."

"Oh."

"Not to worry," she said. "You can reach him in Maui. He's celebrating April Fool's Day there."

The Chip Flip

Jan. 17, 2013

A nd you're surprised?
One of the things that made Chip Kelly the hottest coach in college football was his unpredictability — and his penchant to play fast.

In the end, that's how Kelly on Wednesday ended a glorious run as the most successful University of Oregon football coach in school history: faking a handoff to Athletic Director Rob Mullens — "I'm remaining at the University of Oregon," he told his boss on Jan. 6 — and keeping the ball himself.

Shortly after noon, instead of whisking off to meet Duck recruits, Kelly was on a private jet from Eugene to Philadelphia to be introduced at a news conference today as the new Eagles coach.

Oregon State spawned the Fosbury Flop. Now, Oregon was surprised by the Chip Flip.

Technically, no, Kelly didn't lie. And he made no assurances that he wouldn't entertain future NFL offers. But most of us assumed that "remaining at the University of Oregon" meant for more than, uh, nine days.

But, hey, should anything surprise us about Chip He's always been a high-risk/high-reward stock, a guy whose penchant for winning football games — the Ducks made four straight BCS bowls — gave him a license to call his own shots, whether that meant treating the media as a bother or opting out of booster gatherings.

And in the end, that's what happened: Kelly called his own shot, 10 days after he affirmed he was staying, three weeks before recruits have to commit and perhaps a few months before the NCAA rules on the UO's alleged NCAA recruiting violations.

Is Chip's fake handoff really just a way to end-run having to face the blitzing NCAA? I don't think so. The guy is dying to take his show to the NFL; remember, less than a year ago he had a supposedly done deal in Tampa Bay until he changed his mind.

Instead, Kelly's decision to reconsider a deal with the Eagles after turning them down three days after the Fiesta Bowl says something about his priorities — ultimately, himself — and about college football in general.

That's not easy for Pollyanna types like me to swallow. Some Duck fans undoubtedly feel like Beaver fans did in 1998 when Mike Riley bolted OSU for a chance to coach the San Diego Chargers after he had breathed life back into a nearly clinically dead Beaver program for two years.

If Kelly's departure didn't qualify for love-'em-and-leave-'em status — heck, only Riley, who returned to OSU in 2003, has a longer tenure in the Pac-12 — it was a reminder that college football is, indeed, a business.

The Pac-12 Networks' television contract is worth $3 billion. Coaches have become hot commodities, their salaries dwarfing those of university presidents. And long-term commitments to schools have gone the way of eight-track tapes.

Lane Kiffin bolted Tennessee for USC after a single season, without the class to allow TV cameras to film his rushed going-away press conference.

Kelly's exit wasn't as tacky; at least he met with his players Wednesday morning.

And I've heard no reports of Oregon fans setting mattresses on fire in protest as students did in Knoxville — though some jerk did drive across Kelly's lawn.

Relax, folks. If Lane County has a sky — and with this fog, I'm beginning to wonder — I don't believe it's falling.

Kelly was fun, focused and fanatical; in four years, he went 46-7. Duck fans should be glad they had him. But to suggest that Oregon football is Chip Kelly is to think too small.

Sure, Kelly took the Ducks to new heights. But Oregon football is an offense, a look, a quirkiness, a culture, a brand — and, of course, Phil Knight.

It's Rich Brooks, Mike Bellotti and players such as Joey Harrington, Kenny Wheaton and Dino Philyaw, who raised the bar before Kelly even showed up.

And it's a staff of top-notch assistants that hasn't changed in four years — and, if offensive coordinator Mark Helfrich becomes head coach, might not change much after Chip's departure.

In other words, Oregon football is bigger than Chip Kelly.

I hope he turns 4-12 Philadelphia into a Super Bowl team and revolutionizes the NFL with his no-huddle offense. And avoids getting mugged — or frostbite — in the country's sixth-most-dangerous big city.

Meanwhile, in the words of Chip himself when a player goes down: "Next man up."

Goodbye to S.I.

March 11, 2015

For nearly 50 years, it arrived each Thursday or Friday like a high tide: the latest issue of *Sports Illustrated.*

As a sixth-grader, I can still remember the sense of wonder when

I opened the package containing a note that a subscription had been started in my name. "Merry Christmas," said the card. "Love, Mom & Dad."

The magazine followed me off to college at the University of Oregon, where I honed a sportswriter's dream at the School of Journalism. From newspaper jobs in Bend and Bellevue, Wash., and back to Eugene. From sportswriter to feature writer to general columnist. From son to father to grandfather.

Until now. My subscription ran out in early February and I didn't renew.

My decision was neither made flippantly nor wrestled over for months by pro and con grapplers on the mats of my mind.

I simply decided that the sports world the magazine reflected each week was increasingly a world that I not only wasn't interested in, but in many cases detested:

Blather about lost-touch-with-reality pro athletes who whine about $10 million contracts.

Incessant hand-wringing about Tiger Woods' legacy, as if what's really going to matter on our death beds is how many majors we've won.

Page after page on losers like football coach Bobby Petrino, who left the Atlanta Falcons for Arkansas by taping a goodbye note to a locker, and was fired by the Razorbacks after having an extramarital affair with a 25-year-old woman whom he'd hired as an assistant, all of which came to light after he lied about a motorcycle accident the two were involved in. Which, in the wonderful world of sports, landed him a $3.5 million-a-year job as head coach at Louisville.

More and more, I found myself thinking: Why should I devote my time and money to people who taint the sports I love but are fawned over as if they were gods?

So I quit *Sports Illustrated.*

In fairness, blame for the magazine's weekly sports junk food is as much about the changing culture as it is about *Sports Illustrated* itself; the magazine, you can argue, is only reflecting the values of those who play and coach and watch.

And so it is that we now have huge chunks of the magazine devoted to fantasy leagues— as if the real stuff isn't enough to satiate us. (Reminds me of the young couple I saw on the beach recently: Killer sunset. Sixty degrees. No wind. And they're lost in puffing a joint, making you want to say, Kiddos, if this moment isn't enough for you just as it is, you're in for a sad, sad life.)

Gone is the psychiatrist's eye of Gary Smith, who could peel away the layers of an athlete's soul like no other writer I've read.

Gone is the humor of Rick Reilly.

Gone is the insight from freelancers, whose first-person essays brought a richness and diversity to the table that you don't get from some Ivy League grad writing about playing 18 holes with the president.

What used to be the poetry of sports — Kenny Moore's essay on the beauty of cross-country foremost among it — has become the Pablum of sports.

What used to be the diversity of subjects — I remember being chilled by the series on grizzlies at Glacier National Park and enchanted by a piece on a boat show — has become a fast-food menu of greed, gambling and ego. *You want domestic violence with that?*

True, the magazine's photography has always been great — and, with technology, greater. And computers have revolutionized its use of statistics and charts. But what *Sports Illustrated* lost was its soul — soon after sports began to lose its own.

Which brings me to the third leg of this so-long stool: Me.

At 61 and noticing more intently the scoreboard clock, I find myself increasingly aware of wasted time. And reading about people whose lives aren't much wider than a football field no longer passes my litmus test for such.

True, evildoers are slicing off the heads of innocents and governors are playing loose with our trust — and yet I'm not about to cancel my subscription to *The Register-Guard.* The difference is, as a citizen, I need to keep abreast of the world around me. But as a sports fan, sorry, I feel no such obligation.

So it's time to seek my sports inspiration elsewhere, most recently at a fourth-grade YMCA basketball game in Eugene where a small but feisty player from Mohawk collided with my grandson and both fell to the floor. Instinctively, the kid reached out a hand to help up my grandson.

You won't find that moment in *Sports Illustrated.* Instead, you'll find grown-up athletes acting childish — bullying women, deflating footballs, paying $50,000 fines instead of talking to the press, ad nauseam.

Me? I'll subscribe to the inspiration of the Mohawk kid.

For free.

12.
Ties that bind

Love again

Dec. 7, 2014

SISTERS — It happened nearly a month ago, before snow and cold stilled this part of Central Oregon in the quiet of an early winter.

A young woman. A young man. And one of those weddings that you think back on and find yourself smiling about again and again.

Not because of the beautiful setting: a barn in the golden light of aspen trees, the Three Sisters adorned in new snow as if stylish bridesmaids.

Not because of the people who had gathered in this rustic setting from such faraway places as New York City, Hawaii and South Carolina.

And not because of the role I was privileged to play in it all: the officiant.

No, the reason the memory lingers is because it reminds me of the resiliency of the human spirit. The hope that emerges from hopelessness. And, to quote a line I used from the band Rascal Flatts, the broken road that can lead two people straight to each other.

Perhaps you remember Bethany Smith.

I wrote about her for *The Register-Guard* in May 2012. Girl meets boy, Ryan Smith. After graduating from the University of Oregon in 2009, boy and girl look forward to a lifetime together. But boy gets cancer and is told he has only a few months to live.

A graphic designer at The Duck Store, Bethany had once said she'd hoped to spend a couple of years planning her wedding. Instead, she planned it in three days; nobody knew how much time Ryan had left.

Bethany and Ryan were married at a Bend restaurant on Dec. 11, 2011.

Later, Bethany's father, Stephen Schmidt, told me he'd never experienced anything like it: every drop of joy tainted with the reality that it could not last, every wide-eyed smile etched with mistiness, every embrace between Ryan and friends and family possibly the final one.

He was so sick he couldn't even stay for the entire reception.

Ryan Smith died six weeks later, Jan. 24, 2012.

Bethany stood before guests at the UO's Ford Alumni Center and did something few 24-year-old women will ever do: eulogized her husband of the same age.

When, as a promise to Ryan, she posted wedding photos on the Snippet & Ink wedding blog, the pictures triggered more response than anything the site had ever experienced. Bethany wound up on NBC's "Today" show being interviewed by UO alum Ann Curry.

Then, she returned to her apartment and Boots, the cat she had often sneaked into PeaceHealth Sacred Heart Medical Center at RiverBend to snuggle with Ryan.

How do you start a life over again?

It was a question that came up often as Bethany, my wife Sally and I talked nearly every Tuesday evening on our back deck in the summer of 2012. After the response to my column, I'd approached Bethany about writing a book on her and Ryan. She liked the idea.

Still, it was an often-painful series of interviews, me feeling slightly guilty for having to bring up the past, she feeling the pain of having to relive it. Her beautiful smile only rarely came out to play.

Ultimately, my agent couldn't find a publisher. But the unexpected benefit of the literary defeat was a friendship with one of the most courageous people I've ever met.

Months later, when the three of us were out to dinner, Bethany said it, "I've met someone."

Weirdly, it was someone I casually knew, Garrett Loveall. I'd written about his father David, a pastor at Eugene's ThreeSixteen Ministries, and mother, Nita, who had doggedly refused to give up in adopting a 14-year-old son, William, from Uganda. (See p. 244.)

Later, I wrote a column about the worldwide success Garrett was experiencing from the roll-up tote bags he designs and makes here in Oregon. A refreshingly ambitious young man.

Time passed.

Sally and I saw less and less of Bethany. She moved to Redmond, in part to be closer to her folks. In my old-school estimation, the move did not bode well for the future of Bethany, 27, and Garrett, 28. But last August a phone call came from Bethany.

She and Garrett planned to wed in November.

"Bethany," I said. "That's awesome!"

"And we want you to do the ceremony."

"Me? But Garrett's father is a pastor."

"And just wants to enjoy the wedding as a father," she said. *"Please."*

Over the years, I've been part of hundreds of events as a speaker, but nothing compares to the honor this was.

I had the best seat in the hou—, uh, barn, watching Bethany start down the aisle with her mother and father, the autumn light infusing her with angelic ambiance. A few feet to my right, Garrett's eyes glistened. Garrett, the kid who, in a candid moment with his dad, had once lamented the elusiveness of love.

And now, here came his bride. Two people, one who had overcome a broken heart, the other who understands that she will never completely heal.

I spoke of Rascal Flatts, 1 Corinthians 13:7 ("love always hopes, always perseveres …") and of what gives barns like the one we were in their character.

"The rough-hewn beauty of a barn's exterior wood — its character, its soul, its definition — exists not *despite* the time and the elements it has endured, but *because of* the time and the elements," I said. "The resistance it has faced and overcome has proven its worth. Likewise, the character of your relationship — its soul, its definition — comes from the journey you've already been on. The resistance you've faced and overcome have proven your relationship's worth."

Hours later, when the reception had morphed into wild dancing, I watched Bethany's folks and Garrett's folks join the youngish crowd with who-cares exuberance, video footage of which I could threaten to show their friends.

But what I'll remember most was Bethany's beautiful, non-stop smile.

Back again, after the long, broken road.

Street inspiration

March 7, 2013

JUNCTION CITY — Susan Jones remembers the night that changed everything.

June 2006. She and her family were sitting in the drive-through line at the Coburg Road Dairy Queen.

And there she was: a homeless woman shuffling across the parking lot, pushing a baby stroller with her life on board.

Tall. Gray-haired. Maybe 50.

A woman easily recognized by regulars in that area, even without her usual two white dogs. A homeless woman whom I'd written a few columns about.

"I looked at her," Jones says, "and then just said it: 'That's my cousin Jayne!'"

Jones bolted from the Jeep and wrapped her in a hug. It had been at least a decade since she'd seen the woman whom she'd once idolized. In Jones' younger years, her cousin's many horse-show trophies had given her Scappoose home the feel of an equestrian hall of fame.

But now, as she looked at Jayne, she realized her cousin didn't recognize her. As Jones talked, she noted one brief connection. "It was like the someone I knew was way back there," she says. "There was a distant look in her eyes."

She knew that Jayne, like Jones' now-gone sister, had struggled with mental illness; still, it was frustrating to see her cousin so unnerved by their meeting. Jayne clearly wanted to move on.

"I offered her some money, asked her to come home and live with me, asked if there was anything I could do," Jones says.

Her cousin refused any help and pushed her stroller away.

Later that night, Jones began looking for her cousin. No luck.

The next morning she went to the Eugene Mission and St. Vincent de Paul's Eugene Service Station on Highway 99. Had they seen her? Nope.

Meanwhile, though, Jones was intrigued by St. Vinnie's. Her two kids were going to be on their own soon; she'd have more time. So, she decided to volunteer.

"The side benefit," Jones says, "was if Jayne showed up, I'd be there."

Jones never would find her cousin; she still doesn't know where Jayne is today. Instead, she found herself, which led to a connection of a different kind.

She changed her e-mail address to: inspiredbycousinjayne@comcast.net.

In October, when the church she attended, Eugene Faith Center, started a food pantry, Jones volunteered to head it up.

Six months later, when a Junction City partner agency of FOOD for Lane County was looking for a new director, Jones got the job.

A year from the time she'd met Jayne, she was executive director of Junction City Local Aid, which operates out of a 1,600-square-foot nook on Sixth Street.

"Some of our clients fit the same profile as my sister and cousin," Jones says. "I knew I couldn't reach my sister and Jayne, but I thought 'I can help other people like them.'"

She quickly made her mark. Says Kara Smith, FOOD for Lane County's agency relations coordinator: "Every time I have a new agency interested in becoming a partner, I show them Susan's setup. She runs things so smoothly, almost perfectly."

But the Junction City job quickly proved challenging. When the recession hit in 2008, Country Coach, Junction City's high-end motor home plant that had contributed half of the agency's $40,000 budget, went bankrupt.

Jones didn't retreat, even in a community where more than 20 percent of the population was getting help from the agency. She began working closely with the *Tri-County Tribune* and Tri-County Chamber of Commerce to better get the word out — not only for donations but for potential clients.

"Every flier we hand out has a 'donor' side and a 'client' side," says Jones, 52. "You can't assume which side of the flier people might be on."

Replacement money started coming in. When a $50,000 bequest arrived out of nowhere, the local aid board decided to use it as a down payment to buy, ironically, an old Country Coach service center offered at a tantalizing price.

Perfect, Jones figured, to help fuel her dream of making Junction City's poor less dependent on Eugene services.

The new digs offer five times the space. And the potential, Jones believes, to house other agencies whose focus is helping the poor.

"People in Junction City have a lack of access to programs they need," Jones says.

The building — the plan is to move in before April 1 — could be a catalyst to change that lack of access, she says. "To help us not just throw fish at people, but teach them to fish."

Once, FOOD for Lane County's Smith was meeting with Jones in the local aid's cubbyhole office.

"Who's this?" Smith asked when seeing a photograph of a woman and a horse.

"That woman," Jones said, "is the reason I'm here."

Always our parents' kids

June 19, 2011

On Wednesday night, I was sailing on a brisk wind at Fern Ridge Lake when — sparing you the nautical details — a bolt popped loose, meaning I'd suddenly lost partial control over that really big sail in the middle of the boat.

Not good.

I immediately did two things: Told myself not to panic. And thought of my father.

WWDD: What Would Dad Do?

On this Father's Day — 15 years since the summer he died — I'm reminded that regardless of our age, we are, as sons and daughters, always our parents' children.

It's a premise that some, even if they agree with, might regret. If you had a father who ignored, abandoned, abused or demanded too much of you, I can understand why you'd eschew any such connection.

Like his son, my father was far from perfect, but I still feel an odd assurance when I sense him, most often when I'm involved in one of three outdoor pursuits: sailing, fly fishing or backpacking — the things that connected us, if even tenuously, when I was young.

Our boat, *At Last,* is stem to stern with unwritten signs that say: "Your father was here." He built half a dozen boats; he was good with wood. But his genius lay not in perfection but in improvisation and innovation.

He once lengthened a 17-foot boat to 19 feet. Who does that — lengthens a boat?

He invented a system so you could more easily raise our current boat's 25-foot mast by yourself. When I'm using it, fellow sailors will sometimes stop by and offer a mixture of furrowed brows and wonder.

He could do more with a roll of duct tape than anybody I've known; for years, our mast light was affixed with the stuff.

But his boat handiwork also drives me bonkers. Earlier this spring, I was taking off a piece of teak and, of the 10 screws, six were Phillips and four were flatheads. Really, Dad? You couldn't have just gone with one or the other?

His tattered sailboat tool box — I came close to trashing it last month — is a rat's nest of nuts, bolts, tools, fittings and whatnot that I can hardly open or close, it's so full.

Among the things I shared at his memorial service was a paintbrush ensconced in hardened fiberglass; he was a better starter than finisher.

And yet when I stumble across such foibles, even if I might initially mutter "you gotta be kidding, Dad," I also embrace them as a reminder of a man I loved. And a man who I am more like than I sometimes want to admit.

A few weeks back, I needed to glue a piece of ½-inch plywood beneath a cockpit seat on which to mount a CD player. (My 84-year-old mother loves the wind in her sails with a touch of Jimmy Buffett.) But gravity was working against me. As the resin was drying, how could I exert pressure on the plywood so the seal would be tight?

WWDD? He'd do exactly what I did: use four drumsticks I had lying around — don't ask why — that, when cut to length, propped up the piece of wood perfectly. It worked, its unconventional bent reminding me of the man who had passed on this whatever-works gene.

My father was a simple man. He was fishing jokes and Heidelberg beer and squishy tennis shoes, much of his life spent launching boats and wading lakes and streams with his fly rod.

He was the smell of Prince Valiant pipe tobacco and Old Spice, the cologne of seemingly an entire generation until we Baby Boomers embraced the likes of Hawaiian Surf, English Leather and Brut.

In many ways, he was a loner. Not the guy in the group shot, but the guy behind the camera lens. (He was a commercial photographer.) Not a joiner or the life of the party, but someone you wanted there.

For years, Mom had a cartoon on the refrigerator showing a lone man sitting on a blanket with a sandwich in his hand. Beneath it: "(Warren Welch), self-employed, holds company picnic."

And, finally, he was a scatterer of tools. If you wanted a quarter-inch drill bit, you'd sooner find it beneath a spool of movie film in his photography darkroom or in a fishing creel than on his workbench.

Thus was my confidence at low ebb Wednesday night after I'd lowered the sails and pondered what kind of tool I'd need to get inside a 3-inch space and blindly tighten a bolt. I am, after all, my father's son.

My instinctive thought, of course, was duct tape, but that, obviously, would be no match for the force of a sail. Clawing through Dad's pregnant-with-neglect toolbox, I was beginning to lose hope.

Then I saw it: an L-shaped socket wrench and, after a bit more digging, a socket that fit.

The tool worked perfectly. I refastened the bolt. Raised the sails.

And thus did the father-son voyage continue.

Unconditional love

April 4, 2010

On Thursday night, I found myself in a south Eugene living room with 28 people who had husbands, boyfriends, sons or grandsons incarcerated in some state or federal prison. Or did so until recently.

When it was her turn to share, one woman said: "Our son is 41 and at OSCI (Oregon State Correctional Institute). He won't get out till he's 68, so he has 27 more years. But he's doing good. There've been no lockdowns lately, so that's good."

Among other things, Easter, Passover and spring are about hope. About promises fulfilled. Freedom secured. And warmth and sunshine replacing what we can only hope is winter's final curtain call. (Enough is enough.)

In short, about better days to come.

In this woman's words, I was reminded of the gritty power of the human spirit. And in the people around her, reminded of the strength of encouragement. Both of which help us abide until those "better days to come."

Here was a mother who was anticipating a day when her son would be free — nearly three decades from now, at a time when she might not even be alive. And here were people willing to support her willingness to hang in there.

Inspiring stuff, this. And, for me, inspiring stuff whose timing was perfect.

Let's face it: It's been a dark first quarter. Since January, we've seen Haitian children on the TV news wandering among their earthquake-ravaged homes, searching for parents they will never find. Heard of people we know who have lost jobs or have run out of work. Read newspaper reports of lifted Sieg Heils at Pacifica Forums and fallen football stars at the UO.

Last week, waiting to see a doctor about a nagging foot problem, I couldn't help overhear a man on his cell phone, a little boy at his side. "We have no choice," he told the person on the other end of the line. "We have to file for bankruptcy."

The previous week, I sat in an office at Doyle's Harley-Davidson in Eugene and listened to its manager talk about how "heartbreaking" it was to go through job applicants for menial jobs.

"It brought me to tears," says Victoria Doyle. "I have applications from men who have been laid off from jobs they held for 10 or 20 years and were making $50,000 a year. And they're willing to take $9.50 an hour."

To clean bathrooms. And wash motorcycles.

My job affords me the pain and privilege of seeing people's lives at ground zero. My week, for example, began with ex-KEZI anchor Rick Dancer, who recently learned he has cancer, showing up for an interview only hours after being told his mother had died. My week ended with a group of people grieving for their prodigal sons, some of whom have come home, some of whom have not.

In between, I interviewed Tamie Yarnall, the former Sheldon High drama coach whose horrific accident nearly eight years ago has scarred her so deeply, and her successor and friend, Lynda Czajkow-ska-Thompson, who recently learned she has terminal cancer.

You come to the end of a week like this and feel like a rafter whose craft has bounced and twisted through the rapids; suddenly, it's quiet and smooth. You're twirling in an eddy and think: What have I learned here?

That for all our differences, we're all in the same boat. And that although much of our lives are spent battling each other about health care, highway names, athletic prowess — you name it — we are, in the end, like the folks sitting in that living room.

People looking for hope. People who need encouragement. And people who have stepped up to be that encouragement.

It was one couple's first meeting. "You're not alone," someone told them. "We've all cried at some point or another."

That's how the circle is completed: Someone has the courage to ask for help. And someone has the compassion to say, "You got it."

Not that there won't be more rapids on down the river. But the lesson of this season — and the essence of Easter and Passover — is that you needn't face them alone.

Fathers who father

June 20, 2010

On this Father's Day, a few toasts to deserving dads:
Here's to a Eugene father I know who, as a way to spend more time with his 16-year-old daughter, trained with her for their own two-person triathlon, successfully completing it June 12. (He won the senior division, she the junior, earning a thrift-store trophy for her efforts.)

Here's to the father the two of them saw while doing their half-mile swim at the River Road Pool at Emerald Park: a guy patiently — and painstakingly — teaching his physically disabled son to swim.

Here's to guys celebrating Father's Day today for the first time. Invest in your children now so that by the time they're 3 they can reciprocate by, say, showing you how to download NPR podcasts onto your computer wristwatch or whatever they'll invent by then.

Here's to soccer dads and baseball dads and swimming dads who don't have time to coach but make time anyway. (Remember: Nobody on his deathbed ever said, "I wished I'd spent more time at the office — or on Facebook.")

And here's to fathers who listen to their children practice music — and, regardless of the quality, are convinced the kid is Mozart.

Here's to the father who sat behind me at "Kids Night" at PK Park on May 29 (Oregon-California) — and not only spent half a week's salary on food for his kids but didn't blame them when their animal balloons popped.

And here's to fathers who allow their sons or daughters to bury them in beach sand. On the Oregon Coast. In one of those biting winds that makes your head feel like a snow cone.

Here's to fathers of prodigal sons or daughters who have left home. Never give up on them. Or yourself.

And here's to fathers who yell encouragement from the sidelines instead of ragging on officials and embarrassing their child and anyone else supporting their child's team.

Here's to a friend in San Diego who, while toasting his daughter at her wedding in April, honored her for, instead of speed-dating her way through life, patiently saving herself for one good man.

And to a Eugene father-of-the-bride who, after walking his daughter down the aisle, presented her with a pearl necklace — only to realize that the groom had one-upped him with a diamond necklace that she already was wearing. Not skipping a beat, the father bent down and carefully wrapped it around his daughter's ankle.

Here's to good fathers who care enough to take a Birth To Three class and become even better fathers.

And to fathers who were handed legacies of shame but courageously broke those chains and started a new legacy for their children.

Here's to fathers who, like us all, have blown it with their kids. In the words of the great philosopher Elton John: "Sorry seems to be the hardest word." But it also might be the most powerful.

Here's to fathers who, in a trying economy, are working a job — or hours — they don't particularly like in order to support their families.

And here's to fathers whose dads have passed on. Remember the good times (knee football in the living room on Sunday nights), learn from the bad and, for character-building nourishment, be thankful for both.

Here's to a doctor I know who'll celebrate Father's Day in Haiti — with two of his daughters scrubbing in to help him serve hundreds of patients in need.

Here's to fathers who say yes to crazy stuff — say, snow angels en route home from Bend.

And to fathers who care enough to say no to their children when necessary.

Here's to grandfathers who, because of their own sons' inability to do so, have stepped up to be, in essence, fathers to their grandchildren. In 2007, the U.S. Census reported that 2.5 million men — about 42 filled-to-the-rim Autzen Stadiums — fit that description.

And here's to those who, in a similar vein, serve as mentors to children without a father in their life. There's honor in that.

Here's to fathers who wear the camouflage in Iraq or Afghanistan or somewhere else far from home and, today, will miss their children even more than most days. Thanks for your willingness to be away from your families.

And here's to fathers who are safe at home while their sons and daughters serve in the armed forces overseas. May those children — and the rest of the troops — soon be like him: safe at home.

Here's to stepfathers. There are easier jobs, aren't there? I remember once gently warning mine to have my mother home by midnight.

(Never mind that she was 75 at the time.)

Here's to fathers who have lost sons or daughters, like the man who lost his son in Iraq and, I noticed, left a fishing lure by the young man's headstone at Springfield Memorial Cemetery.

Here's to hip fathers who r trying 2 keep up with their children on the L8tes technology, even if it is 2 little 2 L8.

And, finally, here's to fathers who don't know a tweet from a twit but realize this universal truth:

You don't need a keyboard to say "I love you."

A grandfather's lesson

Nov. 26, 2009

> *As fish are caught in a cruel net, or birds are taken in a snare, so men are trapped by evil times that fall unexpectedly upon them.*
> — Ecclesiastes 9:12

How do you give thanks when, it might appear, there's little to be thankful for? How do you show appreciation for the freedom that's synonymous with America when you might feel like a bird in a snare?

They are questions that Ernest Yamada may have considered on Thanksgiving 1942, hunkered down on the desolate plains of southeast Colorado.

"It has snowed twice," he wrote to a friend back in California. "Sometimes the cold north wind from Wyoming blew so hard that I was chilled to the bone and the knife I was holding blew away inches from where I intended to cut."

Yamada, 43 at the time, was referring to harvesting beets, which, he said, were "froze like rocks."

He, his wife, Lillie, and their two small boys were among 7,000 Japanese-Americans and Japanese interned at Camp Amache, in Granada, Colo., near the Kansas line.

After the Pearl Harbor attack drew the United States into World War II, they had become the enemy back home.

His grandson, Greg Yamada of Eugene, shared the man's story with me.

Ernest was a U.S. citizen because he was born in Hawaii, at the time a U.S. territory. His parents were Japanese.

In 1918, he enlisted in the Army. And afterward earned a degree in marketing from the University of California at Berkeley — not a common thing for Asians amid the racism of the 1920s. Eventually, the family settled in Los Angeles. "Japs Keep Moving," read a sign over a Hollywood area house back then. "This is a White Man's Neighborhood."

Ernest landed a job as a supervisor for a company that distributed farm products to Eastern markets. He married in 1928. And became a father of two boys, one of whom, Ed, would someday be Greg Yamada's father.

After the move to Los Angeles, Ernest languished as the Depression leveled three retail businesses he'd established. He scraped out a living by mowing lawns and cleaning houses. Joined the American Legion and a Methodist church. And hiked and swam with Lillie and the boys.

Then, three months after Pearl Harbor, came the edict: Japanese-American and Japanese people — 120,000 in all — were to be moved to "War Relocation Camps." For the Yamadas, that meant Colorado.

Like other interned families, they lived in a 20-by-25-foot room with bare floors and little furniture. Ate in a mess hall. And were guarded by armed soldiers in towers.

And yet there was no bitterness in his letter from Thanksgiving 1942. "We are thankful for many things and we accept the day in that spirit," he wrote. "We are pioneers, not in the same sense as American pioneers who went through so much physical hardships, but pioneers in a more subtle human relationship, arising out of racial differences, customs and culture.

"If the doctrine of brotherhood is the goal of Christian Religion, and the fusion of different cultures and molding them into that ultimate high ideal which God preaches and democracy strives for, then we shall strive to contribute, however small in measure."

After reading the letter, Greg shakes his head. "I don't know that I could be so gracious. Our generation expects so much, the right to this or that. I find his words pretty amazing, considering where he was in life — his hopes and dreams squashed by circumstances beyond his control."

The family was released in 1943 and, after the war ended, returned to Los Angeles.

Ernest kept records of possessions, including his 1936 Oldsmobile

Coupe, that he had to give up; by the family's return, they had lost more than $25,000 worth of items in today's dollars.

In many ways, says Greg, the man's life was tattered with unfulfilled aspirations — a college graduate who mowed lawns, cleaned houses and, after the war, dabbled in silk-screen and photography.

He died in 1964 at age 65 from contaminated blood after routine surgery. But his legacy endures in the words of a letter Greg sent out last Thanksgiving to extended family.

A reminder of an honor that endured amid evil times.

Together to the end

Oct. 23, 2011

They were nobody special and everybody special — particularly to a Kelly Junior High School kid back in the 1950s.

David and Anne Shulda.

I never knew them. You probably didn't either.

They were relatively obscure folks. Lived out in the River Road area. He drove a truck for Coca-Cola. She was a homemaker.

They were the kind of people whose obituaries you might scan and think, hmmm, then go on to the next one.

Until, that is, you realized — as you might, if you look on Page B4 today — that their obituaries are merged as one.

I suppose I should back up to the beginning. David and Anne were both born in New Britain, Conn., Anne on Oct. 26, 1924, David on May 19, 1927.

They married in 1955 and — along with Anne's 13-year-old son, Tom, from a previous marriage — moved to Eugene, where David had a brother.

Which is where that Kelly Junior High kid comes into the story.

At age 13, Russ Busey never figured he'd someday be the power of attorney for the Shuldas' estate. He just knew that their son, Tom, was his new pal from the East Coast and that the Shuldas were one fun family.

"My dad was 40 when I was born and my mom 30," Busey says, "so while I liked my family, the Shuldas were more fun. Lighthearted. And were just much more outgoing. Anne called me their second son."

David was a Mason, a Duck fan and, along with Anne, a big believer in donating to Third World organizations such as Heifer International and the Eugene-based Makindu Children's Program.

The Shuldas had deep ties to their church, St. Matthew's Episcopal on River Road.

Until, that is, the church was torn down to make room for the new Belt Line Road in the 1960s. But the Shuldas didn't skip a beat. St. Matthew's members merged with St. Thomas Episcopal Church on Coburg Road.

"It was like we were the city mouse and they were the country mouse," says Nancy Muhlheim, a St. Thomas member who became casual friends with them. "Dave and Anne were strong members, all about leadership and loyalty. Both Dave and I became ordained deacons."

When another church member, Mabel Chadwick, died, St. Matthew's was born again; Mabel had donated her estate to rebuild the church at its current location, 4110 River Road.

"Talk about the power of the grave!" Muhlheim says.

The Shuldas attended there for years, then moved on to the Episcopal Church of St. John the Divine in Springfield.

"Deacons are about feeding the widows and orphans," Muhlheim says. "Dave was all about that. He had a passion for the Triangle Lake Camp and Conference Center." Helped promote it. Helped build it.

Meanwhile, Tom and Russ graduated from North Eugene and went on to the University of Oregon. Russ went off on his own, started a family and lived in such places as Chicago and England, winding up in Ontario. Tom never married and lived in west Eugene.

Decades passed. In 2010, at age 65, Tom died of heart failure.

It shook the Shuldas. So did the news that the Episcopal camp at Triangle Lake was closing. "Very hard on David," Muhlheim says.

But he and Anne kept clinging to each other. "With no other relatives alive, the two became each other's support," Muhlheim says. "They were in it for the long run."

With Tom gone, the Shuldas asked Russ, now 69, to be their power of attorney. He considered it an honor.

For years, Anne — she turned 86 last October — had been experiencing health problems. Severe enough that David began making some arrangements with Musgrove Family Mortuary.

But three months ago, David's health started failing, too. He was 84. He ping-ponged from care center to the hospital. "Anne was worried that he'd go first and she'd be lost without him," Busey says.

Meanwhile, Anne bounced between hospital and care center, too, winding up at Sacred Heart Medical Center at RiverBend after a blackout. She then had a stroke and went into a coma.

Muhlheim, who'd been checking in on both David and Anne, got a call Oct. 15 from Avamere River Park rehab center. David didn't have much time.

Muhlheim was with him when he died that Saturday at 10:47 a.m.

Later that day, she went to visit Anne. A volunteer whose voice Anne knew passed on the news that David — they'd been married 56 years — had died.

Nobody knows whether she heard it, but she died less than two hours later.

13.
Christmas

A stolen memory

Feb. 26. 2012

At the state Children's Services Division in Eugene where she worked, Judith Dowe Knudtson placed the new turquoise wallet on her desk.

It was late December 1975.

A younger sister, Karen, of Salem, had given her the wallet, the only present the single mother got for Christmas that year.

Judy, 34, transferred the contents of her old wallet into the new one, then took out three plastic monogrammed letters — J.E.D. for Judith Elaine Dowe — and glued them to the outside.

For a woman searching for an identity, they weren't much, those letters, but they were something. They represented a woman who, like the mothers and children she dealt with at work each day, had lived through some struggles.

When she was three days old her father, a farmer near Salem, had died after being dragged beneath a tractor tire by snagged clothing.

A stepfather later died after being in an automobile accident.

Though an honor student at North Salem High School, Judy quit as a 17-year-old junior to marry a Navy-bound sailor and start life anew in California.

After a divorce 13 years later, she returned to Oregon with two suitcases and two sons. John was 12, Russell, 6. In 1972, they settled in Eugene.

Judy worked in a vegetarian restaurant downtown. Took classes in nutrition and medical management at Lane Community College.

She supplemented food stamp purchases by canning fruit and vegetables given to her by a food bank. The boys bathed with soap slivers the size of potato chips.

Because she had a heart for single moms — certainly she'd seen her own mother struggle — Judy landed a $600-a-month job assisting caseworkers at Children's Services at the southwest corner of West 11th Avenue and Lincoln Street. Still, she sold Avon products on the side to make ends meet.

Now, with the monogrammed letters still tacky from the glue, she left the wallet on her desk to dry — it had no money in it — and took her lunch to the break room around the corner.

When she returned 15 minutes later, the wallet was gone.

What hurt wasn't losing the contents; she had no credit cards and could put a stop on her checks.

It wasn't even the pain of presuming a co-worker had ripped her off. (Clients were off-limits in her area.)

No, what hurt was that this was the one Christmas present she'd gotten, given to her by someone she cared about deeply.

She began to cry.

Thirty-six years later, the phone call caught her off guard. Judy, now 71, lives in the Washington Abbey apartments with her second husband, Rollin Knudtson. The call was from a nephew, Charlie Dowe, whom she hadn't spoken with in years. A newspaper columnist — me — had called him, trying to track her down. Something about a wallet of hers having been found.

On Feb. 8, a crew working for McKenzie Commercial Contractors had found a dirty but dry turquoise wallet while ripping out the floor of a building being renovated at the southwest corner of West 11th and Lincoln.

McKenzie owner Todd Glenz called and asked if I wanted to track down the owner. I like a good mystery. I took the wallet, saw the name on the driver's license, and after a few hours of Googling and phoning, connected with the nephew, who began making calls himself. Two days later Judy called me.

At first, she didn't remember the wallet. Then it all came back.

Over the phone — and with her permission — I described the contents that I hadn't gone through yet: a $5 uncashed check to her for Avon products, a Bi-Mart card issued July 5, 1974, three 13-cent "Airmail" stamps, six 10-cent regular stamps — stuff that brought back memories for Judy.

She had business cards reminding her that she'd had her hair done at the Curl E Que beauty salon on West 11th. Was a member of Radio shack's "battery club." And wrote checks of $8.50 to National Geographic and $37.15 to EWEB.

She remarried in 1991, retired after 25 years at Children's Services and is still mom to John, 52, and Russell, 45 — and sister to Karen, who lives in Salem.

Would she like to see where the wallet was found, I asked. "Love to," Judy said.

An hour later, with Glenz, we were at the office — or the shell of the office — where she had once worked.

In 1975, the year Judy's wallet went missing, a Children's Services office renovation put a second floor on the building; a 16-inch space separated the roof of the old building from the floor of the new part. It's likely that the wallet was dropped between the two before the project was sealed up, because that's where it was found.

Presumably, it was placed there by someone who thought it would never be discovered.

"I had no idea who did it," Judy says. "I didn't feel suspicious about people, I just felt sad."

And now that it's been found?

"It's not the wallet that matters," she says. "It's just seeing it again and being reminded that my sister gave it to me as my only Christmas present."

She paused. "That," she says, "makes me happy."

Christmas cheer

Dec. 13, 2009

Like last year, the money was handed to me in a bank envelope: Twenty $50 bills. One thousand dollars. My instructions: Spread some Christmas cheer. Get the money to the "street level" in a way the giver, who insists on anonymity, wouldn't have time to do.

Which is why I was at the Springfield United Parcel Service warehouse Thursday night, where it was so cold you could see your breath — inside. Workers hustled around in coats and gloves, loading packages as less romantic versions of Santa's elves.

I wanted to reward such an elf. And when I heard about a woman who works two jobs — this one at night — and commutes from a town an hour away, she sounded worthy.

I handed her a $50 bill and explained that this is the second year this anonymous "Santa" has commissioned me to help him out.

She hugged me — by proxy, him.

Not everyone, of course, is as effusive when receiving no-catch money. Take the University of Oregon student at the Greyhound Bus Depot who had just finished finals and was heading for Portland to see an aunt. She took the $50, but with great suspicion.

I headed over to Hawthorne's Cafe & Deli where I gave a woman behind the counter a $50 bill and told her this was for however many customers in line it would cover — after she and a co-worker split a $10 tip.

I wanted to wait around and see people's reactions, but that's not the point. The point is to seed the community with this anonymous giver's good will toward others — regardless of the receivers' reactions.

But let's be honest: Giving feels better when the receiver accepts the gift with a certain graciousness. And yet how can you predict who's going to pay the kindness forward and who's going to use the $50 to get drunk and contribute whatever's left to the USC Athletic Fund?

So, yes, while some of my receivers were random choices — the first Dari-Mart employee I saw in the Harlow Road store — at times I narrowed the playing field.

At UO's Knight Library, open all night during finals week, I thought it would be nice to reward some hard-studying student. I spent 45 minutes walking the library's four levels and couldn't make a choice. Weird, I know.

But though tempted to give it to the kid in the "I Break for Pizza" shirt — obviously a kindred spirit — I wanted to pick someone who would have been my financier's "chosen one." So I returned the next day.

Finally, I found a first-floor librarian who pointed me to a young woman who "studies here all the time."

I handed her the $50. Her face lit up. She is, I learned, a Family & Human Services major who volunteers at the White Bird Clinic. "This," she said, "will get paid forward, I promise you."

I bought breakfast for two young men at The Pump Cafe in Springfield and for whoever paid their bill next at Teresa's Place down the street. Gave $50 to a young father at Target looking to buy his daughter a wooden train set for Christmas. And, at the Gateway post office, hid a $20 bill in the slot for the next person who decides to use an Express Mail form.

At the Eugene/Lane County WorkSource office on Oakmont Way, I gave $50 to a 61-year-old, out-of-work forester. "Thanks," he said. "Not much out there." And tracked down the two guys responsible for putting up the "Peace on Earth" sign atop the Ya-Po-Ah Terrace — one of my Christmastime favorites — and gave them $50 to split.

But the most memorable moment of Phase I came under the Washington-Jefferson Street Bridge when — fresh from dropping

$85.47 at Bi-Mart — I handed two homeless women and a man three sleeping bags, three stocking hats, three pairs of socks and gloves. Plus, $15 each in gift cards from Dutch Bros. Coffee.

"Gloves?" said one woman, her hands bare despite mid-20s temperatures. "New gloves?"

If all you'd seen were her eyes, you'd have sworn it was Christmas morning.

Giving at street level

Dec. 19, 2010

So, there I was Thursday morning, standing at the eastbound exit from Highway 126 onto Pioneer Parkway in Springfield, holding a cardboard sign.

"$10 bills," it said. "1 Per Driver. Just Ask! Happy Holidays."

Giving away money, I was about to learn, is not as easy as you might think.

I was about two-thirds through the $1,000 that an anonymous donor gives to me each year to dole out to people at the "street level" when, I figured: What's more "street level" than this?

I put on sunglasses, wrapped the hood of a hoody sweatshirt around my face and hit the street.

Nothing. Few drivers would even look at me or my sign, even when, with a Vanna White sweep of the hand, I would highlight the "Just ask." Even when I mouthed the words, "I'm giving money to you!"

Clearly, there were no fish in this hole. I left for better waters, soon casting away at the westbound exit off Randy Papé Beltline and Coburg Road, near Costco. (Such exits with left-hand turns allow you easy access to driver-side windows.)

Nothing again, which surprised me. I didn't expect car-after-car success, but I thought my goal — unloading 10 $10 bills in 10 minutes — was reachable.

Desperate, I headed for the eastbound exit of this same interchange, just north of the Heeran Center.

Brian Caldwell, 50, was already working the much-coveted corner but I had leverage. Caldwell, who said he'd recently been laid off work at Sundance Lumber Co. in Springfield, said he was getting about $20 a day in handouts.

I offered him $10 if he'd lease me his spot for 15 minutes. Deal.

Nothing. The traffic was heavier than that at the other two exits, but people weren't biting.

"You know," said Caldwell, "you might do better with the wording you have on the other side of your sign."

On that side I'd written "Free $10 bills: One per driver."

"I think that word 'free' might help," he said.

I paid him a $10 consulting fee and went to work. Bingo. I started getting some action.

"Seriously?" said a woman.

I handed her a $10 bill.

"This is amazing" she said. "I just dropped off chocolate truffles for the homeless. Now I've got money to make more. This is like 'pay-it-forward!'"

The drivers of perhaps one in every half dozen cars would roll down the window. Most said, "What's the catch?"

"No catch," I'd say. "Just spreading holiday cheer."

And they'd take the money and smile.

Just before my 15-minute lease was up, I gave away my last bill, thanks to Caldwell's marketing insight.

There were tougher spots to spread holiday cheer. I bought 20 $2.50 gift cards from Perk and Play Coffeehouse on Crescent Drive to cheer up the long-faced folks in the Gateway Post Office line, which had been 30-people long earlier in the week. Alas, an employee told me that handing out gift cards was against regulations.

I went down the street to the Oregon State Police's Springfield regional headquarters and asked if I could give the troopers and office folks $50 worth of coffeehouse gift cards to say thanks. "That might be against regulations," a woman told me.

She returned a few minutes later with a smile. "The lieutenant says thank you."

Bingo! Speaking of which, earlier in the week, at the Oregon-Jacksonville State basketball game at McArthur Court, I'd decided to give $50 to one of the Daisy Ducks volunteers who sells bingo cards.

Given their involvement in a game of chance, I chose three people and told them I'd give the money to whoever came closest to picking the Bingo letter I was thinking of. Sharon Bowman won — but not before a sudden death playoff in which she correctly chose the "O" that, naturally, I had in mind.

During Tuesday afternoon's wet and windy weather, I passed out $5 Full City Coffee Roasters gift cards to the first five people I saw working outside: a city of Eugene surveyor; two Skinner City Farm volunteers, on bikes, hauling leftovers from restaurants to be composted; and two Living Concepts Landscape Services guys working at 11th Avenue and High Street.

At LTD's Springfield Station I "adopted" all the people in the "G" bay waiting for a bus, handing out 10 $10 bills. (One man declined, saying, "I have a lot of stuff going on" and not elaborating.)

Finally, I stopped by Bi-Mart and bought four pairs of gloves and socks, plus stocking caps, for the homeless folks under the Washington-Jefferson Street Bridge. The temperature on this Friday morning was near freezing.

Suffice it to say that not only did they not ignore my offer, but one smothered me in what — given his size and the empties at his feet — I can only call a beer hug.

"Merry Christmas, man," he said.

Made merrier, of course, by people like our anonymous $1,000 donor — and others of you who quietly help folks at the street level.

Remembering the kids

Dec. 25, 2012

As I left to hand out the second half of $2,000 worth of Christmas cheer given me by two anonymous donors, the tragedy at Sandy Hook tore into the lives of a Connecticut community.

I decided to give away the remaining money in honor of each life lost at Sandy Hook Elementary School on Dec. 14. I would donate only in increments of 26 — in honor of the 20 children and six educators who died.

I had no particular plan. I just went where I felt led, which is why I wound up at Creswell City Hall.

"Can I pay for someone who's behind on some sort of payment?" I asked.

In turned out that this day — last Thursday — was "shut off" day for people who were a few months behind on their water payments. One such place was The Growing Place, which offers a preschool and child care.

Ten minutes later, I walked into the place on North Mill Street. A little boy and girl were playing with Tinker Toy-like thingamajigs, the embodiment of innocence. My mind flashed to Sandy Hook.

I explained to owner Holly Powell who I was and how two individuals had deputized me as their traveling elf.

"I've paid the $209.50 for your preschool's water bill," I said. "And paid ahead $50.50 on next month's bill. A total of $260, in honor of the Sandy Hook victims."

Powell melted into tears and hugged me.

I was still in a "kids" mood when I went to the Creswell Library and donated $260 to the "Catharyn L. Pilaczynski Books for Kids Memorial Fund."

In Springfield, I was drawn to the Animal Urgent Care clinic, 103 West Q St., where I learned a woman's miniature pinscher had nearly died a year ago after eating a foreign object. She'd been making payments, but was still far behind. I paid $260 to help her get caught up.

On Gateway, I was leaving the Dari Mart when a rough-hewn guy asked if I had a cigarette.

"No, but I've got $26 for you in honor of the students and teachers killed at Sandy Hook," I said.

The man took the money and immediately bowed his head and folded his arms crossways to pray for the children and their families.

"Merry Christmas," I said.

In front of Sacred Heart Medical Center at RiverBend, I gave a woman who'd just gotten off a bus $26 and, later, $26 to the crew at Delta Oaks Little Caesars after I picked up a pizza.

At Campbell U-Cut Trees on River Road between Santa Clara and Junction City, I told a worker standing in a downpour that I wanted to pay $26 each for the next two customers' trees.

I handed him $80. "And you can keep the change."

Part of giving is trusting people who might help you pay it forward. But I drove away feeling uneasy.

In Junction City, I saw a woman crossing the Dollar Store parking lot. She was pulling what looked to be her life belongings in a suitcase on wheels.

She turned down my offer of $26. "Give it to someone who's homeless," she said.

Inside the store, I left $52 to pay for two shoppers' totals.

"Hey, this is really cool," said the manager.

Outside the Junction City Goodwill store, I saw a woman and her elementary school-age daughter heading toward their 1972 Chevrolet pickup truck.

"How many people in your family?" I asked.

"Three."

"OK, here's $78 — $26 for each of you."

"I'm in shock," she said.

I left $26 at Nina's Pony Express in Junction City — to pay for $20 worth of drinks for the next few customers and a $6 administrative fee to the barista, then headed for home.

As I drove past Campbell U-Cut Trees, I thought of stopping again to see if — and to whom — he'd paid the money forward for the trees.

Naw. Giving always involves a certain amount of risk; there are no guarantees that generosity will be paid forward.

The next day, I had just started writing this column when I got the phone call. It was from a Eugene woman, Marion Foley, whose husband of 64 years, John, had died shortly after Thanksgiving.

Her son, David, and his wife, Gayle, of Montana, chose to stay on after the memorial service so she wouldn't be alone for Christmas. But even with their presence — and that of their dog, Pugsley — she told me this was looking like a bleak Christmas.

"I was feeling very sad," she said, "and then I went to the Campbell Tree Farm, where my husband and I had gone for nearly 30 years to pick out our favorite tree."

Hers, she was told by a worker there, was free; it had been bought by some columnist at *The Register-Guard*.

"You made my December a little happier," she told me. "Thank you so much."

I might have helped, but the real givers here were the people who donated the $2,000 — and the honest man at Campbell who paid it forward.

Once home, I realized I'd made an error on my spreadsheet and still had $186 to give away.

I figured my two donors would approve. The online payment was to United Way of Western Connecticut for the "Sandy Hook School Support Fund."

14.
Losses

Hope amid the hurt

Nov. 25, 2010

After the losses. After the horrific way in which they occurred. After the headlines and heartache and hollowness, you could understand why, only two months removed from that tragic last day of summer, Jennifer Flannery wouldn't be big on giving thanks.

But on this Thanksgiving Day, I'm reminded of that adage about how crisis reveals character. And how much she clearly must have.

Because Flannery does want to give thanks.

It began with a simple e-mail Tuesday from a friend of Jennifer's, Susan Stafford, with a one-word subject heading: "Gratitude."

"On the night of September 19-20 Aidan and Eryn Rauscher died at the hand of their father," it began.

Flannery, 37, has received such an outpouring of support from the community, the e-mail said, that she wanted to find a way to say thanks.

For the Oak Hill School teachers and families who fed her and supported her nightly for a month, then showed up to help clean out and organize Flannery's house.

For Moira Kilte and Johnna Charbonneau, parents of Oak Hill kids, who spearheaded the organization of the memorial.

And for the volunteers who did so much to make the service so meaningful.

If you follow local news, you know the reason for the memorial service. The story slammed the community like a sneaker wave, one of those this-doesn't-happen-here crimes that happened here.

It was a double murder-suicide. Flannery's estranged husband, Richard Rauscher, 47, shot the couple's two daughters, Aidan, 9, and Eryn, 7, then himself at the house south of Junction City where all had once lived. Flannery had filed for divorce in August and moved to Eugene with the children.

After such an emotional pounding, many of us wouldn't have the strength to see beyond our own pain, much less the desire to make others feel appreciated. But Flannery, who admits she's still "in a fog," wants people to know how much they've mattered to her:

The city of Eugene Planning & Development Department employees, who brought food — "even a homemade cake," says Jennifer

— while work was being done on her 1936 farm house, which is now on the market.

The Oregon Medical Group's Center for Women's Health, whose employees offered food, support and elbow grease in cleaning the house.

And the people of First Congregational Church who have welcomed her.

Oregon novelist Jane Kirkpatrick knows about pain. She's survived a small-plane crash, lost a sister and once received word about a stepson who'd been murdered, his killer never found.

In her book, "A Simple Gift of Comfort," she refers to Margaret Mead on the subject of healing — and those who help us do it.

"She wrote that the earliest signs of civilization are not the tools or bowls uncovered from the dust of time, but the discovery of healed bones found within the caves or graves ... That a bone could break and heal meant someone had to care enough to carry water, bring in food, fend off enemies, encourage, and daily move the injured from their pallets ... "

Clearly, a lot of "someones" have been there for Flannery. Someones such as:

John Fisher, an attorney, and Bobbie Rosenberg, a certified public accountant, who've given hours of no-fee help.

Tiffany Roseboro, who rounded up gift certificates from places such as the Olive Garden and Café Yumm! And Bella Day Spa, which pampered her for free.

That people naturally step up in such situations is hardly a given, particularly when the loss is so traumatic. Scott Wiggins, whose wife, Susan Stafford, is a triage nurse with Flannery at the Center for Women's Health, knows well.

His father committed suicide when Scott was only 4, a death that, because of religious tension, split the family. Instead of supporting his mother, others ostracized her, even blamed her.

"I still remember running to my grandfather in a grocery store and having him push me away," Wiggins says.

So helping out Jennifer — he's done much of the carpentry work to fix up her house — has been, for him, a chance to right the wrongs of the past. To embrace someone instead of shame them.

Others have done the same:

Hardware and home-improvement stores that have donated material.

Cabinet crews and painters and the like who have donated their time.

And "the whole Mainard tribe," Flannery says, friends who painted the outside of her house and helped with the estate sale.

"I had awesomely amazing children," Flannery says. "OK, Eryn could be a troublemaker at times, but in a good way. So, yeah, I've had a horrible couple of months."

She pauses, gathers the gumption to say words I presume aren't easily said.

"But I've also been blessed. This is an amazing place, Eugene. People I know, people I've never met — so many have stepped up."

People such as:

Volunteers from Oak Street Child Development Center, led by Lisa Wilnau, spearheaded the estate sale.

Wiggins, Stafford and other friends, for all sorts of support.

Family members such as her brother, Sean Nobel Flannery and sister-in-law Amanda Nobel Flannery, with whom she now lives. And others too numerous to list.

One Thanksgiving you are a mother of two children, the next you are a childless mother.

"What people have done for me can't take the pain away," Flannery says. "But it does this: It gives me hope."

And hope is something to be thankful for.

The final shot

July 11, 2010

Some people get one last shot in life.

Donald DeLutis' shot came July 3 when, in the second quarter of an international seniors basketball game at Springfield High School, the 76-year-old investment adviser arched a three-pointer from the top of the key.

Swish.

Minutes later, the San Francisco man lay dead of a heart attack.

"He died with his Air Jordans on," says teammate Ira Glick, a professor at the Stanford University School of Medicine.

Who was this player who became a tragic footnote to the nine-day Pan-American Maxibasketball Championship tournament that ended

Saturday?

About twice the age at which the average NBA player retires — and still playing the game he loved — DeLutis was clearly a man for all seasons, basketball being only one of them.

DeLutis was chairman of Orrell Capital Management Inc.

"He was so diverse that he could speak to royalty or to the street cleaner with equal ease," says his widow, Ruth DeLutis.

Literally.

On money matters, he advised such notables as British royalty, the Reagan administration and Charles Schwab, the billionaire founder of the Charles Schwab Corp.

And yet it was also DeLutis who befriended 6-foot-10 Anthony "Bones" Davis, a former Harlem Globetrotters player who was sweeping basketball floors at Kezar Auditorium when the two first met.

"He didn't have a penny to his name," Glick says of Davis.

DeLutis took Davis under his wing, got him involved with the NorCal Sharks senior basketball team, drove him to games, even paid for him to fly to the occasional out-of-state tournament.

"He was very generous," Davis says. "One of the nicest people I've ever met."

"On or off the court, Don always saw the bigger picture," Glick says. "His strategy was maximizing the individual talents of those around him. On the court, he was always advocating for us to set picks for each other, help get the guy open. Same way off the court. Very involved, for example, in Catholic charities."

A saint? No, his widow, Ruth, says. But the type of guy who cast a shadow far beyond his 6-foot-2 frame. A visionary, particularly in his ability to see the big economic picture.

"People would tell him he predicted something 30 years ago and it had come true," says Ruth, who directs an extended-care program for a Catholic school. "And yet the people who've been so devastated by his death have been the everyday people he'd chit-chat with at the Silver Clouds restaurant a few blocks from our house."

The DeLutises have lived on a street heavily sprinkled with million-dollar houses and own a place in Palm Desert. And yet, those who knew him say Don never lost sight of those who weren't as fortunate.

He served on the board of the Salesian Boys and Girls Club of San Francisco for more than 20 years.

"Don could fit into any group he wanted," Ruth says. "His mother was a hairdresser, used to talking to all kinds of different people."

His father was managing editor of the *Rome Sentinel* in New York.

Don DeLutis played basketball at Niagara University, then attended graduate school at Boston College.

He was politically conservative and culturally broad, a regular at symphonies, theater and opera events. And was known to belt out some spirited Italian songs at open-mike restaurants. "He thought he was the new Dean Martin," Ruth says.

"One of the best and brightest," says Glick, a psychiatrist. "One of the smartest guys I've ever met. And extremely competitive."

After decades as an investment adviser — and helping raise a son, Dante, now 35 — DeLutis suffered a heart attack about 11 years ago. But five years ago he decided to return, competitively, to the sport he loved: basketball.

The Sharks emerged as one of the best senior teams on the West Coast, winning Arizona's 75-plus tournament last year. "It was a new lease on life for him," Ruth says.

"And him getting me involved was the same thing for me," Davis says. "He reinvigorated my life."

DeLutis not only played on the NorCal team, he was its captain, travel arranger and uniform designer.

"He was pumped for the tournament in Oregon," Ruth says.

The Sharks were playing a team called USA 75+ in the opening round.

"I gave him a pass, cut right, came back, looked over to the left side of the court and he was slumped over a chair on the bench," Glick says. "He's the only guy I'll ever meet who hit a three-pointer within minutes of his life's end."

"As hard as this is," Ruth says, "if you have to go, this was, for him, the perfect way."

The Sharks forfeited the game and decided it best to withdraw from the tournament.

DeLutis' memorial service was Friday at Saints Peter and Paul Church in San Francisco. Standing room only. "I couldn't handle it," says "Bones" Davis, who said he broke down during the service. "I had to leave out a side door."

Which reminds us: What people really remember about us isn't how we die, but how we lived.

Officer down

May 15, 2011

Shortly before I show up for the interview at her rural home north of Springfield, Kristie Kilcullen finds the words scrawled a few pages into a blank notepad:

"I love you, sweetie."

They were, of course, from him: her husband, Chris Kilcullen, the 43-year-old Eugene police officer who was shot and killed April 22 by a motorist he'd pulled over on Highway 126 in Springfield.

Not far away sits a box of hundreds of letters and sympathy cards that have poured in from strangers. From widows of other officers killed in the line of duty. From school kids — "my favorites," Kristie says. From "sweet little old ladies" who might include a $10 check for her two kids' scholarship fund.

So, on the notepad: a reminder of the man she's lost. In the box of mail: a reminder of the support she never knew she had.

Grief and gratitude amid what she calls the "fog" of instant widowhood.

"I'm not sure 'comforting' is the right word regarding the outpouring because my heart is so broken right now," says Kilcullen, 40. "I'm not sure anything can comfort me. But it's touched me. Deeply."

In some ways, even overwhelmed her: learning, for example, that the University of Oregon had donated Matthew Knight Arena for her husband's memorial service.

On the night before the memorial service, walking into a room at EPD's command center to see dozens of law enforcement officers who'd arrived from around the state to help organize the procession and service. "All these people who gave up a week of their lives and kids' baseball games," she says. "I wanted to hug every one of them."

Seeing, from inside the limo during the procession, a throng of people lined up on the Mohawk Boulevard overpass across Highway 126. Then, after fearing less community support in Eugene, finding herself pleasantly surprised. Among those paying their respects: a man in the Whiteaker neighborhood whom her husband had arrested before, hoisting a beer in his honor.

Opening a bill from McKenzie Disposal. "Our heartfelt condolences," it said. No payment needed.

Hearing the sound of a car outside and realizing it's another daily meal being brought to the family by Lane County law enforcement families; the schedule runs through early July.

Realizing that the May 6 Dutch Bros. Coffee fundraiser brought in $61,000 to fund scholarships for her two children. And that more than 3,200 people have stamped their approval on a Facebook site to have that stretch of Highway 126 named in her husband's honor.

Being surrounded by an entourage of family and friends and Chris' co-workers, there to serve and protect.

All of which feels good, she says, until she sees the Rock Band drum set in the corner of the family room and remembers her husband. "He said he was never going to grow up. He was a little kid in a big-boy uniform."

Until she sees the custom chicken coop he built out back or the Duck football jersey with Chris' badge number, 248, on it, given to her at halftime of the UO spring game at Autzen Stadium eight days after his death; "he'd be over the moon with that."

Until she flips through what she thought was an empty notebook and sees his handwriting.

"I'm still in shock, completely," says Kilcullen, a wad of Kleenex in her hand. "Breathing is my goal."

The hardest moments? "Telling (4-year-old) Katie her dad was not coming home. Or every time she picks a wishing flower and blows on it and says, 'I wish daddy would come home.'"

And how, as an adult, she tries to say something comforting but, deep down, feels just as Katie does. "People say I'm strong," says Kilcullen, who is taking a break from her job as a State Farm claims adjustor in Springfield. "I don't feel strong. I feel heartbroken."

But appreciative. And cautiously hopeful.

That her husband's death will awaken some people to the respect police officers deserve, she says, but don't always get. Say, when officers use force in a situation and some immediately assume it's a case of police overreaction.

"Too many people play armchair quarterback and think we should Kumbaya situations that can't be Kumbaya-ed," she says.

She said as much in a letter that was read on her behalf at the memorial service, a letter that was forthright but, she tells you, actually toned down from the original.

"He goes to work everyday to protect people, puts his life on the line and we sacrifice and miss birthday parties and pagers go off while you're leaving for vacation and he's 100 percent gone during football season and after a while, yes, resentment builds up when you don't feel people appreciate that," she says.

But after his death, she saw another side to the community. Now, she wonders if she misjudged the amount of support there is for the police. Or if Chris' death has inspired such support.

At any rate, she says, Chris would have loved to see the respect paid for a fallen officer.

"Everyone is hurting and coming together and it's mind-boggling," she says. "I'm cautiously optimistic things might be different now. I want families of cops to realize something: If, God forbid, anything like this should happen to your family, this community has your backs."

No, it won't ease her grieving, but she's sensed it in every letter she opens. Every blue ribbon she still sees flying. And in her walk up the Autzen Stadium aisle after the halftime presentation.

Applause from adjacent fans followed her up like a vertical wave. But what she remembers most was one older man whose respect, she'd like to believe, wasn't intended so much for her as for Chris and for every man and woman in blue.

He stood at full attention, hand on brow in full salute.

Enough to just 'be'

Jan. 26, 2012

Here's the mystery of Jason Reynolds, a young man whose memorial service will be Friday in Springfield.

He never held an impressive job. In fact, he seldom left the house.

He never attended a prestigious university. In fact, he never went to a day of school.

He never was a star athlete. In fact, he never walked or talked.

For 23 years, virtually all Jason Reynolds did was kiss the ones he loved and wink and remind us that in a world that celebrates "doing," "achieving" and "acquiring," it is sometimes enough to just *be*.

How else do you explain the eight card tables in the Reynoldses' living room, each spread with dozens of photos of him that his folks, Alan and Gail, were preparing for Friday's 4 p.m. service at Springfield Faith Center?

Or more than 100 businesses and 250 individuals contributing to an "extreme home makeover" done for the family — basically, a $400,000-plus house — largely because of Jason's special needs?

Or a brother, Joel, now a graduate student at Emory University in Atlanta, who claims he is who he is because of the brother who never said a word to him?

"I'd be a fundamentally different person than I am if I hadn't had him in my life," says Joel Reynolds, 26, who earlier got degrees in philosophy and religious studies at the University of Oregon's Clark Honors College. "He gave me not only a deep respect for people who have disabilities, but a deep respect for the value of life, period, and for the unique individuality of every single person."

Jason's father, Alan, remembers coming home one day when the boys were younger. There was Joel, watching TV, his arm wrapped around his little brother's shoulders. His little brother who could barely see the TV, much less know what program was on it.

"When Joel got older and would bring friends home, the first thing he'd do was introduce them to Jason," says Alan, a carpenter. "He once told his mom, 'I've got the best brother in the world. But when it comes to running, I might need a dog.'"

Jason Reynolds never took a step. Never read a word. Never tasted food.

He was fed through a tube in his stomach for most of his life.

"He was like a loving 1-year-old boy," says Gail, his mother.

At age 1 and at age 23 and at every age in between.

When Gail, now 56, and Allen, 57, learned that their new son had something called muscle-eye-brain disease and had a 95 percent chance of dying by his second birthday, a friend came to them. When a disabled child is present, he told them, more than 90 percent of marriages fail. And siblings are almost always thrown off course.

"Where are you going to put him?" the friend asked, referring to a home for the disabled. The Reynoldses decided the living room would be a good spot. That way, they could keep an eye on him and he could keep an eye on them.

Tammy Werth, 47, was among Jason's caregivers. When she started the job, she had a chip on her shoulder and partying on her priority list. "I was a hard-hearted person," she says. "He melted my heart. Because of him, I put the party ways in the past."

He did it without a word. Without a deed. Without much other than facial gestures, which, for Werth, were windows to "his sweet,

sweet soul."

"Working with him, you sensed that he loved you no matter what," she says. "He was an earth-bound angel."

"The thing Jason did was bring people together," says Dan Hill, who was president of the Home Builders Association of Lane County, which, in 2007, built the family a new house — for free. "People captured the vision; at times we had 30 to 40 volunteers out there. And Jason was the heart of the vision."

That he required time, money — about $20,000 a year — and lots of effort is indisputable; Gail's folks, Velora Morton and her late husband, Jack, devoted countless hours to taking care of their grandson.

"I have to say this journey has been difficult for the family," says Velora Morton, 85, "but it's been a great learning experience, too. You learn that the deepest values in life aren't what we traditionally call 'success.' And that God has an interesting toolbox, interesting ways he 'fixes us.'"

For some time, Jason's doctor in Seattle told the family that nobody with this disease had lived as long as their son. But as Christmas neared, Jason's lungs were shutting down.

He rallied with Joel home from school. But after kissing his off-to-the-airport brother goodbye, Jason crashed. Within hours, his lungs congested and temperature soared.

He died a week later, on Jan. 9.

"It was an absolute honor and privilege to be his mom," Gail says.

"We were," Joel says, "blessed to have him."

The ocean taketh

Feb. 8, 2011

YACHATS — Nearly half a century ago, I remember my father walking me at low tide across what our family called "The Bridge," a thick, truck-wide slab of basalt over a chasm just north of Smelt Sands Beach in Yachats.

Even with no water — just sand — beneath it, "The Bridge" imbued in me a sense of reverence and danger.

I remember introducing its high-tide excitement to my own two sons, showing them how waves pounded under it — in extremely high tides, over it — and surged up the narrow slot beneath, then shot skyward in a magnificent geyser of frothy white.

And I've watched my grandchildren awed by a force of nature that you can not only see, but feel: ka-*thump*.

But now "The Bridge" will always evoke not only magnificence, but mournfulness.

For it was here, on Saturday, where two South Eugene High School students were swept into the ocean by a wave and died.

"I was heartbroken," said an e-mail from a brother-in-law who lost a teenage son to drowning.

And so it was for others who might not have even known Connor Ausland or Jack Harnsongkram, two seniors who were among the "Mr. Axeman" pageant contestants in Yachats for a weekend retreat.

The tragedy happened on perhaps the most heavily walked stretch of central Oregon coastline, the 804 Trail that's studded with three motels: the Adobe Resort, just south of the spot, and the Fireside Motel and Overleaf Lodge, just north.

"The Bridge" sits below a distinctive ocean-front cabin that I affectionately refer to as "The Spam Can." It's a favorite spot for winter storm-watchers (there's a bench just above the spouting horn), photographers and cairn-builders, whose summer stacks of rocks seem to pay tribute to the chasm's splendor of spray.

Oregon's surf is beauty, yes, but, alas, the deaths remind us that it is beast as well.

"The sea is unforgiving," says Bill Sheretz, a former Florence-based Coast Guardsman and now the Oregon State Marine Board's boating safety waterways coordinator. "It has no conscience."

Even if it might needle our own.

Talk to those who spend time on the Oregon Coast — or search your own memory — and you might find a time or two when the beast gave you a wake-up call.

Author Bonnie Henderson of Eugene, who has hiked every foot of the Oregon Coast, remembers a time she saw a stump on the beach. "Quick," she said to a friend, "take my picture on it."

She'd barely hopped aboard when the wave hit.

"I fell off and was completely drenched," she says. "Fortunately, I wasn't swept out. But I was soaked and ruined my binoculars, and I remember thinking: 'Why was I doing that?' The ocean is so deceptive. It catches even people who know better."

The loss of the South Eugene boys was all the harder for Henderson because her son, too, had once been a Mr. Axeman.

"Our surf," she says, "is deceptive. It can look good, then, within seconds, you have a tragedy."

Last November, during a raging storm, I positioned myself atop a bluff to shoot video of waves crashing into the rip-rap-fronted bank, then surging seaward to clash with other incoming waves. I made sure I had an escape route if I needed higher ground.

But a wave came in sideways — wasn't expecting that — and I got soaked to my waist, though not pulled out to sea.

Even as coastal veterans, we can naively believe that past performances indicate future results. And, in my case, forget that looking through a video camera viewfinder blocks your peripheral vision.

"The term you invariably hear is 'sneaker wave,'" says Bert Morris, a retired Coast Guardsman who's worked the Oregon and Washington coastlines. "There's really nothing 'sneaker' about such a wave. It's been running a couple of thousand miles across the sea, getting bigger and bigger."

We also might underestimate the force of such waves. "A cubic yard of water might not sound like much but it weighs a ton and might be coming at you at 20 to 25 mph," he says.

I remember a family story about a man with a cabin above the rocks using a garden hose to save someone in the ocean.

But such a rescue Saturday would have been all but impossible. The water temperature, based on a reading off Newport Monday, was probably about 50 degrees; the tide nearly high (7.41 feet at Alsea Bay); and the rocks creating conditions akin to the two young men being in a moat of pounding waves.

Not good conditions for any kind of rescue.

A friend of mine says when he cautions his granddaughter about the power of sea, she says he's being "too serious."

But if any good can come from the deaths of these two young men, perhaps it's just that:

While still appreciating the ocean's beauty, being serious — even "too serious" — about respecting the beast.

Bartender-turned-hero

Jan. 30, 2011

At 62, she died a month ago Saturday, one of those unassuming souls whose standing-room-only memorial service at West Lawn Memorial Park & Funeral Home only hinted at the kind of legacy she had left.

Indeed, if the unexpected death of Willamette Family Executive Director Valorie Michelle "Micki" Knuckles rocked the worlds of those involved in local substance-abuse care, the aftershock has come in the weeks since as word spread around the country.

The online tributes flowed in from Florida, Texas and other places, most with a familiar ring:

"She saved my life more than once."

"(She) gave me a second chance when no one else would."

"(She) never judged me, even when others did."

"One of the most amazing women I've ever known."

So, who was Micki Knuckles?

A former bartender who overcame drinking problems of her own to help hundreds, perhaps thousands, do the same.

"I can't tell you how many people, after she died, told me, 'If it hadn't been for Micki Knuckles I wouldn't be here,'" says Susan Richards, an assessment counselor with Willamette Family, whose main center — there are six — is near the Owen Rose Garden.

Though Knuckles could have worked for treatment centers that dealt with a higher-status clientele, she reached out, instead, to the poor. The outcasts. Mainly single women, many trying to get their lives together with a child or two in tow.

Women like she'd once been.

Knuckles was raised by an alcoholic single mother — a waitress — in California and Albany. She was married briefly; gave birth to her lone child, Robert, when she was 18; and became a bartender.

In essence, she became her mother.

But just as her mother would eventually do, Knuckles quit drinking, joined Alcoholics Anonymous and built a new life.

"We were both convinced men were crazy and swore them off," says Mary Ann Unruh, who roomed with her at the time. "Then along came Mike."

An alcoholic and drug addict, Mike Knuckles had, in 1980, fled Kentucky in the wake of a barroom death threat. He knocked back his last drink at The Embers on Highway 99 in Eugene, whereupon his uncle hauled him off to an AA meeting.

At a later meeting he met a 31-year-old woman — same age as him — celebrating her first year of sobriety: Micki.

They married in 1985.

"She was trying to figure out what to do and I told her bartenders made good counselors, so why not try that," Mike Knuckles says. "I like to take credit that she became one of the best in the state, even if she'd frown at the suggestion."

In 1988, Micki Knuckles became director and, in 2009, executive director of Willamette Family, the bulk of whose 180 employees are recovering alcoholics themselves.

"It's been said that the heart is the hallway between the mind and the soul," says Sue Norse, the nonprofit agency's finance office manager. "Micki was the warm heart of Willamette Valley."

If she had a weakness, some say, it was having too soft a heart; though head of a big operation, she'd stop everything to listen to some client's story — or to find a piece of gum for an employee's 2-year-old who showed up.

"Her favorite movie was *Pretty Woman*," says Jacki Rodriguez, a sister, about a film in which Julia Roberts plays a prostitute who undergoes a rags-to-riches transition. "It was because she could identify with the character played by Julia. She got herself out of a mess."

And then dedicated her life to helping others do the same.

"She had a keen understanding of what young unmarried women were going through and had a real ability to connect with them," says longtime friend Wanda Urban, who went through an internship program at Serenity Lane with Knuckles back in the 1980s.

"She reminded me of TV's 'Maude,' only a little more kinder and less cynical.

"Absolutely driven. But never looking for personal acclaim."

Nobody saw that driven-ness more acutely than Mike, who, as Willamette's head of facilities, remembers how she would run herself ragged putting on the annual Christmas party for employees and clients.

"She burned the candle at both ends and sometimes in the middle," he says. "I admit: I was jealous at times. She'd sit there at home, grinding out a grant proposal, sleeping from 3 a.m. to 6 a.m. She lived on coffee and cigarettes. And she suffered every time she lost a client, questioning herself: 'Did I do everything I could have done?'"

It is a sad irony that a woman whose life was about overcoming addictions learned last spring that she had lung cancer. "She struggled to quit smoking," Mike says, "but she couldn't control that one addiction."

Chemotherapy treatments worked, but the cancer had metastasized into her brain.

"I told the doctor, 'It's like we won the lottery, then walked out and got hit by a truck,'" Mike says.

Micki came home from the hospital on Christmas Eve — a "great Christmas Eve," Mike says — but slipped away in the days that followed. She died Dec. 29.

But, her legacy suggests, not before teaching so many others how to live.

Patron saint of cats

Nov. 7, 2010

Y ou don't ask, but her friends tell you anyway.
They tell you what they think Starly Susan Pupke was doing Wednesday night when she was killed while crossing 30th Avenue near Lane Community College.

"My thought is she saw an injured cat or dog on the other side of the road," Cathy Bill says, "and ran across the road to save it. That's the kind of determination she had."

Ma'Carry Cairo says the same thing. So do two other Pupke friends. And her mother, Gladeus "Sim" Pupke of Cottage Grove.

Pupke, 57, was Eugene's patron saint of homeless cats.

Bill, who worked with her for 12 years as part of the Feral Cat Coalition, estimates that Pupke — pronounced Pup-Kee — saved more than a thousand cats from death at the Lane County Animal Regulation Authority.

"As far as I know, no one individual did more to save cats around here than Starly," says Nancy Sorensen, who called Pupke to trap a handful of feral cats in her Bailey Hill neighborhood. "She not only came and trapped all four cats, but got them spayed and neutered — and kept them while they recovered."

In 2009, a friend of Cairo's was dying of cancer. The woman had two cats of her own and had been "adopted" by a stray that then had four kittens.

"When my friend died I was desperate to figure something out with these cats," Cairo says. "Starly threw me a lifeline. Took them all, got them spayed and neutered. I checked back. She'd found homes for all seven of them. She was an amazing woman."

If she couldn't find such homes, Pupke kept cats on the 5 acres she owned off Bailey Hill Road. She lived in a 1,000-square foot mobile home on the site. Was single. Did maintenance work at apartments. And usually wore jeans and a sweatshirt.

By all accounts, she was poor.

"She always put the animals before herself," says Laurie St. Jacques, who calls Pupke her closest friend. "She made sure they had a nice warm place and a nice, clean litter box. Herself? She lived primitively."

But Pupke never wallowed in her poverty, St. Jacques says. "She was poor but she had a very rich personality."

Says Cairo: "Financially, she was always living on the edge but she'd never turn down a request from someone who needed help with cats."

She favored mackerel to lure cats into her homemade traps.

"People in the know," Cairo says, "have told me Starly was the best cat trapper in Lane County."

Pupke — named Starly after a student her mother, Sim, had taught — grew up on a farm outside Cottage Grove with four siblings.

Her mother taught high school, her father, Ron, junior high.

"At 10, she took it upon herself to take care of the sheep and the horses, before school," her mother says. "She liked to ride horses. And she always had a soft spot in her heart for cats. Her love for cats was in her DNA."

At times, friends say, Starly could be like a cornered cat herself. "She had a huge heart for animals and a huge heart for people, but she could be very cantankerous," Bill says. "Nothing got in the way of her doing her job."

Pupke would testify at public hearings in defense of "no-kill" policies for strays.

In recent years, her mother says, Starly struggled with depression stemming from her bipolar condition. Three years ago, she had to have a double-hip replacement.

"But she had this marvelous group of friends," Sim Pupke says. "Somehow, she always managed to keep her head above water. She was independent. And courageous."

St. Jacques says she last talked to her friend about an hour before the accident. The two were planning to do some endurance horse racing together in the spring.

"We were going to go horseback riding Wednesday night but she called about 5:30 and said she couldn't get away from this job she was working on," St. Jacques says.

An hour later, Pupke was headed west on 30th Avenue, near LCC, when she stopped. It was nearly dark. She left her vehicle's lights on and engine running.

"She'd go places I would never go," Bill says. "She'd crawl into culverts, under horrible, stinky, houses, into attics."

So, the idea that Pupke would pull over and zip across a highway to save some animal is quintessential Starly, her friends all say.

She was struck first by a Honda Civic, then a Pontiac Fiero.

"The news hits you hard," Cairo says. "It's not only somebody you know, but it's somebody extraordinary, someone not known by many people — but somebody who should be."

A camp like no other

Aug. 14, 2011

FALL CREEK — Summer camp: Swimming. Skits around the campfire. The shimmer of sun on a lake.

Kids holding onto candles in the darkness with tears sliding down their cheeks.

A drawing accompanied by the caption: "My daddy jumped from the sixth floor of a parking structure."

A written list of feelings that includes "mad," "sad," "depressed," "shocked," "numb," "scared," "lonely," "overwhelmed" and "guilty."

Boxes of tissues in the activities rooms.

Courageous Kids Camp is like every other summer camp and nothing like every other summer camp.

At the opening gathering last week, Camp Director Kirsten Frazer explained the difference to the nearly 50 kids from around the state — elementary-school aged to high school — who had gathered.

"Look around you," she tells the campers. "Everyone around you has had someone close to them die."

Nobody pins that fact to the kids' shirts like scarlet letters. But neither do the counselors — roughly one for every two kids — ignore the common denominator for this four-day gathering at Sky Camp on Fall Creek Reservoir.

Because, in a sense, that's partly why this is so necessary. "We don't talk about death and dying and grief in our culture," says Isa Jennings, Courageous Kids' program manager. "These kids don't know someone else in their classroom at school who may have lost someone, too. So many feel totally alone."

Until they get here. For them, camp is an oasis, a safe place, a respite where everyone understands all those discombobulated feelings they have. And, what's more, where nobody makes fun of them like at school.

"Its hard to say what I'd be like without it," says Shelly Steward of Elmira, who came as a camper when she was 10 and, now, at 24, is a counselor. (A third of the counselors started as campers themselves.) "Courageous Kids gave me a way to look at my grief in a new way."

Her father, Bob, died in 1997 when crushed by a car he was working under.

"This gives kids some strategies when faced with those situations that others don't understand," says Steward, a Harvard graduate who's now pursuing a doctorate in sociology at the University of California, Berkeley.

"A 'win' is the kids getting the support so they can get to the next step in their grief journey, whatever that might be for them," says Jennings, a green-and-yellow sunshine painted on her face.

But it's almost always a hard-earned win.

"The most common obstacles are misunderstanding or misinterpreting their experiences," she says. Some children, she says, blame themselves for a loved one's death.

What's more, if it was a parent who died, the surviving spouse might be so immersed in grief and starting over that they overlook a child's struggles to cope. Or they sense it but — to prevent having to plumb their own emotional pain — dare not unlock it.

The camp is designed to let such feelings out. It might happen in an art class, a music class, a theater presentation or the nightly candlelight sessions, where kids light candles in honor of their loved one who died.

That setting was off limits to visitors like me. But you can't spend parts of a couple of days here and not sense something special going on. You revel in the children's off-the-wall skits Wednesday night and feel the pain the next morning when a group of elementary kids gather around the same fire to burn their "Yuk Bags."

Among the yukky stuff they've written on pieces of paper: "bad dreams," "sad feelings" and a brother "who tells me he hates me."

The hardest part for me was seeing the younger children; the feet of some 5- and 6-year-olds didn't even touch the ground as they sat on wooden benches around the campfire. And yet here they are, burdened with pain that even adults grapple to overcome.

"When people talk about how they don't like their dad it's kind of hard because at (least) they have one," wrote one child.

"I feel like I'm the only one who understands sad," wrote another, above a drawing of stick people with yellow happy faces on their heads. "Everyone around me is an (artificial) happy face on a body and doesn't know that there are things worse than the pop machine eating your dollar bill."

Counselor Dan Campbell, 16, was coming home from LaPine with his family three years ago when their vehicle was hit head-on near Willamette Pass. His mother, Kelly, was killed.

"I enjoyed the camp so much when I came so I wanted to help kids because I've been through what they've been though," Campbell says.

Campers are referred by schools and pediatricians. Jennings, the program director, thumbs through their backgrounds: "Grandpa shot himself ... mom died of cancer, and this 16-year-old girl was the one taking care of her ... father died of colon cancer, and he feels guilt he didn't spend more time with him ... 13-year-old boy found his father hanging ... ."

Painful stuff, this. But how impressive to see the staff work with these kids, bringing out feelings that need venting and smiles that need radiating. How impressive to see kids who arrive scared and lonely being wrapped in hugs and understanding. And leaving with new friends and tools to cope.

"You get this many broken hearts together with good intentions," says music therapist Mary Ditson, "and great things happen."

The child who made the memory box with "I love Daddy" on top still is without Daddy. But, perhaps for the first time, that child also has a glimmer of understanding. And a hint of healing.

15.
Inspiration

After the fall

April 30, 2013

MOUNT PISGAH — As the entourage made its way up toward the 1,520-foot summit on Saturday afternoon, hikers coming down asked questions.

After all, hiking parties of 65 aren't common on Pisgah. And what was with that "Welcome back Mike!" sign on top?

The curious were soon enlightened: "Mike" was Mike Hawley of Eugene, who on Sept. 16 had fallen 125 feet from near the top of 9,182-foot Mount Thielsen and, against all odds, survived.

The Saturday hike — on Hawley's 59th birthday — was his attempt to make good on a promise he had made himself soon after he had been plucked off Thielsen in a Black Hawk helicopter.

"My goal," he told me in November for a front-page story, "is to hike to the top of Mount Pisgah."

At the time, I remember looking at Hawley in his wheelchair — his foot in a cast, his head pocked with scabs — and thinking: *Really?*

His right foot had been shattered in the fall and amputation was still a possibility.

As November became December, Hawley himself wondered if he'd ever touch the bronze memorial atop a hill he had hiked more than 2,000 times, a hill where he'd come to know dozens of people. None perhaps better than Jorma Meriaho, 65, of Dexter, who had been on Thielsen with him when he'd fallen backward, landed and pinwheeled down the rock-strewn peak like a rag doll.

Hawley remembers staring out the back window of his house on a rainy afternoon in mid-December. He couldn't walk, couldn't drive and, even if he had been able to work, had no job. Ironically, Sherman Brothers Trucking had eliminated his position three days before the accident.

"I was wondering if I would ever get better," Hawley said, "if life would ever get back to normal."

He was doing physical therapy at home, but not much more. Along with his wife, Linda, his hiking pal Meriaho was ferrying him to medical appointments.

Linda, marketing director for Oregon Imaging Centers, remembers those times all too well.

"People had told us it would be a long road back, but at the three-month mark I was really tired," she said. "This was getting old. The days were dark and we didn't see any light at the end of the tunnel."

Slowly came touches of light. On Dec. 22, Hawley drove for the first time.

On Jan. 24, under the guidance of Jeff Giulietti of Eugene Physical Therapy, Hawley began swimming. "I was standing on two feet for the first time since the accident," he said.

In Giulietti's estimation, Hawley needed to be challenged harder to get out of the wheelchair.

"We had to do 'baby steps,'" Giulietti said. "He had to learn to walk all over again."

On Feb. 8, Giulietti encouraged Hawley to walk — at first with Giulietti's hand as guidance, then — at the therapist's insistence — without it.

"I was terrified and thrilled at the same time," said Hawley.

But he did it.

"Jeff's a drill sergeant," Hawley said, "but he's good at what he does."

Hawley's confidence began to rebound. On Feb. 21, now walking with a cane, he had coffee with Capt. Nathan Edgecomb of the Oregon Army National Guard, the Coburg man who had piloted the Black Hawk that plucked Hawley from the mountain five hours after the fall — and just before dark.

"That was awesome, getting to meet him," Hawley said. "Very cool."

He told Edgecomb he was planning to hike to the top of Pisgah on April 27 to celebrate his 59th birthday.

"Mind if I tag along?" asked Edgecomb, 36.

"Would I mind?" Hawley said. "I'd be honored."

A few weeks later, Mike and Linda drove to Salem to meet — and thank — the entire helicopter crew.

He flew to Los Angeles to visit his daughter. Earlier this month, he started a new job as sales director for Eugene-based Cascade Sierra Solutions, a nonprofit agency whose mission is to reduce the environmental impact of heavy trucking.

Meanwhile, his hiking friends fanned out to make Saturday special. "Mike is back" e-mail invitations went out. A flier announcing his return to Pisgah was posted at the trailhead. Friend Rick Kernan, who had been with Hawley on Thielsen, made a sign for the top.

Saturday morning, friends packed champagne, nonalcoholic cider and the sign to the summit. But 20 minutes before the 3:30 p.m. start time, only a handful of people had gathered in the Pisgah parking lot.

Then it happened. A dozen became two dozen and two dozen became four, many of them fellow hikers — "E-Pisgah-palians," Hawley jokes — whom Mike had met in his nearly daily trips to the top over the years.

"Incredible," Hawley said.

Kathy Kernan, Rick's wife, was there; she's the only one to have seen him fall. Also on hand was Karen Daniels, a woman from Bend who had joined the Thielsen party midway up the mountain and was there when Mike had fallen. Along with Meriaho, she and the Kernans comprised the "Fab Four" who were with Mike when the accident happened.

At Pisgah, Daniels got misty-eyed just greeting Hawley. "The last time I saw him they were loading him into a helicopter at 9,000 feet," she said later.

At 3:38 p.m., Hawley offered a "whoohoo!" and the hike began. In his left hand he carried a wooden walking pole inscribed with three things: "Mt. Pisgah 4/27/13," "1,520' or bust," and "7.5 Months A.T.F.," meaning "after the fall."

Halfway up, he looked as if he was Moses leading the Israelites out of Egypt. What started as 55 people crept closer to 70 by the time the group neared the top.

Just short of the summit, like a runner at Hayward Field, Hawley broke a "Happy Birthday" banner that had been stretched across the trail.

Finally, at 4:34 p.m. — just under an hour after leaving — Hawley slapped his palm down on the bronze memorial at the summit.

"Mike is back!" Meriaho said, addressing the crowd, which by now included not only the pilot, Edgecomb, but the medic who had been lowered on Thielsen to help, Sgt. Dan Cleveland; a videographer making a documentary on the rescue; and a friend of Mike's all the way from Seattle.

"Seven months ago, it looked like this day would never happen," Meriaho told the gathering.

He presented Mike with the new "Hawley Trophy," a plastic "high-five" hand given "for doing something stupid and making it back alive to tell about it."

Hawley popped a champagne cork. The crowd offered toasts.

"A toast to Linda!" someone said.

And finally it was time for words from Hawley himself.

"I don't know where to begin," he said.

He paused, his eyes misty, his words stuck.

"To an incredible group of friends," he began. "So many people who did so much for me. Thank you all for coming. This means more than you'll ever know."

Later, after a private barbecue in Eugene, he tried to put it all in perspective.

"I got a do-over," he told me. "My 'do-over' allowed me to turn 59 years old. It also allowed me to continue to be a husband, a father, a grandfather, a stepfather, and be here for the arrival of grandson No. 2 in August — and a chance to try and repay all of the care, grace, kindness and help I have received during this journey."

Next? Perhaps the South Sister, he says. For now, Hawley is happy to bask in gratitude.

"My do-over," he said, "allowed me to learn what friendship is really all about."

All the world's her stage

June 17, 2010

A voice deep in her soul says it. So does a ring on her finger. "All the world's a stage."

For 37 years, Judy Wenger has happily been on that stage, teaching drama and language arts, mainly at Roosevelt Middle School.

Saturday night, at a retirement party at South Eugene High's auditorium that will feature performances by some of her former students, she will take her final bow.

"I honestly believe that 'world's a stage' stuff," says Wenger, who's 60. "This is life. I don't think there's a job you could have that doesn't involve verbal skills, confidence, empathy for others — the stuff theater teaches."

Teachers come and go, and Lane County is blessed with some great ones. But few have touched as many lives as Wenger — she has taught more than 7,000 students since 1972, the oldest now 55 — or touched them so deeply.

"Absolutely she influenced my decision to become a teacher," says

Ceri Gipson, 34, who teaches eighth-grade language arts at Junction City's Oaklea Middle School. "I was a shy sixth-grader but her theater class completely changed me, gave me the confidence to speak in front of people."

Wenger is part Carol Burnett (she's been known to use whoopie cushions as teaching aids) and part moviedom's Mr. Holland (a dozen former students are performing at her 6 p.m. retirement party, which will feature dessert for a thousand people).

"She pulls on kids' heartstrings to get them to achieve at a higher level," says Roosevelt Principal Eric Anderson.

On the lighter side, Wenger was the inspiration for cartoonist Jan Eliot's "Stone Soup" character "Mrs. Wingit." On the grittier side, she battled through ovarian cancer in 2000, hardly missing a class.

"God wanted me there," says Wenger, who jokes about her more conservative faith playing out in an area of Eugene not known for such.

Wenger instilled confidence in kids without much of it. And knocked down a notch those with too much.

Josh Daugherty, an actor in Los Angeles, remembers being "cocky" going into a play, even though Wenger knew he didn't know his lines. "She made me go on stage holding my script," says Daugherty, now 35. "The most humiliating experience of my life. But now, every time I prepare for a movie or TV show or commercial, I remember that.

"Some teachers today might still give you the trophy; you know, 'everybody's a winner.' Judy wasn't one of those teachers. She wasn't going to let the cast and crew suffer because of my being unprepared. She wasn't going to let something get in the way of teaching a lesson."

Wenger has been smitten with theater since seeing Shakespeare's *Twelfth Night* in middle school. She realized she wanted to teach when, at Sheldon High, she was asked to leave the classroom for smart-mouthing a teacher.

"I didn't like that. My audience was gone. So I decided if I wanted to be able to talk when I wanted to, I needed to be a teacher. Plus, I love school supplies, especially paper clips."

She wound up teaching drama, yearbook, Shakespeare, writing, poetry, even sewing.

"We do costumes ourselves so I called the class 'Behind the Seams,'" says Wenger.

She used puppets to help teach writing and created a "QUEEN

OFARTS" T-shirt to emphasize careful proofreading. "You might think it's no big deal if the space between 'of' and 'arts' gets taken out," she'd say, "but, believe me, it changes the sentence completely."

In 2004, Wenger received one of 144 national Teacher Recognition Awards from the U.S. Department of Education after being nominated by Presidential Scholarship winner Jenny Nissel, a former student.

Michelle Koehn, a friend of Wenger's whose two sons had her as a teacher, says Judy has always had a heart for middle-schoolers. Koehn's husband, Chuck, once told Judy he admired her teaching despite those kids being in their angst-ridden teen years, says Michelle. "Judy said: 'No, I teach at that level because of that, not despite that.'"

Wenger's Shakespeare plays and elaborate spring musicals became her trademark over the years. She loved taking kids to the Oregon Shakespeare Festival in Ashland — not the drama "naturals" but the kids who'd never been on a stage.

"I do theater in everything I do," says Wenger, whose Halloween costumes seldom repeated.

"If sports were harder, it'd be theater," says Wenger. "In theater, you have to perform well, look well and sound well. In sports, you only have to perform well."

Among her most touching moments? In the early '90s, a student in *Charlie and the Chocolate Factory* with a brain tumor was given a special pre-show curtain call; he was too sick to perform. "He died the next week," she says.

In 37 years, she's seen girls' hemlines go up, guys' pants sag down, even had a mother plead for Judy to check her daughter's belly-button ring — off limits to mom — to see if it might have caused an infection.

"I've known her for 30 years and not even in the deepest, darkest corner of a cafe has she ever said anything negative about her job, the school or a child," says Koehn. "Totally positive."

Wenger leaves with a ton of memories, 106 unused sick days and the words of Michael Gross (Alex P. Keaton's father on TV's "Family Ties"), who took her aside while on a Eugene visit and said, "What you do is important."

As the curtain closes on her career, it's clear Wenger never forgot it.

A gutsy call

May 9, 2013

You're the 22-year-old editor of the student newspaper at a small Christian college in Dayton, Tenn.

The administration announces that a professor is leaving to "pursue other opportunities."

Meanwhile, you've learned, through an FBI press release and a county sheriff's report, that the professor has been arrested on charges of attempted aggravated molestation and child sexual exploitation after allegedly attempting to meet a "minor child" at a gas station.

And that the professor was arrested as part of an FBI Northwest Georgia Safe Child Task Force operation after "coming to the attention of undercover officers on the Internet."

You tell the administration you want to publish a story about this. The administration says no.

Do you publish it?

To me, it sounds like one of those contrived situations we'd be tossed in a journalism ethics class at the University of Oregon.

But it's real, and Alex Green's decision to publish the article — in his own way — is why he's being honored today as winner of the UO School of Journalism and Communication's 2013 Ancil Payne Award for Ethics in Journalism.

Bravo to Green for having the courage to publish the story. Bravo to the UO for honoring his conviction.

"The whole country was just coming off the Jerry Sandusky situation at Penn State," said Green — editor-in-chief of the school paper, *The Bryan College Triangle* — in a phone interview Tuesday from Tennessee. "If this had become a big story, I could just see people looking at Bryan College and saying, 'Wait a minute, you mean to tell me they knew and didn't say anything about it?'"

Last summer Green was in only his second month as the paper's editor and was a student — and huge fan — of the professor, David Morgan.

"But I am the editor," he wrote after the incident. "I cannot protect the people I like when they do wrong ... It's policy for *Triangle*: When a faculty member leaves, *Triangle* explains why."

It's not policy to run stories past the administration of the private school before they're published. Nevertheless, Green alerted the school president. The editor suggested that, yes, the story would hurt, but like "ripping off a Band-Aid," would ultimately be best for all.

"I expected push-back," Green said. "I got it."

Don't publish it, he was told.

Initially, he abided by the president's decision and did not print the story as planned in the school's Sept. 21 edition. But a few days later, a guest lecturer at Bryan — a journalist from Germany — shared an anecdote about his days as a student journalist. The administration "spiked" his story about a janitor who, the lecturer said, "was striking students."

The journalist told the class how he'd made photocopies of the story and distributed them around campus.

Green was inspired. "If I passed the buck," he said, "I realized there was nobody there to take it."

He had 300 copies printed and placed them in various locations on campus, the story bracketed between his byline and an editor's note explaining that this was an article the administration hadn't permitted him to publish.

"What if there were victims who feared coming forward?" he said after the incident. "Could I live out my life with the thought that I contributed to their pain? Would I turn my head? I could not."

Beyond the visiting professor, Green said he was inspired by the Old Testament story of Shadrach, Meshach and Abednego (Daniel 3:1) who refused, under threat of being thrown into a "fiery furnace," to bow down before an idol instead of worshipping God.

"I just felt this was a principle I couldn't walk away from," Green said.

In an accompanying column, he said some people undoubtedly would read the article and compare Bryan College to Penn State, where officials are alleged to have covered up on-campus incidents of Sandusky, later convicted as a serial child molester.

"Printing this story will not cause a Penn State situation for Bryan," he wrote. "I believe it will prevent one. That's why I'm dispensing it. 'We are Penn State' was their approach. 'Christ above all' is ours."

UO Journalism Dean Tim Gleason, chairman of the eight-person judging panel, said Green's approach to the story was "beyond what we might typically expect from a student journalist."

"We applaud not only his courage in reporting the story but the thought process he shared with us about his ordeal."

Though the Bryan College administration did not discipline Green, he took plenty of shots after the story appeared on the popular journalism blog of Jim Romenesko and exploded on the Internet.

"Has it ever been so glorious to be the person who places the scarlet letter upon the chest of a fallen man?" wrote one person.

But Green wasn't out to punish his professor; "I loved Dr. Morgan. I still love him." What's more, this was not information Green overheard at the student cafeteria; his source was an FBI press release and a county sheriff's reports — public record information available to all.

And anyone thinking the accused's reputation or school's reputation were pre-eminent here — a common theme among detractors — are forgetting about the minor children who never get a say in these situations.

Though he calls the Payne Award "a huge, huge honor," Green says he feels undeserving of being rewarded. "People are quick to knight the hero and demonize the bad guy," said Green, who hasn't heard directly from the school president or Morgan, who is out on bail as he awaits trial. "It's not that simple. There aren't good people and bad people. David Morgan's not a 'bad guy' and I'm not a 'good guy.' I'm just a guy who did what he thought needed to be done."

A son worth the wait

March 3, 2013

The plane touched down at exactly 3:16 p.m., noted some among the 50 people waiting at the Eugene Airport last Sunday with the "Welcome Home" banner and the red, white and blue balloons.

All for David and William and, soon joining them, Nita.

David Loveall, pastor of Eugene's threeSixteen Ministries, was home from Uganda with William Biyinzika, the 14-year-old boy whom he and his wife, Nita, hope soon will be their adopted son.

The two-year journey was over. The journey that Nita had begun. And that David had ended, making good on a promise he had made to William nearly three months before when he arrived in Uganda — to continue hacking through a jungle of bureaucratic red tape to allow the boy from the orphanage to come to America.

"I'm not leaving without you," he said.

The Lovealls' story with William began two years ago when Nita, a hygienist, was invited to join a dental team on a missionary trip to Uganda. The offer came at a time when Nita and David, both now 52 and living in Springfield, were just settling into their empty-nest years with an air of expectation. Beyond his freelance photography business, David recently had launched a new church near Willagilles-pie Elementary School, its name derived from the "God so loved the world ..." verse: John 3:16.

Son Garrett, now 26, and daughter Mikayla, 22, were essentially on their own.

At work one day, Nita was seeing a patient out the door — after sharing about the Uganda trip possibility — when the "older woman" placed her hand on Nita's, along with a check for $40.

"I always wanted to do something like that," the woman told her, "but I never did. So I want to live it through you."

"That gesture is why I went to Uganda," Nita says.

Months later and nearly 9,000 miles away, in a Masaka orphanage with no water or electricity, Nita saw the tears slide down William's face after he'd had some teeth extracted. So brave. And so thankful.

Nita showered him with all the encouragement she could. "Nobody ever showed me such kindness," he told her.

When she later hugged William goodbye, Nita said she would come see him again. Another promise.

Once home, her connection with the boy intensified. "I felt God telling me to bring him home," she says.

But God didn't seem to be telling David that.

"I'm thinking, 'This is our time. We can travel. The house is nearly paid off.'"

On the other hand, David couldn't deny how much this boy's welfare seemed to mean to Nita.

"Every time she'd mention his name," he says, "she'd cry."

So the couple went to see an immigration attorney. No problem, they interpreted the response. The reality that unfolded? Problems upon problems.

Together, they flew to Uganda in September to file for legal guardianship.

William's father was dead. His mother had remarried, had numerous children, and was not interested in parenting the boy.

But the system, they found, was rife with bribery and corruption.

An attorney told them a judge wanted approval from the father's family.

Just pay someone to pretend to be an uncle, he said.

"I preach a lot about telling the truth even if it leads to death," David says, "even if doing so ruins your reputation. Tell the truth. Do what you say you're going to do."

They would not lie. But told they needed more documents, they had no choice but to leave.

Nita cried most of the way home. Still, after 26 hours of travel, when son Garrett picked them up, they immediately began phoning whoever might be able to help. They found a woman in Salem to do a "home study" that they hoped would prove they were trustworthy parents. Other documents were secured.

On Dec. 2, David returned to Uganda.

Holdup after holdup. The judge, despite David having a court date, left on vacation. David got the venue changed. He and Nita were approved to take William.

Then came snag after snag at the U.S. Embassy. Days became weeks. Christmas came and went. January became February.

Back home, Nita got U.S. Sen. Ron Wyden's office involved.

Phone calls. $330 DHL package deliveries with documents. Thousands of dollars spent. Weekly Skype updates from David to his church on Sunday mornings.

On Feb. 14, David wrote on his Facebook page: "I now have in my hand a U.S. government APPROVED I-600 FORM, the last step in the process!"

But to secure it, information had to get uploaded into the embassy's computer in the capital city of Kampala. The information, the couple learned, was in Dallas, then Missouri, then New Hampshire.

It would be sent the next day, they were told. Nope. A blizzard hit; the one woman who could send the information could not get into work.

Finally, success. A U.S. Embassy official in Kampala City confirmed the information had been received. William got his visa.

But at the airport, custom officials refused to allow David through until he showed a batch of documents, including not only his passport but a certified copy of his passport. Stymied, David, a diabetic, panicked momentarily, then found a copy zipped inside his insulin kit.

Home free. Thanks to God, say the Lovealls, the prayers of many and an amazing assist from Wyden's office.

As soon as the adoption is finalized, William will become their son.

"If something is good, you must fight for it," says William, the now-smiling beneficiary of a promise kept.

How terribly cool to be 70

Oct. 9, 2011

Musician Paul Simon turns 70 Thursday and his old friend, Art Garfunkel, does the same three weeks later.

Which makes me think of that song Simon & Garfunkel released in 1968, "Old Friends." It was about old geezers sitting on park benches "like bookends," "lost in their overcoats" and "silently sharing the same fears."

The key line: "How terribly strange to be 70."

The two were 26 when the song came out. Now, 44 years later, here they are at the same age that their song suggests they should be lacing up their "high shoes" with the "round toes" — if they can avoid throwing out their backs — and watching newspapers blow through the grass, while basically waiting to croak.

But hold everything.

Either Simon & Garfunkel overstated the grimness of life at seven decades, the world has changed since 1968 or folks out West age better than those in New York, where the two lived when they released the song.

Because here is life for a few 70-plus folks with whom I'm familiar: At 70, Becky Sisley of Eugene won seven medals at the World Masters Athletic Championship in Finland two years ago, including gold in the heptathlon, 80-meter hurdles and pole vault.

At 90, "Band of Brothers" soldier Don Malarkey of Salem has, in recent years, offered inspiration to F-15 Oregon Air National Guard fighter pilots, met Prince Charles in Buckingham Palace and given a pep talk to the football team of his alma mater, the University of Oregon.

At 89, Jake and Marcie Egger of Tigard — their daughter, Kathy Sherwood, operates Custom Orthotics in Eugene — drove 1,900 miles last summer, most of it on the Alaska Highway, to celebrate

Jake's soon-to-be 90th birthday with relatives. Kathy flew home. Jake and Marcie drove.

At 80, Sister Monica Heeran serves as the interim executive director of the Eugene-Springfield Volunteers in Medicine organization.

At 70, Judy Jernberg of Eugene leads seven Bible studies a month and reads 80 to 100 books a year.

At 91, Earle Foley of Junction City not only drove his Mercedes 450 SL across the country a few years ago but recently took ownership of The Time Out Tavern in Springfield, where he works five-plus days a week.

At 93, the oldest living Hall of Fame baseball player, ex-Boston Red Sox Bobby Doerr of Junction City, has made appearances in Cooperstown, N.Y., been a guest on Eugene Emeralds radio broadcasts and, of course, still fishes his beloved Rogue River.

At 85, former Lane County resident Alma Lou Cline Stubbert went sky-diving in Molalla last July.

At 70, former Eugene Mayor Brian Obie owns and operates one of the city's premiere shopping sites, the Fifth Street Public Market.

At 80, Harvey Lewellen of Springfield set three world, and five American, records in masters track and field weight events. Now 82, he retired three years ago after 53 years as a high school football referee.

At 72, George "Billy Goat" Woodward, who basically lives on the Pacific Crest Trail, has hiked 45,000 miles since retirement, roughly two loops around the earth.

At 71, Al Grapel of Eugene kayaks an average of once a week, leads classes in the sport for the City of Eugene and routinely does Class III rapids — and, "with some amount of terror" — occasionally Class IV.

At (soon-to-be) 70 (Jan. 11, 2012), Eagle Park Slim still plays his soulful blues music at 25 to 50 gigs a year and will be featured in the new Blueseum section that opens Oct. 15 at the Lane County Historical Museum.

At 90, petroleum and alternative energy expert Walter Youngquist of Eugene continues to warn the media of the evils of overpopulation.

At 104, Thelma Doak published her memoirs of life on the plains of eastern Colorado during the Depression, did a handful of book signings and then passed away. (What a great way to go!)

At 78, Cheshire artist Sarkis Antikajian paints nearly every day, leads workshops and exhibits his work in galleries. "I am," he says, "far happier at 78 than I was at 19."

I've undoubtedly missed a couple of million examples; somewhere, I'm sure, there's a 107-year-old bungee jumper that I'll hear about Monday morning. But you get the idea.

It was simple finding these examples. In fact, while finishing up the column, my 84-year-old mother called to let me know she'd arrived safely in New Mexico for the Albuquerque International Balloon Fiesta.

I understand that not everybody has the health or money to do some of things the folks on this list have done. For others, what's terribly strange isn't to be 70, but to sit on the park bench of life and not live with passion.

Regardless of one's age.

The music of their lives

June 21, 2011

We are the melodies and the notes of your opus. We are the music of your life.
— A former student of teacher Glen Holland in *Mr. Holland's Opus*

On April 12, in the fellowship hall at Westminster Presbyterian Church, a former Sheldon High School choir director stood in front of them again for the first time in decades; some had not been a student of his since 1970. With a touch of hesitation, he raised his baton. The 37 people in the choir came to attention.

"I was a little nervous," Glenn Patton later would say. "I wasn't sure what would happen on the downbeat."

Patton scanned the faces of people who, back in the '70s when he sometimes sported a white belt and matching shoes, had been teenagers. Now they were in their 40s and 50s, roughly the same ages he'd been while at Sheldon.

But compared with the 85-year-old Patton, they were like yearlings on the ranch he'd grown up on in Montana, where he'd first discovered music.

Oh, well, it was time. In a quick slash, down came Patton's baton. And, in that moment, he recalls, it was as if the stick, in a single swoop, wiped away the years, the decades.

"Like we'd been transported back," he says.

"It was literally as though time stood still," says Candy (Floyd) Troutman, class of 1976.

Such rehearsals, all part of the Sheldon High School Choirs Reunion, will culminate Saturday night when Patton leads nearly 90 of his former students in a free concert at Sheldon.

It is part TV's "Glee" and part "Mr. Holland's Opus," the film starring Richard Dreyfuss in which his former students surprise him at year's end by gathering in the auditorium, handing him a baton and having him lead the orchestra in the opus he's written.

The idea for the reunion came up last July when Patton and his wife, Jean, were meeting with a couple of his former students for some chit-chat. After a casual mention of a reunion, Julie (Follmer) Holmes ('76) recalled being mildly surprised at how enthusiastic Patton was about it.

"The idea," he says, "had crossed my mind."

Now, that idea bounced forward with the cadence of fast-beat jazz. Holmes is a go-getter. So, too, are a lot of Patton's former students. Within a week, a committee had formed, met and started making plans.

The first challenge was connecting with people. But a Facebook page quickly started drawing interest from dozens of people, mainly from the Northwest but some from as far away as New York, Texas and the Carolinas.

The second challenge was getting commitments; this, after all, was for more than an evening of wine and cheese and "remember-the-time-we ... " recollections. It was time, money and knowing your parts before this Thursday, when the three-day event begins, and being willing to spend Friday and Saturday in intense rehearsals.

But soon 50 people were committed and now it's well more than 80.

After people in the Portland area decided to start holding practices up there, Patton and his wife of 50 years — "she came to every concert we ever did," says Troutman — drove north to be part of the sessions.

After nonlocals expressed interest in fine-tuning their parts, Mike McCornack ('71) turned them on to music notation software, Sibelius, that allows them to hear, say, the alto part of one of the 10 songs the group will perform.

After Patton initially scratched his head at some of the high-tech approaches, he learned Facebook, e-mailing, the works.

Soon, beyond rehearsals, plans include a meet-and-greet on Thursday; a catered buffet dinner, followed by open-mike performances, on Friday; and, of course, the grand finale Saturday night in the Sheldon auditorium.

What, exactly, is it that inspired such an unlikely event, a reunion that took nearly a year to plan?

"I don't think I've enjoyed getting together with people for anything else as much as for this," says McCornack, a choir director and technology coordinator at Willamette High. "Music programs help you get to be friends with people on a different kind of level than you get in the regular classroom. You become a community. You bond. You make something that you once only imagined."

Then, of course, there's Glenn Patton.

"It's been fun reconnecting with old friends and, yes, we want to re-create that special sense of belonging and community that centered on making great music together," Troutman says. "But the bottom line is we want to honor Glenn Patton. No other teacher has had the impact on my life — and I know every one of his students feels the same way."

Patton, as is his nature, is quick to point out that this is about music and singers and old friends reunited, not about him. But, clearly, he's the main reason this is happening.

"He's an icon," says Holmes. "He was very demanding but treated us with a certain maturity I don't think kids get much of today."

Talk to his former students and you hear how he got them through difficult times. How he helped them love music in a way that they've now passed on to their own children. How he could be tough and tender, but usually chose the right moment for each.

"When people were being silly, he knew how to be firm," says McCornack. "When people were worn out, he knew how to inject some humor."

Over time, his students craved his approval.

"When Glenn Patton had to look up or sideways because of an off note, you only hoped it wasn't because of you," Troutman says. "We always wanted to make him proud of us because when he heard 'it,' when we had mastered a difficult spot in the piece, the look on his face — the sheer delight in the beauty we had all just created together — was all the reward we wanted."

Patton grew up so deep in southeast Montana that the family's ranch stretched to the South Dakota line. It was there that he fell in love with music — from a piano-playing mother, a saxophone-playing father and a high school band teacher known as "The Prof."

"I remember our tuba's valves freezing up during football games," says Patton, who played the trumpet.

He earned an undergraduate degree in music from the University of Montana, taught for three years, then came back to UM for a master's in music.

He returned to teaching, taking jobs in Reedsport and Prineville before opting for work as a partner in a music store.

But teaching, he discovered, was in his DNA. "I'd call on band directors and always left with two impressions: either 'If I had 15 minutes with that group I could help them a lot' or 'That's a great idea. I'll sock it away.'"

When offered a job at Madison Middle School in Eugene, he didn't hesitate. After six years he moved up to Sheldon in 1969.

"What I love about music is the connection with people," says Patton, "The Lord has given me a feeling for something I need to share with others."

He helped Sheldon win state contests. Took choirs to Europe and, in 1976, to Washington, D.C., to represent Oregon in bicentennial celebrations at the White House and the Kennedy Center. (Hard to say which was more stunning, getting to sing an unplanned version of "The Star-Spangled Banner" as President Ford waved from an ascending helicopter, or the choir's red, white and blue outfits.)

But, mainly, he inspired his students to play great music — and make something of their lives.

"I was shy and through his support he inspired and sparked what I was holding back," says Marie (Luckey) Gilbert of Beaverton ('75).

"His love for life and music was contagious," says Carla (Jensen) Reprogle of Springfield ('72).

She remembers that after he retired — in 1986, after a short stint at Monroe Middle School — he returned part-time to work as a bus driver. Her son was getting off his bus one day when Patton gently stopped him. "Is your mother's name Carla?" he asked. He nodded yes. "I was your mother's choir teacher in high school. Would you give her my love?"

Over the years, Patton has attended weddings, graduations, even funerals of former students and their families.

Some of his students have gone on to professional singing careers, including Candice Burrows, who was a professional opera singer and now teaches in North Carolina. Some married folks sang in the choir, including Candy Floyd and Scott Troutman ('77), and Jeanie Lanzarotta ('76) and Steve Halberg ('71). And about half of the 80-plus students who will attend the reunion have already been gathering for the practice sessions in Portland or Eugene in anticipation of Saturday's concert.

"It's been a blast," says Heidi (Hahn) Behrends of Eugene ('79). "Singing and laughing and watching a lot of over-50s still being a little intimidated by Mr. Patton saying, 'Stop! Go back to Measure 20 and I didn't hear the tenors' is so much fun. We all sit straight in our chairs and stand when we're told to."

"The experience has been surreal," says Patton. "I've been truly amazed at the response."

In some ways, nothing has changed, though he has ditched the polyester zip-up-the-front shirts. His students still call him Mr. Patton. "I just can't bring myself to call him Glenn," says Holmes. And he still thinks of them as his kids. "It's true," he says. "I'll be talking to one of them on the phone, an adult, but seeing them in my mind as 17."

He's not alone.

"We've all gone back in time," says Gilbert, "to a place that makes our hearts smile."

The courage to forgive

Aug. 16, 2011

The incident happened July 22 just as Callan Coleman was merging, ironically, onto Martin Luther King Jr. Boulevard.

"Hey, nigger!" yelled the driver of a car that had cut off Coleman, possibly a Jeep Cherokee.

Coleman, who is black, and his wife Shelley James, who is not, were heading with their 21-month-old daughter Eva for a reggae concert at the Cuthbert Amphitheater — an amphitheater, by the way, where the two of them opened Saturday night before more than 5,000 people for the Satin Love Orchestra, of which they're also a part.

Coleman, 42, admits that revenge sprang to mind. "He shamed me in front of my wife and you don't want your little girl to go through something like that so, yeah, I wanted to be protective."

But he says he said nothing and did nothing in response. "I wasn't going to let him drag me into his swamp for a knife fight."

What Coleman did instead was mentally knead the incident like bread dough over the next few days. What could he learn from it? How could he grow from it? How could something good come from it?

I heard about his response from someone who'd read his blog and notified me. Intrigued, I contacted him.

"This had never happened to Shelley and me," he told me. "And so I just prayed, 'God, if I get angry and let myself get pulled into his world, that guy wins.' If I'd gotten out of my car, he wins. I didn't want him to have power over me."

As a release, he turned to his blog, warning readers regarding his use of "nigger" that "I don't normally use this word, and don't approve of it other than in proper context ... like books such as 'Tom Sawyer' or when the stupidity of it is being mocked."

This was a case of the latter.

First, he put the incident into perspective. It wasn't about black people being good and white people being bad. After all, he pointed out, it was a black person who'd stiffed his family in a business deal.

"There is no color to wrong," says Coleman, who has a master's degree in counseling psychology from the University of Oregon and spent more than 10 years as a school counselor.

It wasn't about his being a victim, his deserving pity.

"I'm reeling for all of the people on Earth who have to go through much worse pain than one moment ... of one human degrading another," he wrote.

And it didn't mean Eugene is filled with racists. "I could have said Eugene sucks, Springfield sucks, but that's silly," he told me. "One person does not taint all of the other thousands who would never do that in their lives. This is my home."

He wondered, in print, about what the man got out of hurling the word his way. "I wonder if his life is better because he tagged a nigger?" he wrote. "Many niggers have fought and died for his flag so he can live a sweet life here in America.

"Did his kids give him an extra long hug and kisses before they went to bed, telling him how proud they were of their big, tough, nigger-calling dad?

"Will his cable company call and tell him they will be giving him a monthly discount for being such a warrior?

"Is he going to tell his church congregation how much he served the Lord by making sure a nigger heard that word?"

Ironically, Coleman did tell his congregation, Eugene Christian Fellowship, where Shelley leads worship and he plays bass guitar.

Between songs, Coleman mentioned the incident to Pastor Gary Clark, who encouraged him to share it with the congregation.

"The incident," Coleman told them, "brought new meaning to the Bible verse about, 'Father, forgive them for they know not what they do.'"

On his blog, Coleman said he is praying for the man. "I am praying for his family, that his kids aren't scarred from growing up in a house where (their) dad is so insecure he has to harass others to make himself feel better."

He also said it had inspired him in numerous ways:

"It lights my fire to be a better husband and father.

"It lights my fire to be a more loving Christian to everyone, even those whose heads I'd like to rip off in a moment of rage.

"It lights my fire to be the best professional I can be and make so much money that I can bless others." (Coleman is a real estate broker.)

"It lights my fire to honor veterans who don't care the color of the soldier next to them who is risking their lives to save ours.

"It lights my fire to care more about people (whose) lives are not as blessed as mine."

Not that the incident, he admits, hasn't caused him some sadness.

"I feel nothing but sadness," Coleman says, "for him."

The long road home

May 3, 2015

SEATTLE — To those who saw us in the Thai restaurant on this April night three weeks ago, we might have looked like father and son.

Nobody could have imagined the real story.

How before this night, I'd last seen — and *first* seen — the 44-year-old man when he was 15. He was a long-haired, drugged-out cocaine dealer scooping ice cream out of a gallon carton as I interviewed him for the now-extinct *Journal-American* newspaper in Bellevue.

How, back then, I'd asked him, in response to his world-by-the-tail attitude, where he honestly thought he'd be five years from now. He'd mumbled something about owning his own island with "fast cars, fast boats and fast girls."

How he'd wound up in prison and how a bizarre twist involving his father turned his darkness even darker.

How the two of us had corresponded by letters for years. Decades. Through incarcerations in Washington, Oregon, California, Arizona, Oklahoma and Minnesota. And how I'd once promised him, when he was finally released, "dinner on me."

And how this was that dinner.

I won't use his name; as with Jean Valjean in Victor Hugo's fictional *Les Misérables*, our culture isn't quick to forgive just-released prisoners.

It was August 1986 and I was a 32-year-old columnist — I'm now 61 — when a man called with a column idea: Did I want to write about a teenage cocaine dealer? The kid lived with his family on the opulent East Side, across Lake Washington from Seattle, in a $250,000 hillside house that'd be worth $750,000 today. A Porsche and Ferrari graced its garage. The kid pulled down $2,000 a week.

"But last night," the man said, "he tried to kill himself."

"How do you know so much about him?" I asked.

"Because," he said, "he's my son. One summer you're watching your kid hit .700 in Little League baseball, the next summer on an operating table, having his stomach pumped."

The father was a go-go-go salesman who made big money. His son, he told me, was trying to keep pace.

The man blamed the system for his son's troubles. The father had tried to get the state to give his son a tour of a nearby prison in hopes of scaring him straight.

"They said no," the father said. "Maybe waking up the community to what's going on with our kids will help. Maybe a story will help."

I interviewed the boy in their home as the father looked on. "I don't even remember it," the boy-turned-man said to me over dinner. "It was all foggy then."

The column ran, triggering some intense community discussion about young people, drugs, cops, courts and prisons. Three years later, I moved to Eugene.

In 1992, I learned the young man had been imprisoned. In September, I wrote him a letter of encouragement and said I'd love to hear from him. He responded within a week.

He apologized because he figured he had "disappointed" me. "But a little voice inside of me tells me our paths will cross again," he wrote.

His father began writing me, too. His identity had been wrapped up in money, ego and big-boy toys. "If I knew then what I know now," he wrote, "I most definitely would have lived my life in a different manner. The nine Porches and the Ferrari were wonderful for the ego but they obviously mean nothing as it relates to what is real in life."

Then the letters from both of them stopped.

In 1994, a *Journal-American* reader sent me a short article that she called "the saddest thing I've ever read in a newspaper."

The young man, who'd been released from prison, had been arrested again in a drug bust. Not only that. So had his father.

On the night before the two were to appear in court, the father called his son, told him how much he loved him, drove to the rural property where he'd spent his childhood and put a bullet through his head.

Blurred by booze, the son was nevertheless crushed.

I've never met a father and son who loved each other more but hurt each other more.

The young man, by then 23, returned to prison, where he'd been sentenced to 15 years that would become even more. His letters resumed. He talked of books he'd read. He talked about realizing God was real. He talked about his dad.

"The kid that always wanted to be like his father now had a father that wanted to be his kid."

I sent him books I'd written. He read them and talked about them in return letters.

In 1997, out of the blue, he phoned me to say hello. In a subsequent letter, he asked if I'd be willing to write a letter to a judge to help ease his sentence. I did so. The judge did not ease the sentence.

California. Arizona. His letters kept coming, even as he lived a life far different from mine. For example, his included boredom, race riots, guys hanging themselves and prisons meant for 400 men that were housing 800.

He sent Christmas cards. Father's Day cards. Thank-you notes. "I so appreciate your letters," he wrote. "Tell your family hello for me."

Finally, in 2009, he was released from a Minnesota prison on five years' parole, and required to live in a neighboring state, near a relative.

"I'll get you a Starbucks gift card," a friend told him.

"What," he asked, "is Starbucks?"

She gave him a cell phone. "How in the world does this work?" he asked.

He was Rip Van Winkle with a record.

Last December he officially became a free man and moved back to the Puget Sound he loved. The first thing he did was drive to Port Angeles and smell the salt air.

He's been sober seven years. He goes to Alcoholics Anonymous regularly.

Twice, he's been named "salesman of the month" where he works. He and his significant other just bought a $310,000 house. And, from time to time, he stands by his father's grave and wishes he could start over.

"Your father," I said to him, "would be proud of you."

He nodded his head gently, as if unworthy of the compliment.

Two days later, at a writers conference, I told the story about the man. Afterward, a woman told me I'd made a mistake by going back to see him. I was putting myself in harm's way. "People like that," she said, "don't get better. Trust me. I've lived with one."

It reminded me of a line sung by Javert, the police inspector, to Jean Valean in *Les Misérables*: "Men like you can never change."

Let's face it, most people *don't* change, regardless of whether they've served time. But some do.

The humble, clean-cut man whose path did, indeed, cross again with mine was not the cocksure boy I'd met 29 years before.

"I never thought I'd make it," he said.

I raised my glass in his honor. "You did. Bravo!"

And watched as he took a long, satisfying pull from his Sprite.

16.
Close to home

Smokin' hot columnist

Dec. 4, 2011

When the smoke had cleared — and I mean that quite literally — the incident last week reminded me of why I put off home-improvement projects.

Alas, the microwave oven I'd installed 15 years earlier had lost its zap and gone to the great kitchen appliance recycling center in the sky, presumably to commiserate with other devices whose digital faces had also gone dark.

In retrospect, I probably should have stayed away. After all, I had a history with this area of the kitchen. Like some 1930s jungle explorer with no respect for a native culture, I had, in an earlier time, messed with the home-improvement gods' sacred spaces. I should have considered that revisiting the tomb might evoke their wrath — say, send hot lava spewing from our blender.

It was 1996. I was finishing a six-month remodel of the kitchen that would have taken my contractor buddy six days. But on Labor Day weekend, all I had to do was slide a new stove into its niche and I would be finished.

From my perspective, the stove was too big. Others might suggest that my brain was too small. At any rate, despite measuring and remeasuring months before, I was somehow a quarter-inch short of being able to fit the stove in.

The only fix was to take a grinder and shave a quarter-inch off the entire 20-by-36-inch plywood side of some cabinets, the equivalent of emptying Fern Ridge Lake with a Dairy Queen spoon.

But I borrowed an industrial-size grinder and began. Within five minutes, our kitchen was so clouded with sawdust it looked like Yakima after the Mount St. Helens blast. I could hardly see the grinder in front of me.

She Who Had Been Patient With a Dysfunctional Kitchen Since Groundhog's Day made a happy face with her finger on a dust-coated dinner plate.

I took the hint. To contain the sawdust, I grabbed an old bedsheet and strung it around me, from the ceiling, as if I were working in a phone booth.

That proved to be the kitchen equivalent of a stunt I'd pulled off years before: trying to unclog a pipe with a bike chain and coat hanger, and getting them both stuck.

Within minutes of me firing up the grinder, the bedsheet somehow got wound into the grinder. The power tool lurched to a stop. The kitchen's power shut down. I screamed in frustration.

When She Who Waits last saw me, I was running down the street — seriously — like a madman. I was so close to finishing this run-on project and now was going the other direction, like a football team sniffing the goal line and, after a rash of penalties, winding up facing fourth and goal from midfield.

Eventually, I got the stove in place. Now, 15 years later I was testing the gods again.

Our microwave rests above the stove and beneath some kitchen cabinets. To install a new one, I needed to drill a 2-inch hole into those cabinets to get the power cord through, the plug being in a different place than the one on the old oven. But with a dull blade and little leverage, I wasn't making much progress.

"Why don't you lie on your back on the stove?" She Who Thinks of Everything said.

I did her one better. I decided to lie on my back, but also on top of my foam backpacking sleeping mat to prevent scratching the surface of the smooth-top stove.

Much better leverage, though the dull blade was taxing the power drill. Smoke started coming from the wood. The drill was wheezing. The smoke got worse and started smelling almost as if something synthetic was burning. But I kept at it. Nothing could stop me.

Except, perhaps, She Who Noticed Smoke Coming from My Back yelling: "You're on fire!"

I scrambled off the stove. Beneath me, one of the elements glowed red-hot. Coincidentally, the foam pad had a melted circle on it the same size and shape.

Somehow, while positioning myself on the stove, an elbow or knee had flicked on one of the four elements.

I had, in essence, tried to grill myself.

I burst out laughing. She Who Saved My Backside laughed harder. Somewhere, amid the smoke, the home-improvement gods must have laughed, too.

They realized they didn't have to boil me in water for disturbing their sacred spaces, I was more than capable of doing the modern-day equivalent of that myself.

I know it could have been more serious. I don't take safety lightly. But once the new microwave was in place, I came to believe that my amazing home-improvement feat had elevated me to almost godlike status.

Thus, will I forever refer to the incident with the brevity of an oven setting:

Bob on high.

The loneliness solution

April 5, 2011

I didn't wish death upon our old cat, the orange-colored Nesbitt, but it seemed like death was at her door. And, unlike with the appearance of an unwanted solicitor, I wasn't about to hide and pretend I didn't hear the knocking so the visitor would go away.

In cat years, she was something like 1,859 years old. It seemed as if my wife and I had had her our entire lives, although it had been only 18 years. But, as they say, time flies when you're having to haul stained carpets to the dump.

But even if she'd overcome that bothersome bladder problem, she now meowed with the incessant annoyance of a leaf blower. Day. Night. In the house. Out of the house. When we were home. When we weren't home, based on word from family members who would feed her.

She sounded like the senior citizen version of that old Meow Mix commercial, which includes a song whose inspired words are: meow, meow, meow, meow, meow, meow, meow, meow, meow, meow, meow, meow, meow, meow, meow, meow ...

I casually asked a vet friend how you know when it's, you know, time. After asking me to describe our cat's looks and behavior, he told me it wasn't. Argh.

"She's driving me crazy," I'd say to She Who Loves Her Cats With a Fervor.

"It's because she's getting a drink," she'd say, as if I should recognize my obvious oversight and immediately excuse the cat.

"She can't get a drink without meowing?" I'd say. "Plus, she meows whenever she's *not* getting a drink."

That triggered a look whose bubble caption said: "Don't go there, pal."

When the cooling-off period had ended, I reiterated my original point: "She's driving me crazy."

"It's because she's lonely," said She Who Endures Me.

"How can she be lonely? We're here."

No, she explained, lonely for another cat or cats. "If she had another cat around, she'd stop meowing." Yikes.

We have had cats our entire 36-year married life. Twenty years ago, we were up to four but, one by one, they have passed on to the great celestial beyond, where the streets are paved with fur balls.

Now, mulling the passing soon of Nesbitt — all our cats have been named after soda pop, including Pepsi, Dr Pepper, Fanta, Fresca and RC Cola — was like seeing a cloud with a vibrant silver lining.

After all, I could argue, she had lived a long, cozy life. And, meanwhile, I had served admirably for nearly four decades in The Feline Wars: Letting them out; then, three minutes later, letting them in. (Repeat.)

I had dutifully replaced the 1-by-4 outside door molding that Nesbitt had all but shredded to sawdust with her "let-me-in-or-else" claws and whose replacement board had been reshredded to a similar state. I had awakened early to write — at times, a lonely feeling — and found editorial comments on my manuscript in the form of whatever regurgitated food the cat had eaten the night before. (Not good for the confidence.)

As time went on, I sensed that even "She Who ... " was coming to the realization that it was time. Then, two weeks ago at *The Register-Guard*, I got the fateful phone call about Nesbitt.

"Can we get a kitty," said She Who Always Hopes, "so Nessie won't be so lonely?"

I couldn't have been more surprised if I'd seen the Lane County commissioners embrace in a group hug.

"Uh, well — "

"I want to take (granddaughter) Avin out to the humane society and have her help me pick one out."

This wasn't fair; already, I'd pictured my granddaughter cuddling a kitten, my heart warming like the born-again Grinch. But, I reminded myself, don't let yourself be swayed by emotionalism, pal. Think "meow."

"But — "

"Please."

You get married. Start a family. Acquire pets, which come and go as if you're the landlord and they're the tenants. (Tenants from whom you should have required a larger deposit, considering how they left the place.)

But, of course, they become more to us. And how can you can argue with the idea of making people — maybe even a cat near death's door — happy?

It's a boy. Gray with subtle striping. Ten weeks old. Named Squirt.

He keeps me company when I get up early to write, and hasn't left a single editorial comment, which I appreciate. Instead, he watches, with seeming amazement, as the letters and words appear on my laptop screen. He bounces across the keyboard, leaving paws prose — "[[[[[[[[=lopu89yyg54esq1" for example — that's far better than some of the literature you see these days. And, after singeing his whiskers on the nearby candle, will fall asleep on a blanket next to the laptop, his head not far from the "save" key.

Which is appropriate. For, as She Who Knows All predicted, Nesbitt no longer meows; Squirt saved the day.

It's not as if the newbie has infused the old cat with the gumption to, say, bungee jump from the staircase railing. But for the first time in years, she seems to be at peace.

Especially, it appeared, the other night when Nesbitt was fast asleep on She Who's lap. Squirt, tuckered out after chasing his tail for 20 minutes — guys can be so self-absorbingly inane — leaped upward like LeGarrette Blount hurdling a defensive back.

In moments, he had snuggled up close to the older, larger cat and fallen asleep. Nesbitt opened a single eye and returned to sleep, implying reluctant permission. And, nearby, the Grinch was left feeling all toasty inside.

The family comes home

Aug. 22, 2010

The phone call I'd been waiting for since June — the call that would lead to one of those magic moments of summer — came late Wednesday afternoon.

You've experienced such moments, I'm sure, the unexpected intersecting of time and place and people, the result being a summer memory for the ages, at least in your own mind.

The call was from my younger son, Jason. The 28-year-old new father. More significantly, at the moment, the manager of the Not-Yo-Cheese co-ed softball team, a collection of his workplace colleagues at IDX Inc., a software company in Eugene that plays in the Rec 2 League.

Could this be it?

For two months, I'd waited patiently as this half-my-age manager texted invitations to other people, filling lineup vacancies created by vacations and injuries. My older son, Ryan, had been called up, friends of Jason's, total strangers.

But, no, not me. And the season had only a single game left.

Never mind that my last moment of glory was Corvallis' Colt League All-Star game in 1966; I was ready to suit up.

Then came the call. IDX's CEO had broken three ribs in the previous game, sliding into home. "Dad," said Jason, "can you fill in for us tonight?"

Have sweeter words been spoken? Though, uh, sorry about Jason's boss, it was like Ray Kinsella, in *Field of Dreams*, asking his father to play catch with him. I proudly stepped out of the cornfield.

I was to play right-center field, flanked by Ryan's wife, Susan, also a fill-in. Deena, Jason's wife and only six weeks into motherhood, was at first, and Jason at shortstop.

Meanwhile, in the Ascot Field East stands, She Who Watches was on triple-header grandchildren duty.

I exhaled as the umpire called "Play ball." I'd been given my chance, now I had to prove I deserved it.

What a strange place to be: After decades of my sons thinking they needed to live up to my expectations — they should have shot higher — I was suddenly petrified about living up to theirs.

Never mind that this was slow-pitch, co-ed softball and I was playing for a team called Not-Yo-Cheese, the pressure weighed on me like an overstuffed backpack.

Ping! The first batter popped a looper to shallow center. I bolted forward, eye on the ball. It gyrated back and forth in a way I don't remember a ball doing when I was 12. I didn't have a good feeling about my attempt to catch it.

The feeling proved warranted. I slid awkwardly, trying to basket-catch the ball, but it bounced off the heel of my glove.

Error. Failure. Disappointment.

Later, at the plate, I did something akin to getting skunked at a fish hatchery: Struck out.

The next time up, I had two strikes on me. I could read the opening line in my obit: "Bob Welch, believed to be the only person to strike out twice in slow-pitch softball, died Friday ... ."

The pitch came, as if dropped from a helicopter. Whatever happened to pitches that came straight at you and were more easily hit?

I swung. Connected. The ball, just above eye-level, headed down the third base line with less zip than a dog on a hot afternoon. Somehow, though, it got past the third baseman's glove, inside the chalk. Clean hit. I stood on first base as if I were atop Mount Everest.

But the drama was just beginning. Ryan followed with a single, then Deena walked, sending him to second and me to third. The bases were loaded — loaded with Welches — and Jason was up.

Over the years, like fish stories, the length of his hit to left field will be exaggerated. By the time he tells his son Keaton's children, it will probably have landed just this side of Fern Ridge Lake.

Suffice it to say the ball was well struck. The historic home run had the statisticians scurrying for the record books to find out the last time the four people who scored on a grand slam were all from the same family.

The game ended. We hung on to win. Then, after nearly everyone had left, our family gathered at home plate for an iPhone photo.

It will be the image I remember best from the summer of 2010, an image that, in retrospect, I'd find no less beautiful had I struck out twice or Jason grounded out to the pitcher.

Three generations. Nine people, including the quiet hero who, you might say, triggered a seven-person rally:

She Who Watches, aka Sally Jean Welch.

And, as of today, my wife of 35 years.

Dear Cade and Avin ...

April 6, 2010

Dear Cade & Avin,

Another year. Another grandfather's letter. Another reminder that Harry Chapin's song "Cat's in the Cradle" is following me through time like the shadow of a vulture. "I don't know when, but we'll get together then ..." Same words that unsettled me as a father, now unsettling me as a grandfather.

Because of my being too busy, we spent too little time together in the past year. Which is why I so thoroughly enjoyed the lump-sum payment I've been afforded since Friday, thanks to your folks going on their first vacation without you — and Grandmoo and I being part of the medley relay team taking care of you.

Cade, how can I forget Sunday night in Yachats, how you blushed when guitarist Tony Kaltenberg broke into the "Happy Birthday" song as the Drift Inn waitress gave you a candle-crowned ice cream scoop in honor of your turning 5?

And, Avy — nearly 3-year-old Avy — that melt-my-heart grin when you peeked around the corner of the cabin and proceeded to nail me with the icy spray from your 26-inch Water-Blaster Tube? (So thoughtful of your parents to leave such presents for you each day.)

Together, you and I and Cade changed the course of history on Tuesday. Remember? Shovels in hands, we rerouted a 3-foot-wide beach creek as I yammered on about the power of imagination.

You were particularly impressed. Hearing me expound such noble thoughts, you asked, "Bob-bob, can you do this?" Then licked the Nutty Buddy ice cream off your lower lip.

And, Cade, what a blessing it was to explain the nuances of life to you, like when the water-meter reader showed up Monday morning.

"What's that man doing?" you asked.

"Seeing how much water and electricity we've used," I said.

"Why doesn't he just ask us?" you said. "We've used a lot, that's how much."

What a week. Oregon baseball Friday night. The Ducks' spring football game Saturday. And three days at the beach.

Cade, you've fallen in love with baseball; "actually" — to use your favorite word — with foul balls. Oh, sure, you briefly got excited about the free pizza promised fans Friday night if Duck pitchers struck out 10 batters and they ran the number to nine. But, for the most part, it's all about fouls balls for you.

That's because you got two in your first game. I explained that life isn't normally this giving, that to get even one foul ball is amazing, that your grandfather isn't likely to ever again climb over that fence and crawl on his stomach under a ramp to get a ball for you.

But when you win two lotteries on the same day, it's hard to not expect more, especially when your hero is Buzz ("To Infinity and Beyond!") Lightyear.

Thanks, Cade, for the lessons you've taught me, among them: Never assume that if your grandson begs you to teach him to body surf on a day when the air and water temperature are each 54 degrees — and that should you be stupid enough do so — he will be stupid enough to follow suit.

My favorite moment with you was when we shared a beach fire Monday night and you bit into your s'more with the tenacity of the shark in *Jaws* taking a chunk out of Quint's boat. You looked at me, your cheeks pasted with marshmallow, and smiled big.

And, Avy, you taught me the essence of compromise after your grandmother said it was time to brush your teeth. "Let's do it tomorrow," you calmly suggested.

My favorite moment with you came early Wednesday when everyone was asleep. Indeed, it seemed the whole world was asleep, just the two of us sitting in the window seat, watching morning break on the frothy surf.

During the night, a high tide had washed out our diversion dam and returned the creek to its original — and terribly boring — flow. But we can always say that for one day, kiddo, we changed the world, complete with your feather-festooned castle.

I pointed out the light of a boat on the far-off horizon and a lone sea lion playing off the rocks.

"And look," you suddenly said. "In that cloud: A dinosaur. And over there, his sister!"

Why, of course.

All the things we miss when consumed with planes to catch and bills to pay.

Love, Bob-bob

Faith, hope and charity

May 22, 2011

D ear Cade, Avin and Keaton:
In a three-month swath ending in July, you all will have turned a year older.

Time for my seventh annual grandfather letter, which begins with a question:

Cade, on my iPhone's InstaMapper app, what's that "device key" blank they want me to fill in? Some sort of password? Please text me an answer ASAP.

At age 6, you already make me feel like iStupid when it comes to computers, though I can still beat you in basketball, even if, in a recent free throw contest, when my final shot meant victory or defeat, you started yelling gibberish and waving your arms wildly to unnerve me. (Love that competitive spirit, kid.)

You love fishing, sports, camouflage, camping, computers and foul balls.

Your favorite place to camp, you told me, is in Central Oregon, from which you get great views of the Three Sisters mountains.

Which is a good metaphor for what you and your sister and cousin are to me: Faith, Hope and Charity, the original names early settlers gave those mountains.

You, Cade, are Faith, the guy who believes when nothing suggests you should. You believe you'll catch fish and you do. (As long as you're with your other grandfather.) You believe you'll get foul balls at every baseball game you attend and you usually do.

You got five balls last year in six games but, as I told you as we walked to our opener earlier this month, life doesn't always work so wonderfully.

Which is about the time a Eugene police officer walked up and handed you a batting-practice ball that had cleared the right field fence.

Keep believing, Cade. It works.

Avin, you are Hope, aka the Middle Sister.

I see it in your heart-melting smile a promise of the goodness of life.

In your eyes when you boldly walk the balance beam in gymnastics. (At times, stopping midway to offer a fast-motion wave to us fans.)

And in your imagination, which is profound. (If you become a writer, will you digitally inscribe your first Kindle piece for me)

Soon to be 4, you love princesses, sand castles, babies, kittens and to one-up your brother with the occasional hole-in-one at putt-putt golf.

You are staunchly independent, particularly when it comes to refusing most foods except for ice cream and gummy worms. "I am," you once said, "not hungry this year."

Meanwhile, you dream a fairyland world that, I confess, I've never dreamed. But for you I'm willing to try, even if it involves tea parties.

I remember the night at Papa's Pizza when, amid the blur of amped-up kids ravaging the plastic play structure, you said: "Bob-Bob, dance with me. Be my prince."

When you're 57, stuffed with pizza and wearing jeans and a "Metaphors be with you" T-shirt, it's not easy being a prince. But we danced — I was honored to have been asked — and it was more fun than the pool of plastic balls.

So, keep dancing, Avin. And keep hoping, preferably in something or someone more noble than a pepperoni-breathing prince.

Which brings us to you, Keaton. Charity. The name for the youngest of the three mountains, the South Sister, appropriate since you are the youngest of my three musketeers.

You are, at nearly 11 months, a bundle of love. Expressive, your eyes telling epic stories in each nuance. Generous, not yet sullied by the gimme-gimme game that growing up seems to instill. Willing to be picked up, burped, changed, the works.

And so charitable that you gladly serve as a Ducks good-luck charm even in games involving your mother's alma mater, Washington State.

Remember? Oregon hadn't lost a single football, basketball or volleyball game of the nine you'd attended when WSU's heavily favored men's basketball team came to town Feb. 3.

But with you in the crowd, the Ducks ripped the Cougs 69-43, extending your win streak and all but ruining your mother's birthday celebration.

You love a stuffed monkey named George, any object that can be grabbed and food of all types, including some baby-food mixtures that look like Cream of Yuck. (Trust me, it gets better.)

You are in that stage of firsts: smiling, standing up, dipping your toes in the Pacific Ocean, which instantly turned your quarter-sized eyes into the size of sand dollars.

The latest "first": crawling. You explore the ankle-level world with the gusto of someone who realizes adults are missing the really good stuff.

Keep exploring, Keaton. Just remember, as you grow older, to go not only where your imagination is leading, but to where your charity is needed.

So happy birthday, to all three of you kids. And as you journey through life, if you should ever need help along the way, please don't hesitate to see Cade.

He can probably download an app for whatever you need, right buddy?

Love, Bob-Bob

My favorite grandchild

April 10, 2012

Dear Cade, Avin, Keaton and — as of 10:23 p.m. Friday — Lincoln Robert Welch:

First, an apology. Had you been the grandchildren of someone else, say a financial investor, you might get stock options every year. Instead, you get this traditional yearly letter from your columnist grandfather.

What's more, with the addition of each sibling or cousin, you each get a smaller piece of the column pie.

Cade, you turn 7 in three weeks and once amassed column inches like LaMichael James did yards. Alas, you now must share the backfield with three others; fewer carries for everyone. Sorry.

But you're maturing into the type of young man who can take it. Sunday night, your father — around a backyard fire — said, "Cade, now that you've got two little cousins, you need to be a good role model for them. Can you handle that?"

You nodded an earnest "yes," then crammed a few more sweet-potato fries in your mouth and headed off for the swing set. Responsibility on the run.

You live your life on the run. Camping. Fishing. Sports.

In Portland, you watched four NCAA basketball games in a single day, even if it took a small bribe to get you through the last one. You desperately wanted a miniature basketball from the Rose Garden gift shop.

"But, Cade," your father, Ryan, said. "You have lots of basketballs at home."

"But that's the problem, Dad" you said. "They're all at home."

Your logic worked; he caved.

Cade, as you keep growing up, take your father's advice and be a good role model for your sister and two cousins. And always remember this: Of all my grandchildren, you're my favorite.

Avin, at 4, you are a budding soccer player/princess/lover of life. Your smile softens my heart, the earnestness of your words melts it.

"Bob-Bob, I'm going to play soccer," you recently announced. "And I want you to come to my first practice."

I close my eyes and think of you at Disneyland, your princess dress topped off with a pair of running shoes. Oh, Avin, don't ever grow up.

I try to forget another memory of that trip: the morning at the Embassy Suites when you and Cade were playing in the enclosed courtyard featuring two glass elevators.

Suddenly, Cade rushed to our breakfast table with the frenzy of a hummingbird.

"Avin got on an elevator and it went up with her and nobody else!"

Avy, you had a meltdown at the idea of going on the Peter Pan ride; I knew taking a see-through elevator up 14 floors, alone, wasn't your idea of a good time.

After some quiet panic, we found you on the sixth floor, clinging to the iron bars of the rail, face wet with tears.

Please, never leave us again — because, Avin, of all my grandchildren, you're my favorite.

Keaton, you're now the 21-month-old big brother. Weird, huh? Seems like just yesterday I was changing your diaper. (Wait a minute, it was just yesterday that I was changing your diaper.)

In the last year, you've come from being a quiet, reserved little baby to being a walking, talking commentator on the world around you. You not only notice everything, you announce what it is: baseball game ("bay-ball game"), helicopter ("hay-copter"), motorcycle ("mo-cycle").

It took me a half-century to figure out computers; it took you 21 months. For weeks, I've been wondering how to get a report on an electronic newsletter I sent out; the other day, after you fiddled with my iPhone, there was the report — accidental, of course, but there. Thanks, kid.

Later, I was quizzing you on drawings of trucks in your favorite book. I came to one that stumped me. "Keat, it's the one with the big scoop on the —."

"Ex-ca-vator," you interrupted.

With comebacks like that, it's no wonder that of all my grandchildren, you're my favorite.

Lincoln, you turn 4 days old today. Just as our apple tree blossomed last weekend, so did you burst onto the scene like a harbinger of spring: all fresh and new and filled with possibilities.

Your big brother Keaton held you in his arms — until you started crying. "All done," he said. "All done."

And later: "Brother cry. Brother cry."

As you screamed your welcome to the world, I held up my iPhone so your great-grandmother in Corvallis could hear you and she was crying, too. And that is a good thing — the raw emotions of new life and what it does to all those around us.

You weren't even an hour old, and already you were bringing out the best in us, humbling us with your presence, in essence, changing the world.

I know you're young. I know you only know me as that guy in the Duck shirt, the guy with big earlobes and moist eyes, but I need to let you in on a secret I've never told anyone. Until now.

Of all my grandchildren, Mr. Lincoln, you're already my favorite.

The last grandkids' letter

May 9, 2013

D ear Cade (8), Avin (5), Keaton (2) and Lincoln (1):
   Last weekend at our four-generation shindig in Yachats, one scene stood out above the rest:

Watching the four of you revel in nothing but sand and a small creek that you had dammed up into your personal Fern Ridge Lake — with nearly as much water as in the rain-starved reservoir itself.

Cade, you engineered the project and did much of the heavy (rock) lifting.

Avin, you seemed to be Chief Architect and Vice President of Theatrics, at times morphing into imitations of dogs digging holes.

Keaton, you offered play-by-play of everything that was happening — and a lot of things that weren't.

And, Lincoln, you lent a certain "don't-worry-be-happy" spirit to the project, waddling around all wet and coated with sand like a snickerdoodle in diapers.

As I begin my annual letter to you, grandkids, I want to focus on this sliver of time because it offers a lesson about being content.

Stumped by that word "content"? The dictionary says it's being "satisfied with what one is or has; not wanting more or anything else."

And the reason I'm asking you to indulge me on this topic is because, in life, the choices you make will largely be made based on how content you are.

If you're content, you won't feel the need to lord power over others or prove yourself worthy or try to impress people.

Because though people may pretend otherwise, contentment is about the inside stuff, not the outside stuff.

You can't buy it. You can't make it. You can't steal it from someone else who has it.

You find it in how you live: by being thankful for what you have. By thinking of others. And by forgiving a cousin even if he's accidentally splashed you in the face.

Why are so many powerful people discontent? Because power is never enough.

Why are so many wealthy people discontent? Because money is never enough.

Why are so many famous people discontent? Because pride is never enough.

That's how wars get started, because leaders think "If we just had more." (Land, oil, etc.)

And the payoff never equals the price that's paid.

Remember, Keaton, when you politely asked Lincoln, "Can I have the shovel, Linc?" — as you simultaneously ripped it out of his hand?

Lincoln kept his cool. You moved on to other things. And the shovel was no longer an issue.

The momentary discord vanished faster than a whiffle ball fouled into a cluster of shore pine.

Why? Because you refocused on the stuff that mattered: the beach.

The moment. The people around you. And the grandeur of it all.

You see, it's all about perspective — that's what you're teaching me.

One person walks onto the beach and says: "Too much wind. Sand is gunkin' up my shoes. I'll take Hawaii."

Others walk onto the beach — you guys — and see more. You see dams and castles and — remember, Cade? — the washed-ashore buoy marked "Flicka."

You see adventure and intrigue and possibilities, all tied together with occasional laughter.

Your sand play brought your 86-year-old great-grandmother back to the days when she first came to this beach. She was 9.

"It's nice," she said, "to see kids playing on the beach just as I played on the beach."

For all she could tell, it might have been 1936 again.

But it was 2013. Never before in our world have we had more choices, more conveniences, more technological ways to connect us to each other and, ostensibly, to ourselves.

More distractions.

But if there is no smart-phone app for contentment, you remind me that it's not necessary.

You still need nothing more than your imaginations to find contentment on a beach.

And perhaps that's the best lesson you've offered me over the last eight years: It's all about how we look at the world.

Your perspective reminds me of how easily I can lose mine. Can forget what really matters. Can start reaching for a sand shovel that belongs to someone else.

Instead, I need to immerse myself in the extraordinary scenes like I was privileged to witness last weekend: You four so utterly "satisfied with what you had, not wanting more or anything else."

Just sand. Time. And the imaginations to dream what you can make of it all.

Thanks, kiddos, for the inspiration.

Love, Bob-Bob

The new adventure

July 20, 2014

CORVALLIS — On a forested hill in the northwest corner of town, a neighborhood is losing its "witness tree."

In surveying, the phrase describes a large tree so situated that it can serve as a reference point to the land around it. And that's what my mother has been here since 1965.

But now, after nearly 50 years in the house where I spent my teen-age years, she is moving.

The woman who played host to the neighborhood potluck for 47 years.

Who listened to the clack-clack-clack of 2x4 skateboards being ridden down 1960s sidewalks by children who are now grandparents.

Who watched families come and go as the neighborhood changed like a beach transformed by the ebbing and flowing of tides.

Who, from the kitchen window, once saw a high school girl heading for the bus stop and said to me, "Well, she's sure cute. Who's that?"

Marolyn Welch Tarrant, 87, managed to get two children through their teen years and off to college from the staging area of this alpine-green house with the deep orange door. She twice walked back through that door after visits to death's door. (Car accident, 1977, and boat capsizing in which four people drowned near the Galapagos Islands, 1998.) And twice returned to a silence that ached, after my father's death in 1996 and her second husband's death in 2006.

We moved to the two-story house on Norwood Street in September 1965 when I was 11. The lot cost $3,500, the house $20,000. Two stories. Daylight basement. And a darkroom for my father the commercial photographer.

Just down the hall was my room, home of a story that my sons still laugh about with gusto: my getting busted for smoking — not because mom smelled the smoke that I had blown out my window but because she smelled the entire can of air freshener I had sprayed to mask the cigarette smell.

I had one of those moms who loved me enough to force me to smoke the entire cigarette right in front of her, so I'd "get sick and never smoke again," but also let me wallpaper my room — literally every inch of all four walls — in *Sports Illustrated* photos.

And was totally cool when a sixth-grade pal and I — Craig Morris, who could stick nickels in each of his nostrils — slid down the staircase on a chaise-lounge pad.

Great memories, these. But if a son from afar might greet the news of his mom selling the house with a touch of nostalgia — I wrote my "Man from U.N.C.L.E." novel from that basement bedroom in 1966 — the move is a good thing for my mother.

She's moving to an apartment downtown that overlooks the Willamette River. Though she still active enough to sail regularly with me at Fern Ridge Lake, she has decided a 2,249-square-foot house is too much. When my sister, Linda Crew, learned of the new complex opening this fall, Mom loved the idea.

"It's a new adventure," she said in an exclusive interview. "Close to restaurants and the Majestic Theater. I'll miss the kids in our neighborhood but there will be kids in the river park across the street."

And being on the river is especially satisfying for her because the dowtown-river link in Corvallis has been elegantly bridged with a park — and four decades ago my folks fought the proposed riverside highway bi-pass that would have gone in instead of that park.

Given her enthusiastic anticipation for the Sept. 2 move, she might as well be an off-to-college freshman gushing about how she's going to decorate her dorm room.

"It might sound selfish, but what I like about this place is that it just fits me," she said. "This is where I am in my life. I had a house for a family and now it's just me in that big house."

The three-mile move will be the farthest she's ever made. She was born in Corvallis and never moved more than two miles between dwellings, more than half of her life having been spent on Norwood Street.

Ours was the third house in a new development, which was then reached by a gravel road. It's now among hundreds of houses interlaced with asphalt. But deer still mosey into the backyard to nibble beneath the oak and firs.

As the sentinel of the neighborhood—none of the original homeowners still lives on the "loop" — mom has seen it all: triumphs and tragedies.

During the evening, she used to hear a kid around the loop practicing his trumpet. Chris Botti, then a middle schooler, is now 51 and the most recognized trumpet player in the world, worth a net $8 million and, for a while, romantically involved with TV journalist/talk-show host Katie Couric.

That teenage girl Mom thought was so cute used to babysit little Chris. Now she babysits our five grandchildren.

Yup, I married the girl up the street after I interrupted a summer bicycle ride she and her sister were taking. Sitting on our front lawn, the two of us talked deep into the warm night — so deep that close to midnight her father came after her like a cow punch who'd lost his prized calf, all but lassoing her and taking her home in his Olds 88.

"Mom," I said after my folks returned from a camping trip. "I'm going to marry that girl."

The neighborhood wasn't always so warm and fuzzy. I remember the family on one side of us being seriously hurt in a car accident. And the 29-year-old daughter of the family on the other side of us getting caught up in a horrific Silicon Valley tragedy in 1988; when she repeatedly refused to date a coworker, he opened fire with a gun at her software workplace, injuring her and killing seven.

For the most part, though, it was like any other Wonder Years neighborhood: People helped each other during snowstorms. Kids played street football. And the little boy across the street spent hours watching my father build boats in the driveway, peppering him with questions as if fired by a batting-cage pitching machine.

"Someday, when you die, Mr. Welch, I'm going to come to your funeral," the boy told my dad.

And he did.

It was a good neighborhood to come of age in: The sound of a distant trumpet. My first (and only) true love. My last cigarette.

All of it made special by our neighborhood witness tree, soon to be transplanted to a forest all her own.

Scrapping the scoreboard

July 4, 2013

I backed the pickup to the scrap-wood pile at Lane Forest Products and started unloading what used to be my deck and fence.

And there it was, near the bottom of my load: the "Welch Stadium" scoreboard I'd made for the boys back in the early 1990s — the boys who are now 34 and 31 and have children of their own.

I didn't think it would be this difficult, this letting go of a tradition. And yet in the letting go, I was reminded of a lesson appropriate for a day like today, Fourth of July, so steeped in repetition:

Now and then, it comes time for new traditions.

Not that the transition is always easy. This wasn't just a sheet of plywood with peeling white paint. It was the keeper of backyard whiffle ball memories, complete with poker-chip indicators for balls, strikes and outs.

Four wooden disks, each numbered 0 to 9, would be revolved by the hand of the next-up batter to indicate the score. The board could handle any whiffle ball game in which neither team went beyond double digits, which was almost always the case. (In one extra-inning marathon, I think the final was 112-111, and I had to impersonate 37 bullpen pitchers, including a dozen variations of "Sidearm Sammy.")

Ever the sentimentalist, I had hesitated even loading the scoreboard into the pickup.

How can you allow a staple of your young fatherhood years to be turned into fiber for a paper mill or fuel for some physical plant?

Couldn't it be made to work again?

Alas, wood warped by the rain of 23 Oregon winters trumps sentimentalism.

It was time.

I picked up the scoreboard in my gloved hands and carried it to the pile of other people's leftovers, other people's memories.

Then found myself lost in my own.

The rare and magnificent "Effie Ball," with which a batter was honored if he or she ripped a shot beyond the left-field fence, over the street and into the literal upper deck of the Widow Effie's duplex.

The night our two boys and the two boys across the street held an "all-star" game. (Surprisingly, all four of them made one of the two teams.)

The time Michael Jenson — a friend who played on the Kidsports team of my younger son, Jason — spent the night and the boys played whiffle ball forever, running the bases backward. (Another tradition.) The next morning, in our Kidsports game, Michael hit a sharp grounder and took off without hesitation — for third base.

I dropped the scoreboard onto the pile, surprised at how forlorn it looked on the mountain of discarded wood.

I was halfway home before I was reminded that throwing away a piece of rotted plywood wasn't throwing away a tradition. Wasn't a signed-and-sealed mandate to forget about something.

The scoreboard was a symbol of good times now gone, but only that: a symbol.

The memories remain. The only way I discard those is by my own choosing; otherwise, I can return to them as often as my mind allows.

With a new generation now coming to bat — our oldest grandson is 8 — I've been thinking it's time to start new traditions.

With the grandchildren's permission, of course, I imagine a green scoreboard in the Fenway Park tradition tucked tight to the left-field line against the new fence. (OK, so I'm starting a new tradition with an old tradition, Fenway's scoreboard being a classic.)

Instead of running the bases backward, I imagine a $100 college fund prize for any kid who can, with batted ball, hit the brass cow that crowns the new arbor in deep center field. (The owner of this cow, She Who Protects All, isn't as hot on this idea, despite my well-reasoned argument that "it's just a plastic ball.")

I'll propose that the Effie Ball be replaced by the Wyatt Ball. Effie moved away and died years ago.

Two years ago, on the prairies of Manitoba, Canada, a little boy named Wyatt was born to a young couple I know. He died less than nine hours after birth.

In a letter to me, his ex-Eugene mother wrote, "We wish Wyatt could have been on your baseball team and learned to crank some Effie Balls."

And, so, in honor of Wyatt and his parents, when anyone homers into the street it will hereafter be known as a "Wyatt Ball."

Change, you see, is inevitable. You can appreciate the old days, but if you cling to them, you'll miss the new days. You'll miss a new generation stepping up to the plate to offer traditions of its own — which, come to think of it, is what we well-seasoned types once did.

Everything that now seems so old was once new. Every past had a present. Every hymn was once new — and often met with sky-is-falling woe from parishioners who thought the newfangled song impossible to sing.

And so I reconciled the discarding of the "Welch Stadium" score-board.

When I returned an hour later to dump another load, it already had been obscured by someone else's discarded wood.

But that's OK. I can still see it.

Goodbye, Register-Guard

Dec. 6, 2013

Column writing, it's been said, is a little like running in front of a combine in a farmer's field: exhilarating, exhausting and fun — until you trip just once.

After 14 years as a columnist, 24 years at *The Register-Guard* and 37 years in the newspaper business, I've grown weary of trying to outrun three deadlines a week.

Today is my final offering as the newspaper's general columnist.

Though I'm leaving the paper, I'm not forgoing my passion for trying to inspire people through written and spoken words. I'm excited about writing books, speaking at events and teaching my Beachside Writers Workshops and at the University of Oregon's School of Journalism and Communication.

But for the past two decades, my life has read like a series of CliffsNotes condensations. I zip from one event to the other without immersing myself in each with much depth — and without enjoying the journey as much as I should be.

It's time I did.

It's time to slow down and smell the roses — should the Ducks ever again settle for a pulse-numbing week in sunny, warm Pasadena.

To hole up in Yachats for more than a weekend.

To see my grandchildren — four of them, with a fifth on the way — not just at family functions but across the restaurant table from just me, their mouths ringed in waffle syrup.

To hop in the car with She Who Loves to Wander (aka Sally) and head east with no idea where we'll wind up.

And, finally, to look back at nearly 2,000 columns and be reminded of what a privilege working at this paper has been.

In June 1976, the day after I graduated from the University of Oregon, I left to work at *The Bulletin* in Bend with one ultimate goal: to someday return to *The Register-Guard*, where I had spent three years working part-time in sports.

In September 1989, after seven years in Bend and six at a now-defunct Bellevue, Wash., paper, I got that chance. And I've never taken it for granted — stints as a features reporter, features editor and, beginning in November 1999, columnist.

"I see myself as something of a tour guide," I wrote in my first column. "If I'm leading this day hike three times a week, I do so as both teacher and student."

As expected, the people I've written about have taught me much: That life is short. Courage is required. Change is necessary. And risk brings rewards.

Thus, it's time for a new adventure — my "second life," as I call it — while still appreciating the one I'm leaving behind.

"You have a dream position," a reader told me after my first column.

I believed her then; I believe her now. In fact, I still have the Post-It stuck to my cubicle wall, a reminder to never take this job for granted.

I've had the freedom to share some humor, whether it was inventing Eugene-related words that aren't in the dictionary but should be — "hydrospine: the line of spray that forms vertically on the back of a fender-less bicycle rider" — or, in Yachats, trying desperately to listen to a Duck football game that was fading in and out with other stations. "I started getting worried," I wrote, "when (quarterback Jason) Fife threw a long pass to Lucy in the Sky with Diamonds."

I've been able to honor the people we lost; among the ones that hit me hardest was Mario Miranda, killed in an automobile accident in 2000 and one of the high school students I led as head of the 20Below team, a group of young writers who used to contribute stories to the paper.

"I am young, Hispanic, compassionate, sensitive, non-Protestant and certainly not rich," he wrote in one of his 20Below essays. "In fact, after I pay the $70 for my Advanced Placement history class credit, I will have a net worth of $7.50."

I've been able to tell the stories of people who don't pine for the spotlight but deserve it. The people who inspire us with their resilience, such as Katie Barr, the Pleasant Hill High School teacher who lost her husband, daughter and dog in the split-seconds of an automobile accident but rebounded to start a foundation to help the slip-through-the-cracks kids that her school-counselor husband had so passionately believed in.

The people who inspire us with their courage, such as Kayleen Johnston, a bartender at Shooter's Pub & Grill who gave up a kidney to a stranger.

And the people who inspire us with their commitment, such as the 100-plus men and women we featured in our December 2011 World War II series, the most profound journalistic project I've worked on.

So, thanks to *The Register-Guard* for three canvasses a week on which to paint — even if, at times, I slipped outside the lines. (Sorry about the Eugene-oriented haiku — "Better head for Jerry's" — and the mock interview with Smokey Bear; they seemed like good ideas at the time.)

Thanks, editors, for allowing me to climb that crane above Autzen Stadium during its 2002 addition. To take readers along with me on the Pacific Crest Trail by building a special website from which they could follow the journey online. And, after I wrote "I don't get hunting," to go on a weeklong elk hunting trip on which I was thrown from a horse with the dude-ranch name of "Rusty."

Thanks to those who allowed me to tell their stories and their families' stories. The trust between subject and writer is often tenuous. I still remember former UO President Robert Clark's reluctance to let me interview him; at 93, he was ashamed of his forgetfulness. When, after gentle coaxing, he finally relented, he flawlessly recited Robert Frost's "Stopping by Woods on a Snowy Evening," among my most precious newspaper moments.

Whether as a columnist or features writer, I've always favored stories about those who toil with tenacity in the shadows, far from the press conference spotlight. I count it an utter privilege to have spent afternoons with the delightful Barbara Bowerman in Fossil; the courageous Myrlie Evers, wife of slain civil rights leader Medgar Evers, in Central Oregon; and the indefatigable Lewis L. McArthur, editor of the *Oregon Geographic Names* book that his father first had published in 1928, in Portland.

Thanks to the handful of "holiday angels" who, since 2008, donated the $10,500 that I've handed out in random acts of kindness; I sometimes felt guilty getting credit for the sacrifices you made.

To those of you who've sent me questions for the 164 Q&A columns I wrote; together, we answered nearly 1,500 questions about this quirky and quacky place we all love — well, most of the time.

And to those whose ideas were often the underground spring from which many of my columns flowed; for example, I would never have known about Mike Hawley's 125-foot fall from Mount Thielsen — and amazing rescue — had Univeristy of Oregon sociology professor Patricia Gwartney not notified me about the harrowing incident and the friends who helped him survive.

And, finally, thanks to you, dear readers; you've encouraged me when I've succeeded, taught me necessary lessons when I've failed and withstood more references to sports metaphors, s'mores, "It's a Wonderful Life" and hot chocolate than UO's new football complex has flat-screen TVs. (Whoops.)

Together, we convinced the federal government that it should name that prominent notch in the Coburg Hills Hayworth Saddle, came up with 300 names for rain and had a racist sign removed after a Brownsville man aimed it at his Hispanic neighbor. (Thanks to a reader who ripped it off the offender's fence and personally brought it to me.)

My 86-year-old mother, the subject of a few columns herself, has told me we enjoy an experience three ways: by looking forward to it, experiencing it and looking back on it.

In that spirit, I'll long cherish our racing together across the farmer's field, staying one step ahead of the combine.

ALSO BY BOB WELCH

52 Little Lessons from A Christmas Carol

Nuggets of wisdom from Dickens' holiday classic

52 Little Lessons from Les Misérables

The power of grace and integrity to change the course of lives

ALSO BY BOB WELCH

52 Little Lessons from It's a Wonderful Life

Blessings of inspiration from George, Mary and Bedford Falls

Cascade Summer

Adventure on Oregon's 452-mile Pacific Crest Trail

ALSO BY BOB WELCH

My Oregon

RG columns from
1999 to 2004

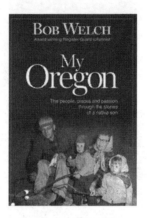

My Oregon II

RG columns from
2004 to 2009

ALSO BY BOB WELCH

Pebble
in the Water

A nurse's death in WWII.
A journalist's book. An adventure galore.

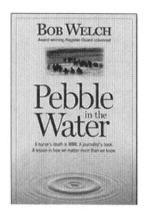

BOB WELCH AS A SPEAKER

"Hands down, the most impressive speaker we have heard in years. The response was nothing short of remarkable."
— **Alex Rankin,**
Archivist, Boston University

"I've never laughed and cried so much during one speech. Welch is a master story teller."
— **Rosemary Garagnani,**
President, Oregon Association of Collegiate Registrars and Admissions Officers Bend, Ore.

"He was absolutely superb! Mesmerizing, motivating, challenging."
— **Clara Richardson,**
Director, Purdue University School of Nursing

"Bob is funny, nostalgic, sentimental, inspirational, poignant, and absolutely prolific as he hit the ball out of the park. Forget raising the paddle; Bob motivated the group to raise the roof."
— **Bev Smith,**
Executive director, KIDSPORTS

WELCH CONTACT INFO

Phone: 541-517-3936
Email: info@bobwelch.net
Web: bobwelch.net
Mail: P.O. Box 70785, Springfield, OR 97475

Made in the USA
San Bernardino, CA
24 September 2018